Advance Praise for

The Creativity Choice

"In this groundbreaking book, Zorana Ivcevic Pringle shatters the myth that creativity is an innate gift reserved for the fortunate few. Instead, she unveils a powerful framework that reframes creativity as a series of deliberate choices that anyone can make. Whether you're tackling an ambitious project or seeking fresh inspiration in daily life, *The Creativity Choice* equips you with the tools to transform your ideas into impactful action and meaningful accomplishment."
—Marc Brackett, bestselling author of *Permission to Feel*

"Consider this book your creativity coach: it shows how anyone can embrace creativity in their everyday lives. A must-read for all who want to grow their own creativity, support the creativity of a team, and lead for creativity and innovation."
—Scott Barry Kaufman, coauthor of *Wired to Create*

"As a scientist-turned-biotech CEO, I never thought of myself as 'creative' until I read *The Creativity Choice*. This book challenged my views and beliefs, illustrating how small decisions and persistence can lead to transformative ideas and actions, much like scaling a start-up. Pringle masterfully blends personal stories, cultural insights, and the role of emotions in daily life to illuminate the science behind turning ideas into action. She offers an inspiring and practical guide for anyone who seeks to harness creativity."   —Marina Udier, CEO, Nouscom

"A must-read for anyone who values creativity. A thought-provoking book that is rooted in science, storytelling, and daily realities. I enjoyed the insights that will allow you to find your own creative influences."   —Kim Schaefer, CEO, Museum of Illusions

"As someone who's spent a career helping innovators and entrepreneurs bring their ideas to life and into the public domain, I'm grateful for Pringle's work. I've never read a clearer, more thoroughly researched, or more thoughtful framework for why to be creative, and how we can all nurture creativity as a skill set. In the age of AI, when the last thing that will set humanity apart from machines is our creativity, I cannot think of a timelier moment for this book."

—Kate Goodall, cofounder, Halcyon, and
managing partner of Halcyon Venture Partners

"I am always impressed by the creativity of Pringle's research on creativity. In a scientifically based book that is very readable, Pringle marshals evidence from the psychology laboratory, interviews with especially creative people, and real-world settings to provide hope that we can all be more creative. You will enjoy reading this book and, more importantly, it will impact your life!"

—Peter Salovey, Sterling Professor of Psychology
and president emeritus, Yale University

"While the outcomes of creativity can be beautiful, enervating, inspiring, even life-changing, the process of creativity is often messy, frustrating, confusing, even painful. Pringle's insightful approach takes away the mystery of creativity and offers pragmatic strategies for reclaiming it as a skill that can be cultivated and practiced. Creativity should bring joy to our lives, and this book helps readers reclaim it has their own."

—Anne Fullenkamp, senior director of creative experiences,
Children's Museum of Pittsburgh

"I've seen the impact of creativity in helping over one thousand ODF startups launch and raise over two billion dollars. *The Creativity Choice* will help those seeking to overcome rigid or stifling environments and turn ideas into action." —Julian Weisser, CEO, ODF

The Creativity Choice

The
Creativity
Choice

The Science of Making Decisions
to Turn Ideas into Action

Zorana Ivcevic Pringle, PhD

PUBLICAFFAIRS

New York

PublicAffairs
Hachette Book Group
1290 Avenue of the Americas, New York, NY 10104
www.publicaffairsbooks.com
@Public_Affairs

Printed in the United States of America

First Edition: May 2025

Published by PublicAffairs, an imprint of Hachette Book Group, Inc. The PublicAffairs name and logo is a registered trademark of the Hachette Book Group.
The Hachette Speakers Bureau provides a wide range of authors for speaking events. To find out more, go to www.hachettespeakersbureau.com or email HachetteSpeakers@hbgusa.com.

PublicAffairs books may be purchased in bulk for business, educational, or promotional use. For more information, please contact your local bookseller or the Hachette Book Group Special Markets Department at special.markets@hbgusa.com.

The publisher is not responsible for websites (or their content) that are not owned by the publisher.

Print book interior design by Sheryl Kober.

Library of Congress Cataloging-in-Publication Data
Names: Ivcevic, Zorana, author.
Title: The creativity choice : the science of making decisions to turn ideas into action / Zorana Ivcevic Pringle.
Description: First edition. | New York : PublicAffairs, 2025. | Includes bibliographical references and index.
Identifiers: LCCN 2024049053 | ISBN 9781541704329 (hardcover) | ISBN 9781541704336 (ebook)
Subjects: LCSH: Creative ability in business. | Creative ability.
Classification: LCC HD53 .I87 2025
LC record available at https://lccn.loc.gov/2024049053

ISBNs: 9781541704329 (hardcover), 9781541704336 (ebook)

LSC-C

Printing 1, 2025

Contents

To my grandparents

Introduction

Picture it. A *New Yorker* cartoon. A party scene with two couples talking. A woman says, "Did you know it was Harry who came up with the idea for the daiquiri?" At the surprised looks from the group, she adds, "He just never did anything with it."

Of course, we laugh at the joke.

But if we reflect, we can also imagine Harry's inner monologue when he first got the idea for the daiquiri: "Who am I to create a drink?" "What does a lawyer [management consultant? scientist? architect?] have to do with inventing a cocktail?" "Are my friends going to think this is silly and that I should just get back to my day job?" "What if real bartenders think it's a ridiculous idea?"

We can imagine the voices of the parents, teachers, peers, coworkers, and leaders from Harry's recent or not-so-recent past becoming one in his mind, nagging at him. Now Harry faces a choice: Should he heed these doubting voices and let his idea fizzle or carry on despite them and start testing recipes? Let's imagine Harry prevails and decides to go for it.

Then when he tries to mix the imagined drink in his kitchen, he realizes it doesn't taste quite right. He tries again, but it's still not what he wanted. This impasse sparks more questions and uncomfortable feelings. "What possessed me to think I could do this?" "I don't really know how to mix drinks." "This is so frustrating!" Naturally, he wants this discomfort to end. Again, facing the choice of whether to act on his original idea or not, Harry turns away from it. His idea for a daiquiri becomes a passing anecdote he shares with friends and colleagues. If the drink ever becomes popular, he can remind them, "I thought of that years ago! Remember when I told you about it."

Chances are, each of us knows a Harry. A person who does not lack ideas but lacks whatever it is that helps transform those ideas into something tangible.

If we are honest with ourselves, we can find plenty of times when we were Harry. Times when we had creative ideas, ideas that had potential, but we did not follow up on them and let them fizzle, half developed. So, the idea stayed just that—a thought only.

If not developed, every creative idea remains locked in the realm of fantasy.

———

Creative work in itself is stressful and riddled with anxiety-provoking uncertainties. It takes resilience to persist through these challenges. It takes willingness to endure and overcome obstacles, from the internal voices of doubt and self-criticism to scarce material resources to difficulties in getting support for ideas. How are creative people able to do what others cannot? How do they transform the challenges and difficulties that original ideas are riddled with into actions and achievements?

As a senior research scientist at Yale University, I study the personality traits of creative individuals across many different domains, from painting and sculpture, to scientific research and mobile app design, to business ventures. I explore how people think of their own creativity and who is most likely to believe they are creative. I examine how creative thinking changes throughout childhood and adolescence. I study the role of passion in creativity at work, how supervisors and leaders create a climate that enables and supports creativity, and the conditions under which stress hurts or does not hurt creativity.

The big question behind all my research, however, is how some people manage what others fail to do—namely, to move successfully through the process of transforming creative ideas into something tangible. Anyone who ever participated in a brainstorming session will know that most of us do not lack ideas. Hundreds of ideas can emerge in a single session as sparks of inspiration fly and sticky notes accumulate on the whiteboard. Yet, most people never breathe life into their ideas; nor do most teams and organizations move to develop and implement them. There is a vast gap between the many ideas we have and the substantially fewer actions, products, and innovations that arise from them. And this isn't just because we're discarding poor or unworkable ideas—plenty of ideas with great potential, in fact, are routinely left undeveloped, most eventually to be forgotten.

As a young researcher poring over books and journal articles in search of what it really takes to make a creative idea tangible, I found that, by far, most research is concerned with the ins and outs of *coming up with* ideas. The neuroscience of creativity, for example, maps brain structures involved in generating creative ideas. Cognitive scientists have shown us how people draw on their knowledge and memory when generating new ideas. Similarly, multiple decades of research have shown that *positive activated moods* (the technical description for emotional states such as happiness and joy) boost creative thinking. Although we have learned much about creative thinking, neither neuroscience nor cognitive science addresses the long process of developing ideas outside the laboratory and building them into original and effective products or performances.

Although we know that when people feel happy, they are generally more original and flexible in their thinking, researchers have also found that the benefit of these moods does not go far. It turns out that if people work on generating ideas for longer than four minutes, whether they are happy or not makes no difference: their creative ideas become similar in both their quality and the quantity, regardless of mood. Creativity that results in performances or products that make our lives better or easier does not happen in a few minutes. It takes anywhere from hours to days, sometimes many of them, for an artist to create a painting or a musician to write a song; months for designers and engineers to create a new mobile app; and years to develop a movie or an innovative new consumer product.

Ideas are certainly important. But having ideas is not enough.

I found that another prominent line of research studies *who* the creative people are. Do they have traits that make them into outliers, different from the rest of us? How could we describe creative individuals? After decades of study, we know that the central trait of those who are creative—artists and scientists, entrepreneurs, and innovative organizational leaders—is openness to experience. Being open to experiences means being curious, valuing aesthetic experiences, enjoying hearing about new ideas, having a vivid imagination, relishing thinking about things, and striving to carry conversations to a higher level. Open people are passionate about their interests, prefer variety to routine, are not attached to conventional ways of doing things, and embrace change.

Interviews with eminent creators, from business leaders to prominent artists to Nobel Prize–winning scientists, point to another key feature of creative individuals' personalities. They embody contradictions. Creative individuals hold traits that usually do not go together. They have great energy, especially when their work asks for it, but also often have periods of inactivity. They are playful but also disciplined and responsible. They have immense powers of imagination, yet are rooted in reality. They are passionate about their work, but they retain the ability to step back and look at it with detachment, which allows them to critically examine and further develop it. They have a capacity for both extraversion and introversion; they are able to engage with a broad range of people yet are also attracted to solitude and quiet. They recognize the creativity of their accomplishments and are proud of them. However, they do not tend to focus on their past achievements. The focus on their next idea or project keeps them humble.

But again, although openness to experience and the ability to embody contradictory traits are important for creativity, they still don't fully explain how ideas are turned into performances and products.

In my continued pursuit of answers to this question, I learned something especially heartening: the science of creativity is clear that rather than being an innate gift of the lucky few, we can *learn* to be more creative at any point in life, and creativity can be nurtured by others around us—parents and teachers, mentors and workplace leaders. Perhaps even more surprising, just learning what creativity is and how it works can help our own creativity. When we know the inner workings of creativity, we know that the difficulties are not uniquely ours. We understand that we are getting frustrated not because we are not capable of being creative but because the creative process is *supposed* to be challenging. We can also develop strategies to encourage both choosing creativity and recommitting to it, even when the going gets tough (or boring or infuriatingly frustrating). And we can learn where and how to look for sources of support.

As I noticed something was missing from the existing research, I started doing my own. I focused on how people approach their creative work. What do we actually *do* with an idea to transform it from an exciting "thing" in our heads to something tangible that enriches our lives, makes them safer or healthier, or changes how we go about our daily activities?

When my son was young, a picture book, *What Do You Do with an Idea?*, posed this exact question. It told a story of a child who one day had an idea. The child was not sure where the idea came from and wondered what to do with it. The idea was fragile at first, and not knowing what to do, the child walked away from it. But the idea kept reappearing. The child worried what people would say about the idea, whether they would find it strange or silly. In spite of others' reactions, the child decided to care for the idea. To protect it and nurture it. And the idea grew and transformed and became visible in the world.

This story illustrates a crucial fact about creativity and the secret for understanding the difference between ideas that make it and ideas that don't: making an idea happen starts with a choice. You have to choose to act—despite any physical, material, or emotional obstacles—until ideas take shape. This is what I call *the creativity choice*. Alas, it is never a one-time thing. Rather, the creativity choice has to be made again and again, as many times as it takes until your creative idea(s) come to life.

Creativity is hard work. The process of creative work includes times of discomfort and doubt and frustration. It takes persistence in the face of obstacles, from bumps in the road to full-blown creative blocks. But it also includes times of great excitement and joy.

One thing about creativity is clear. There is no formula into which we can plug our thoughts and ideas. No way to unequivocally arrange and process what we start with to get to the final solution. The paths to creativity are as numerous and unique as the people who embark upon them. That is why six- or ten- or twelve-step programs of the creative process cannot live up to their promises, as appealing as they might sound. So, let me be clear from the outset: this book does not promise a blueprint or a roadmap for getting your creative ideas out of your head and onto the page, canvas, platform, or store shelf, whatever the case may be.

This book does promise to walk you through the hidden parts of the creative process—from making the initial decision to go for it, to choosing which ideas to pursue, to persisting when you inevitably encounter difficulties along the way. Ultimately, you will learn how to bridge the gap between having the first spark of an idea to turning it into something visible and tangible. When you come along the journey of this book, you will learn how to make the creativity choice as many times as necessary to bring your ideas to life, whether they are works of art, performances, stories or books, curricula, new products, innovative practices, or groundbreaking discoveries.

This book is built on the foundation of the science of creativity. I draw on research in psychology, design studies, entrepreneurship, and organizational behavior. Along the way, I describe what we know about the creative process and how it works. Science is a collective and a cumulative endeavor. As a scientist, I am clear that no single study tells the whole story. And I know that any individual study does not make for reliable knowledge. There is appeal and temptation in unique pieces of research that tell something surprising or counterintuitive. But only taking them together, when the same results emerge time and again, can we consider them trustworthy. This book is based on such results.

Finally, to bring the research to life, I interviewed dozens of creators about their work—artists and musicians, entrepreneurs and management consultants, scientists and educators, production designers and designers of complex digital systems, and innovators who have built organizations small and large. I share many of their stories. They show us how what scientists study in the lab is lived out by people for whom creativity is both a choice and a necessity.

I will not be teaching you creative *thinking* or how to generate creative ideas. Many books have been written on that subject already. Our business here is much more interesting and challenging. We want to explore what distinguishes those who make the decision to follow through on their creative idea(s) from those who do not—and how you can learn to do the same.

THREE LESSONS OF THIS BOOK

This book teaches you three groups of lessons: how to make the first creativity choice and get started, what psychological and (surprisingly!) emotional tools you need to navigate the creative process and stick with the creativity choice, and what you need to make creativity happen in our social worlds (because creativity is social even when it does not seem to be).

The first part of the book examines what shapes the initial creativity choice. We might consciously desire creativity, but we are implicitly also biased against it. This bias is not conscious, but it nevertheless influences our decisions. Creative work exposes people to discomfort—*Can I figure out how to make this idea happen? What if people don't like it?* These are risks to contend with. Yet, some of us find ways to walk into that uncertainty. We may not necessarily like or enjoy these risks, but we accept and tolerate them.

After this initial willingness to bear the personal and social risks of the creativity choice, we ask ourselves whether we can do it. *Can I be creative?* Often, we are less than sure.

We pick up messages from the world around us. Portrayals of creativity in the media often talk about revolutionary discoveries or individuals who won Nobel Prizes or MacArthur Fellowships (sometimes called "genius grants"), and it can be difficult to imagine ourselves in their company. We learn lessons from what our teachers said and what they did (which are not always the same) or what leaders in our workplaces acknowledge or encourage.

Alas, the initial creativity choice is not enough. We also need tools that can help us move from deciding to get started to actually doing and persisting. The second part of the book is all about these tools. In our world that declares itself solution focused, creative individuals are instead problem focused. They spend time and effort exploring and framing problems and remain open to revisiting and reframing them.

Creative doers know, sometimes intuitively, that the creative process is an emotional roller coaster, and they are skilled at harnessing the power of emotions, both positive and energizing ones and those that are more challenging. They do not push away frustrations and distract themselves from them to feel better but choose to face them and work around them or with them.

The final part of this book examines how the people around us—parents and peers, colleagues and leaders—influence creativity. If you find yourself not making the creativity choice, you have likely been swayed by others around you. Likewise, when you do make the creativity choice, there are always ways, visible and invisible, that others have nudged or supported you. Our social environment creates the physical and psychological infrastructure for what we can do, making creative work more or less likely to happen and succeed. In the long run, this can make the difference between a one-hit wonder and repeated hit-making. Knowing how to recognize the influence of others can help us examine our environment, and it can inform the search for a new one when change is necessary.

The research on which this book is based is full of surprises. Chief among them is that creativity requires courage—not bravado or brashness but real, lasting courage, the kind that is hard won. Creativity requires the courage to decide to pursue our original ideas, even when we cannot be sure they will work or do not have the slightest notion of how to make them a reality. It requires the courage to persevere when the road is bumpy, uncertain, and uncomfortable and to keep going until we create the results we want, even if that means starting over multiple times. And it requires the courage to share our ideas with the world, even when they hold risks to our reputation.

Your creativity journey will usher you toward something that only you could ever dream of and invent, something for which the world could very well be waiting. So, let us begin.

PART ONE

Choosing Creativity

Creativity Is a Choice

D o you want to be creative?
   No, really.

Are you *willing* to be creative?

I was in first grade when I first considered this question, even if not in those words. Creativity was not part of my vocabulary, but when I saw it, I recognized it in the manner of "I want what she's having."

In art class at my elementary school in Croatia, the teacher asked us to make drawings to celebrate the national holiday that was coming up. It was the Day of the Republic, the holiday commemorating the country's founding. A "flags flying across town and in shop windows" kind of day. In schools, it was a tradition to hold an assembly, with students showcasing their talent and hard work—reciting poetry, performing skits, the choir singing, the mandolin orchestra playing.

Our teacher gave us an open-ended task. We could decide to draw anything we wanted to show the spirit of the holiday. And I did not know what to do.

So, I looked around at what my classmates were doing. What was Dinko working on? And Toni, Vinka, Nikolina? It seemed that everyone around me was drawing the same scene of a flag-clad main town square and fort. Feeling reassured, I drew it too.

When our teacher hung all the drawings on the classroom wall, I was amazed that twenty-odd students had drawn the same picture. Flags flying. Venetian fort. Fishing boats in the harbor of our little town in the Adriatic.

Except Branka. Decades later, I remember that she drew students at the assembly standing in front of a microphone.

I wanted to be like Branka. I wanted to make an original drawing like Branka. I wanted to dare to do something different.

But honestly, I was not *willing* to be like her. I had plenty of ideas, and I liked to draw—at home. At school, I decided that I wanted to please my teachers and my parents. Which meant doing all that was expected. Not venturing into the unexpected.

All these years later, I still think about that experience from time to time and wonder if that was the spark that nudged me, decades later, on a path to study creativity.

I remain fascinated by the gap between the many ideas we have and the not-as-many actions that arise from them. I was not willing to be original and creative in my first-grade classroom. I did not make the decision to do something that I was capable of doing. Thoughts of what my classmates and teacher would say and a sense of self-consciousness were louder.

WHAT IS CREATIVITY?

Scientists like to start any discussion by clearly defining what they mean by the terms they use. After seven decades of research, there is broad agreement that creativity is the process of making something that is both original and effective. As you'll see, it is not just a *physical* process of making something—a design, a book, a new consumer product, a novel organizational system—but also a mental and emotional process of building ideas into products and performances. Creativity's "end product" is *original*: it results in something that has never before existed. And it is *effective*: it solves a problem, sparks a new insight, brings aesthetic delight, changes how we communicate or interact with others, or even alleviates suffering. Creativity's end product can be nearly anything, and it can happen in any area of life. Creativity is as much about answering scientific questions, designing products or buildings, or devising improvements in work processes as it is about painting, sculpting, or composing music. Have you made something original and effective? Then you have been creative.

Once you read what creativity actually is, it might seem obvious. Yet, we often don't think of creativity in this way. Rather, we tend to associate it narrowly with thinking or with particular kinds of work. And it turns out that the first associations we have with the word "creativity" can have important consequences for how we think of our own creativity, what we create, and even whether we make the decision to engage in creativity or not.

Social psychologist Vlad Glăveanu examined people's mental associations with "creativity" in two different ways. First, he asked people from their teens into their sixties to come up with the best symbol of creativity and to explain their choice. Not surprisingly, the top symbols represented art—a paintbrush or a palette. The next category of symbols stood in for abstract thinking. By choosing the yin-yang symbol, for instance, study participants wanted to communicate that creativity exists in bringing together apparent opposites, which complement each other and reveal a little something of one another.

To get another perspective on people's associations with creativity, Glăveanu examined the first 500 results returned by Google Images for a search on the word "creativity." After excluding multiples of the same image, he found the most common symbols were a lightbulb, a brain, a paintbrush and colors, a computer, a toy, a musical note, and children's drawings. He then presented these symbols (as words) to study participants and asked them, on a scale from 1 to 7, how well they represented creativity.

The paintbrush and colors most often got the perfect 7. A child's drawings, a musical note, and a lightbulb were also considered good representations of creativity. Just as in the first study, when people could freely think of any symbols that came to mind, the symbols of creativity people agreed with the most were about art, complex thinking, and expressiveness or childlike spontaneity.

Finally, participants were asked whether they considered themselves to be creative, and if so, what their creative achievements were. Most often, people described themselves as creative if they had *artistic* achievements—if they painted, drew, wrote, composed music, or danced, for example.

This "art bias" is seen far beyond the psychologists' laboratory; in our daily discourse this bias is visible in who gets to be described as creative, using the noun form of the word. Although the term "creative" as a noun is not a recent invention—in English it dates to at least the 1930s—these days the word seems to be everywhere. Certain people are described as creatives, and others are not. This implies that some professions, mostly those in the arts, culture, design, and advertising, engage in creative work and can accomplish creative deeds. The rest of us don't get such a title.

Research by Glăveanu and others shows, however, that our intuitions about creativity and how we talk about it can lead us astray. There are two big problems with assuming that creativity is primarily about the arts and culture or about spontaneous expression. First, it turns out that unrestrained, free-flowing creativity is, at best, rare in real life. Rather, creativity requires great effort and must work around (often frustrating) constraints. And second, if we believe creativity is free-flowing, playful, and even effortless, we may take the obstacles and impasses we encounter as a sign that we lack creative ability—which is enough to make many people give up.

Of course, people are not wrong that the arts are creative. Those who paint, write poems, or compose music that gives us goosebumps are making something new and having an effect on how others feel or think. They have the power to delight us and make us cry, to outrage and disgust us, to make us feel awe, and to give us different perspectives on the world.

But art is just one form of creativity. Creativity also exists in our everyday activities and interactions and in our professional lives. When I moved halfway across the world to attend graduate school and was missing everything dear and familiar, my best friend Tatjana sent me an envelope full of grass she picked in front of her house. The envelope had a one-line note: "Green grass of my home." That was both original and effective, and thus creative. Close to twenty-five years later, I still tear up just thinking about it.

And creativity is virtually everywhere in the world of work, from delivering original and effective presentations in project meetings, to talking to potential funders, to devising new products that make life easier or more fun, to drawing out the best from team members with different skills and experiences. I grew up in a family of engineers and, by the luck of the draw, have many friends who are engineers. Complex problem-solving is at the core of their work. However, they rarely refer to it as creative and tend not to believe they are creative (often mentioning family members who are more artistic as having gotten the "creativity gene"). If you look for creativity in one specific place, you will overlook it in all the others.

ALL THE FACES OF CREATIVITY: FROM MINI-C TO BIG-C

Creativity exists not only in just about every area of human activity and life but also in forms small and large. Often, when we hear the word "creativity," we think of the Albert Einsteins, Agatha Christies, Nikola Teslas, Steve Jobses, and Coco Chanels who have enriched our world with their magnificent creations. If these were the only creative people, it would be easy to get discouraged and decide it is not worth embarking on the creative process. We know we are not going to be able to fill those shoes. Luckily, the Albert Einsteins, Agatha Christies, Nikola Teslas, Steve Jobses, and Coco Chanels are not the only creative ones. The rest of us can be creative in ways tiny, little, and large, each enriching our lives and making a difference in distinct ways.

Psychologists distinguish four levels of creativity, each with their own characteristics and effects. The most basic form of creativity is personal creativity, or "mini-c" creativity. This is creativity found in the learning process and in making original and meaningful connections between concepts and ideas. Think of children's drawings or finding methods that make learning something new easier to remember. Mini-c creativity is original, usually just for a single individual. When I was in school, I would record myself on a cassette tape (oops, dating myself!) saying vocabulary words in Latin or German and then testing myself by pausing the tape, saying the word, and checking whether it was correct. Chances are, I was not the first person in the world to devise this studying strategy. But no one taught it to me. It was both original for me personally and meaningful, two highlights of mini-c creativity. I learned those vocabulary words, and it was less unpleasant than staring at the textbook.

Mini-c creativity is not limited to childhood. This kind of creativity exists at work when you devise a way to organize all the materials you, as an office manager, need at hand on a daily basis or when you find a way to connect your personal experience to what you are doing, leading to a new and original idea.

The most common form of creativity is everyday creativity, or "little-c" creativity. Think of writing a personal travel blog, making your work colleagues feel truly seen and appreciated, or coming up with just the right way to teach or explain a work process to a colleague or an intern. These can be forms of self-expression, little surprises that brighten and enliven relationships, or solutions to everyday problems.

Little-c creativity denotes something original that is appropriate for a particular everyday situation or problem. Whereas mini-c is personal, little-c is shared with others. An original birthday gift for a friend is truly creative if they genuinely love it—if it succeeds in delighting the friend and making them feel cared for. Acts of everyday creativity are often shared only with a select group of others, like coworkers, friends, and family. Research shows that this kind of creativity contributes to our own well-being and the well-being of those immediately around us. Everyday creativity helps us experience a sense of growth and makes life more joyful or our work easier.

When creativity is shared more broadly and requires specialized skills, psychologists talk about "Pro-c" or professional creativity. This kind of creativity requires substantial learning or expertise (and thus earns a capital letter), such as building objects of practical or decorative use, scaling business ventures, and conducting scientific research, among infinite other possibilities. Pro-c creativity is original and effective in achieving its goals—getting a reaction from an audience, solving complex problems, or being usable and useful. This is the creativity of designers designing, architects drawing plans for structures of our built world, mathematicians solving long-standing problems, product engineers developing hardware and software for new gadgets, leaders turning around organizational cultures, and entrepreneurs bringing their ideas from prototypes assembled in garages and living rooms all the way to publicly traded companies. This book primarily focuses on this kind of professional creativity.

At the highest levels of creativity are the creators and creations we can readily name as having changed our culture or the way we live. This is double-capital "Big-C" creativity, and it is the realm of the very few. There are only a handful of psychotherapists—for instance, Sigmund Freud, Carl Jung, and perhaps Carl Rogers, but likely not many more. It also includes Thomas Edison and Steve Jobs as technology innovators, and Billie Holiday and Ella Fitzgerald as the great jazz singers. There are other Big-C technology innovators and jazz greats, but the exhaustive list is not very long. Not only have these individuals made something so original that it changed a whole area of work, but their influence continues even beyond their deaths.

FROM ONE LEVEL TO THE NEXT

Different levels of creativity coexist in individuals.

Albert Einstein was a Big-C physicist who revolutionized how we understand the universe. But his violin and piano playing can best be described as little-c. He largely played for his own pleasure, was known to improvise, and occasionally accepted invitations to perform at benefit concerts where he was attractive more as a famous scientist than as a musician.

We see more examples daily in the world of work. In my work as a scientist, designing research studies requires expertise and professional know-how. That is Pro-c work. But coming up with strategies for how to motivate people to take part in research is little-c creativity.

Similarly, business leaders use all levels of creativity in their work. Ben Silbermann is the founder of Pinterest, a visual discovery platform where users collect and save images they find. Images on their boards can be a means of self-expression, a way to visually imagine their future, or a means to help with planning or problem-solving. This multibillion-dollar company is a major Pro-c achievement. But the idea spark for it started as a mini-c kind of creativity, a form of personal connection. Ben thought of his childhood passion for collecting and made a mini-c insight: the internet needs its place for collecting finds from online searches. This insight helped him recognize the value of the idea, its potential, and the importance of persisting on the long road to its realization.

Our peak creativity can progress and develop from one level to another as we build expertise and experience. I like baking but am not a big fan of strong cinnamon flavor. So, I choose to reduce the amount of cinnamon and add some cardamom instead (it makes me think of summer and wonderful, faraway places). When I first started baking, this was the only deviation from the recipe I would dare. It was personally meaningful to me, even though my family and friends for whom I baked might not even have noticed it. My peak baking creativity was at mini-c level.

Once I became a better and more confident baker, I started introducing bigger changes to existing recipes or even combined recipes. And I started becoming known as a party baker. I am still not an expert, but I have a reputation in my circle of friends as the person who will bring interesting and delicious cakes to every occasion (and have at least one that people have not tried before). My peak baking creativity reached little-c level.

Sometimes little-c creativity grows into Pro-c or expert creativity. One of my favorite food websites, Smitten Kitchen, started as Deb Perelman's personal blog. It evolved from a blog about her personal life into one about making and eating food. As it gained readers among eager cooks and eaters, Deb realized that she had something valuable to offer, got more practiced, and became a professional food blogger. In addition to blogging, she built expertise in recipe development and published three cookbooks. Similarly, Marques Brownlee started making videos reviewing technology products that he already owned when he was in high school. These were works of little-c creativity, lacking in professional lighting and editing. But he persisted and grew to become a celebrated Pro-c creator. His main YouTube channel has just shy of 19 million subscribers, he has been on the *Forbes* magazine list of the top "30 Under 30" social media creators, and Vic Gundotra, former senior vice president of Google, called him "the best technology reviewer on the planet." Gabi Logan, meanwhile, always loved to travel. After college, she worked in nonprofit and corporate settings but also tried to write about travel whenever she could. She finally left her job to focus professionally on travel writing. Freelancing for travel magazines grew into a coaching business for writers. She wrote a book and is now teaching others through online courses, webinars, and personalized coaching about how to build sustainable travel-writing careers.

Even the greats of Big-C creativity have to start somewhere smaller. Julia Child became a celebrated chef, cookbook author, and TV personality. But she did not think much about food until her husband, Paul, introduced her to French cuisine when they moved to Paris after he got a job with the US Foreign Service. In her autobiography, Julia describes their first meal together in France, sole meunière, as "a morsel of perfection" with a "distinct taste of the ocean."

She decided to build on this newly discovered revelation of what food could be and enrolled in the famous Le Cordon Bleu culinary school. She graduated on the verge of her forties. She joined an exclusive women's culinary club in Paris, Le Cercle des Gourmettes, where she met Simone Beck and Louisette Bertholle, who were busy writing a French cookbook for the American market. They invited Julia to join them and help make the cookbook appealing to Americans. This was the start of an informal test kitchen and cooking school, L'Ecole des Trois Gourmandes, where Julia became an expert recipe developer and communicator. Their book, *Mastering the Art of French Cooking*, not only became a best seller when it was first published in 1961 but is still in print more than seventy years later. After publishing eighteen books, hosting television shows that spanned from 1963 to 2000, and inspiring others (from *Saturday Night Live* to *RuPaul's Drag Race*), Julia Child has had an enduring influence on American food culture. She built a budding interest in food into a profession and, ultimately, into Big-C creativity.

We cannot all be a Julia Child, changing a culture with the force of our creativity. Still, there is a lot that we can all do. We can all decide to build and develop our interests and skills and take on new challenges. These decisions can lead to having insights of mini-c creativity, playing with little-c creativity, and engaging in Pro-c creativity by applying our professional expertise toward creative goals. Your creative work can start small and grow to eventually solve important problems, advance your career, improve lives, and build new capacities in communities around you, spreading like ripples from stones skipping on calm water.

HOW CREATIVITY IS STUDIED AND MEASURED

Creativity scientists devise ways to measure how people think and what they do. When they examine details of creative thinking and how such thinking is affected by the way tasks are presented (e.g., whether people are explicitly asked to be creative) or by mood, researchers ask study participants to come up with ideas or solve problems in the laboratory. For example, they might ask them to list all the ideas they can think of for how to use common objects or to imagine what would happen if hypothetical scenarios, such as people being able to read others' thoughts or become invisible at will, came true. These tasks might seem removed from real-life creativity, but they are not dissimilar to thinking about the consequences of the widespread application of artificial intelligence (AI), for instance, which is very much a question facing thinkers and societies in our time. And indeed, how people do on these kinds of tasks is related to their creative behavior and achievement in everyday life.

Other creative thinking tasks that researchers use in their studies can be very similar to problems that designers or business consultants encounter. Participants could be asked to think through how to improve educational experiences at institutions of higher education, how to put together an advertising campaign for a sports team, or how to design a new waste-disposal system for passenger trains. Then, researchers can observe how people think through these questions either individually or working with others.

After study participants complete these design or problem-solving tasks, researchers evaluate the creativity of their solutions. Harvard

Business School psychologist Teresa Amabile had a fundamental insight about how creativity can be measured in a most meaningful and reliable way. She realized that it is difficult (probably not even possible) to identify the specific features of products that make them creative. Is that painting creative because of the striking horizontal line in the midst of a landscape? Or because of the contrasting colors and a particular composition? It is at best not clear.

But Amabile realized that when people deem something creative, they tend to agree in that assessment, even if they cannot explicitly pinpoint why. Scientists apply this observation in judging any and all kinds of creative outputs, from ideas, to hypothetical problems, to haiku poems written in the laboratory, to designs of consumer products. They show any products to experts—artists when judging art, designers when judging new designs, managers when judging solutions to business problems—and ask them to independently evaluate how creative these products are. Judges tend to agree, indicating they are capturing the ineffable attribute of creativity. When I describe studies in which participants generated ideas, solved problems, or created something, I speak of creativity evaluated in this way.

Because much of creativity happens at work, this book pays special attention to creativity in the workplace. Organizational behavior scholars measure creativity at work in two main ways. One is to ask people directly a series of questions that taken together assess how creative they are in what they do. People answer how often they have found new uses for existing methods or equipment, identified opportunities for novel products or work processes, come up with and suggested new work-related ideas, or solved problems that caused others difficulty. People know best what they do at work and can provide valuable information. Alas, this information is not without flaws. Sometimes people can be overly optimistic about how original or useful their ideas are or how significant their contributions are to the projects on which they work. Other times, they might not recognize the importance of what they have done.

Another way to measure the extent of creativity at work is by asking people's immediate supervisors. Supervisors are familiar with employees' work and can have a broader picture of the importance of different contributions. These judgments have important practical consequences, such as rewards or new opportunities for those judged as creative. As those with decision-making power, supervisors, managers, and leaders can champion ideas they consider creative, making them more influential. However, they can also be biased. For instance, supervisors tend to evaluate women as less creative than men and be swayed by behavior intended to impress.

Throughout the book, when I speak about creativity in the workplace, I refer to one of these two kinds of measurements that assess creativity.

CREATIVITY IS FULL OF DECISIONS

I was a doctoral student when Robert Sternberg, one of the greats in psychology whose work I deeply admired, published a paper titled "Creativity as a Decision." In this brief commentary, he made a basic assertion that one thing all creative people have in common is a decision to engage with the creative process and purposefully pursue something that is original and can be effective in solving a problem or fulfilling a particular goal. But in this article Sternberg did not identify individual and social influences that contribute to making this decision or examine factors that contribute to successfully following up on this decision and persisting from the initial intention through action and its execution. This book unpacks these crucial details.

Creativity is a choice both metaphorically and literally. Anyone who has ever made decisions in life knows that we need information when facing choices. We also know that some choices are exciting and others anxiety provoking. Creativity is no different. It also benefits from collecting diverse information and weighing it before committing to a creative idea, and throughout the process we often experience many emotions, from stress and tension to excitement, that we have to manage and cope with.

Creative work is also literally a series of choices. From our first vague ideas all the way to completed projects and products in hand—businesses launched, books written, new app prototypes developed, or whatever else can be imagined and made—we have to make decisions that shape what we do. What is worth pursuing? Is this idea ready? Do I need to develop it more? What do I need to make it come alive?

Although the creative process is full of decisions, this does not mean that being creative is a simple "just say yes" matter. Rather, our creativity choices are influenced by the messages we absorb from the culture around us and the spirit of the times in which we live; by our thoughts, which are shaped by knowledge and experience; by our feelings and how we deal with them; by our relationships with others; and by the environments in which we work.

At the very beginning, the most basic decision is whether to engage in the creative process or not. Agatha Christie wrote about it vividly. "There is always, of course, those terrible three weeks, or a month, which you have to get through when you are trying to get started on a book. There is no agony like it. You sit in a room, biting pencils, looking at a typewriter, walking about, or casting yourself down on a sofa, feeling you want to cry your head off. . . . And yet it seems that this particular phase of misery has got to be lived through."

It is easy to relate to the angst and distress when facing the blank page, canvas, or screen. If Agatha Christie, one of the best-selling authors of all time, who wrote seventy-five books, was feeling it so strongly—if she was biting pencils and pacing frantically—it is not strange that we go through this misery too.

Nevertheless, she continued to make the decision to embark on the creative process, even knowing how difficult it would be, and the world is richer for it.

Making that first decision is only the first step. We make the creativity choice over and over again, often unconsciously. We do not necessarily pause and make a list of pros and cons, as we might when choosing between competing job offers. Decisions we make can become apparent only in retrospect, when we realize that we could have taken different courses of action. In the middle of work, we might experience it as simply doing. But behind that doing are hidden decisions. An artist starts their creative process by deciding what they wish to portray. Next, they make decisions about the structure of the artwork, usually developed through drawing many preliminary sketches, choosing to combine them, deciding to pick some and discard others. As the outline of the painting emerges, they fine-tune it, adding layers to the canvas and choosing what features will make the idea come to life most effectively. Finally, they decide on the finishing touches—those textures or colors that first attract us to a piece of art.

Artists are not unique in having to make choices in their creative process. Scientists make decisions about the ideas they want to study. The creativity choice at this point means choosing more original over less original questions. Are we willing to ask questions that others have not asked? Do we want to risk being criticized for challenging the prevailing wisdom? Scientists also have to decide how to examine their questions. Are we going to choose methodological approaches that are not popular but could provide original insight? Sometimes original questions require new ways of measurement or observation (which might not exist and require additional work, potentially delaying our progress).

Similarly, business start-ups begin with an idea. Founders make decisions about the features to include in a prototype. They balance desires with financial and design constraints, making more decisions in the process. And they test different ideas before choosing some and discarding others, finally making their products available to all users.

Whatever your area of work, you will face at least two major groups of decisions when you choose to start on a path of creativity.

The first set of decisions is about what aspects of the problem, question, or product to focus on and what angles to examine. The second set of decisions addresses how to cope when you encounter obstacles and criticism.

THE JOURNEY OF CREATIVITY FROM
HAVING AN IDEA TO BREATHING LIFE INTO IT

Unlike the (fictional) Harry from the *New Yorker* cartoon who had the daiquiri idea but never did anything with it, the historical inventor of the drink offers lessons about not only coming up with an idea but also deciding to do something with it and bringing it to the world to enjoy. Jennings Stockton Cox was an American metallurgic engineer in Cuba at the end of the nineteenth century. Cox was the general manager of the Spanish-American Iron Company, situated near the village of Daiquirí in the Sierra Maestra Mountains, about fourteen miles from Santiago de Cuba. He was overseeing a group of American engineers, and the task of keeping them happy was not easy. The work of mining was difficult, they were far from home, and they were exposed to risks, such as contracting yellow fever. So, in addition to generous pay, the perks of the job included tobacco and alcohol rations. This being Cuba, the readily available alcohol was rum.

We will never know exactly when or how Cox got his idea for the daiquiri, but from his actions, we can conclude that he thought he could be creative and develop a new cocktail. This confidence is at the core of creativity choices. Importantly, such confidence does not imply absolute certainty and the absence of any self-doubt. Rather, it means mustering enough conviction to summon the courage to decide to embark on the creative process. Cox did.

We also can tell that Cox knew that creativity does not come out of the blue in a spontaneous burst of inspiration. He did not simply sit down to write the cocktail recipe when he was struck with a great idea. Rather, he identified the problem of keeping his engineers happy. Cox was curious about his Cuban workers mixing rum with coffee. He used this curiosity as a spark that got him experimenting with mixing drinks on his own. Getting to the final recipe took time and effort. It meant he kept making the creativity choice again and again, each time a recipe wasn't up to snuff.

Then, one evening he was at it with another engineer, Giacomo Pagliuchi, and they used what they had at hand. It turned out to be just right, and Cox recorded the recipe in his diary. "For six persons, mix the juice of six lemons, six teaspoons of sugar, six cups of Bacardi Carta Blanca rum, and two small cups of mineral water. Shake well. And serve with some ice." He named the cocktail after the town where the mine was and where the drink was concocted.

The story of Jennings Stockton Cox and the daiquiri would not be complete if we ended it with him writing the recipe in his diary, however. If that were the case, we might not know of it today. And he did not invent the daiquiri as a lone genius. Or make it popular completely alone.

Cox was an outsider in Cuba, a country that already had a rich cocktail culture, which made people receptive to new and original mixed drinks. Being an outsider provided him a way to see possibilities that insiders could not and to embark on the route of experimentation. He was fascinated by what he noticed around him but not so bound by traditions as to miss new opportunities. Cox found inspiration from casual relationships with Cuban miners, and they cheered him on when he introduced the new cocktail. And his partner in mixing was there to keep him going when another recipe was not quite right.

The evolution of the daiquiri continued after Cox settled on the recipe. He would bring the cocktail from the town of Daiquirí to Santiago and then to Havana. In the 1920s and 1930s, the bartender and owner of the bar El Floridita, Constantino "Constante" Ribalaigua Vert, developed the frozen daiquiri. Ernest Hemingway tried the daiquiri and loved it so much that he became a regular at El Floridita.

He wanted his drink with double rum and no sugar. From this, the Papa Hemingway daiquiri evolved (and is still served at El Floridita); it includes rum, lime juice, grapefruit juice, and maraschino liqueur.

The choices Cox made set his actions into motion. He made them in spite of uncertainty about what exactly to do and whether he would succeed. We turn next to examine what it takes to choose to pursue creative action when the path to making our ideas into reality is not clear.

Creativity Takes Risk

Max Miller is an American YouTuber with more than 2.5 million subscribers and author of the *New York Times* best-selling cookbook *Tasting History* (with Ann Volkwein). Max always loved history. Not the long lists of dates and battles and rulers and how they changed world maps that you learned about in school. Max wanted to know how people lived. Who were the people in first and third class on the *Titanic?* How did medieval peasants spend their days? What was life like in the trenches of the US Civil War and World War I?

Max did not know what to do with his interest in history. He considered writing historical fiction and at one point even got started on a novel, but that did not work out. Back in college, Max had studied vocal performance and performed on Disney cruise lines, but neither did performance prove to be a viable career path. Instead, he took a job at Audible as an audio producer and then worked in marketing at Walt Disney Studios. It seemed that history as a creative direction would fall by the wayside.

Then, as chance would have it, Max was at a Disney resort with a friend when she became suddenly ill. He kept her company as she watched *The Great British Bake Off* in her hotel room. Max watched, delighted, as the bakers made wonderful cakes and cookies, pastries and custards, breads and pies, and built show-stopping creations that told a story through sculpture-like edible marvels. All of this happened in a collegial atmosphere, in which contestants were learning and teaching the audience along the way. But what really got Max were the breakaway segments about food history, which took viewers back in time to learn the origins of specific dishes.

Swept away by what he'd seen, Max started to bake at home. He also researched the various recipes and where they came from. Food is to be shared, so he brought his baked goods to work and told the stories that went along with them. At the 2019 office Christmas party, a colleague suggested that he make these stories into YouTube videos. The idea for how to bring together his passion for history and love of food was born.

Max bought the necessary videography equipment and started making videos. He posted the first video, "How to Make Medieval Cheese," in late February 2020. Only twelve days later, the World Health Organization declared the COVID-19 pandemic. In just over a week, the governor of California issued a stay-at-home order, and Max was furloughed from his job at Disney.

That's when Max started making videos for the *Tasting History with Max Miller* YouTube channel full-time. Each video re-created a dish from the past—from Roman snails to seventeenth-century Korean pancakes, from Japan's Edo-era noodles to Aztec pozole, from the diet of Marie Antoinette to an American school lunch during the Great Depression—with a generous serving of history. When he started, Max could not have imagined that four years later his videos would have been seen more than 200 million times.

When Disney called to give him back his job, Max had to make a decision: go back to a good and safe job or continue as a professional YouTube content creator. He went for the latter. A year later he had a contract for his first book of recipes and history, and as I write this he is working on the second.

CREATIVITY IS ROOTED IN PSYCHOLOGICAL RISKS

Told like this, Max's story of success seems inevitable. The truth is that getting started is much less straightforward than it might appear. Max doubts that he would have started his YouTube channel if he had not purchased the rather costly recording and lighting equipment before he was furloughed from his day job. Making those purchases when out of a job would have seemed much more of a financial risk. But financial risk is not the only kind of risk. There are also the psychological risks.

The psychological experience of risk is based on uncertainty. We cannot be certain of our ability to do something we haven't done before and do it well. There is no way of being clear about what comes between the idea and its realization. Nor is there any way of being sure about how our work will be received. In spite of what self-help books might profess (and how much we may wish for assurance), creativity cannot be reduced to a set of surefire steps that eliminate uncertainty and risk.

Scientists studying the effects of uncertainty have found that we tend to look for anything to reduce it. Uncertainty can mean danger, and we often jump to that conclusion. The problem is that if we eliminate uncertainty, we preclude creativity. Creative pursuits, by their very nature, take us into the unknown. And this is a big part of the reason why we can passionately speak about the importance of creativity—then turn around and not act on our ideas. We cannot mentally bear the uncertainty and the sense of risk creative work entails.

It was uncertain whether Max could really build a successful YouTube channel. Objectively, he did not have the skills when he started and never would have been hired by an established TV history or food channel. Max was not a chef or a historian and did not know how to script, film, or edit videos. He did not know when to post, how to tag videos, and generally how to make them attractive to a potential audience. Would he be able to figure it out? This is the first kind of psychological risk important for creativity: intellectual risk. When we take intellectual risks, we are asking questions and attempting to learn new things and acquire new skills, even though we cannot be sure we will be successful in doing it. Max stared down these uncertainties and went for it.

Max also had to contend with another kind of psychological risk: social or reputational risk. Taking reputational risks means putting ourselves out there and sharing our ideas and our work, even though we are uncertain how people will react. For every YouTube channel that goes from a casual hobby to a successful career, an unknown (very large) number do not. Encouragement from Max's friendly coworkers wouldn't necessarily be an accurate indicator of interest from YouTube audiences. What would viewers say in the comments? Luckily, Max didn't let this risk stop him either.

TAKE INTELLECTUAL RISKS

Pablo Picasso described taking intellectual risks when he said, "I am always doing that which I cannot do, in order that I may learn how to do it." This approach to life and work might seem like a difficult philosophy. When challenging ourselves to take intellectual risks, we accept the possibility of failure, primarily in our own eyes. Doing what we do not know how to do is uncomfortable. Doing what we cannot yet do demands that we acquire new skills and try new approaches to problems. In creative work, taking intellectual risks means choosing and pursuing original ideas, even though we cannot be sure we can develop and build them. It means taking a leap. Going into uncharted territory.

A team of international researchers set out to examine how being willing to take intellectual risks helps creativity. They asked three groups of questions of more than 800 people, ages eighteen to seventy-nine. First, they asked how likely they were to take intellectual risks, such as doing something new, even if they were not good at it and might make mistakes in the learning process. Next, they asked how confident people were in their ability to be creative. Did they believe they could solve problems creatively? Finally, researchers presented participants with a long list of creative activities, from writing and music, to cooking and humor, to science and invention, and asked participants to indicate what they had accomplished and any recognition they had received, from praise from friends or family to receipt of national or international awards.

The results showed that intellectual risk taking was related to both creative confidence and creative behavior. In other words, those who were willing to take intellectual risks were more likely to believe that they could be creative, to engage in creative work on an ongoing basis, and to garner more creative achievements than those who were not willing to take intellectual risks.

The researchers found there was a threshold of minimal intellectual risk taking necessary for creativity. Below this threshold, even when people believed in themselves and were confident in their ability to be creative, they did not end up acting on this belief. You may think you have creative potential, but if you are not willing to take the intellectual risk required to create, that belief won't translate into action. You need to be willing to take an intellectual leap to transform the conviction that you *can* do something into *actually* doing and achieving it.

The good news is that the threshold for how much risk you need to take is rather low. You don't need to be willing to take great risks or be a true risk taker. Rather, a measured willingness to take risks helps creativity. You do not have to challenge yourself to do each day something you cannot yet do, like Picasso did. Instead, when creative work requires learning a new skill or developing a novel idea, consider how to take the first step. Max did not know how to edit videos, how to title them, or how to create appealing thumbnails, but he could find YouTube tutorials on it. Find a place to start and a way to take the sharpest edge of risk off, and you can step over that risk threshold.

TAKE REPUTATIONAL RISKS

Being willing to take intellectual risks is not enough. We also need to be willing to take some social or reputational risks when we share our original ideas or work with others. Because we can never be sure how people will react to our ideas, sharing them exposes us to the potential for criticism or even public failure. Have you ever spoken your mind about an unpopular issue at a meeting? Or openly made a suggestion that challenged prevailing wisdom? Or proposed something that was outright rejected? If so, you know how deeply uncomfortable and even threatening situations involving social risk can be. In creative work, taking reputational risks means voicing our opinions and ideas, even though we are not sure they will be popular. It means asking people to come with us where they have not gone before.

The anxiety that arises from a social or reputational risk makes the decision whether to pursue a creative idea, much less share it, difficult. There is a conundrum in judging the value of ideas. The social value of creativity is clear. Societies benefit from technological innovations and scientific breakthroughs that make our lives easier and keep us safe. Our lives are enriched by creative works of great art and music. And educators and organizational leaders alike acknowledge that creativity is important. On its list of the top ten skills crucial for the jobs of the future, the World Economic Forum includes five groups of skills that are related to creativity: ideation; originality and initiative; complex problem-solving; critical thinking and analysis; and innovation. And these skills have only been climbing up the list in their importance.

However, when it comes to the individual—just us alone with our ideas, riddled with doubt and uncertainty—it is less obvious whether

pursuing creative ideas is worth the trouble. Despite its social importance, and despite the near universally espoused value of creativity and innovation in mission and value statements, we too often
receive rather different messages in the environments in which we
spend much of our lives—namely, schools and workplaces. Educators
pressed to follow elaborate curricula might allow little opportunity
for open-ended creative projects. Managers pressed to reach specific
performance metrics might prefer to play it safe and not venture into
something original. Thus, the personal decision about whether we
should consider creativity as worthy of our time and attention is less
than clear-cut. The problem is that without deciding that creativity
matters—and that it matters so much we are willing to endure the
discomfort of standing up and standing out to champion untested or
even unpopular opinions—we are unlikely to attempt it.

The Power of Social Pressure

Social pressure can have a dramatic influence on what we do. Psychologist Solomon Asch conducted the now classic experiments in
which he showed people a set of three lines that were clearly different in length and asked them to match another line to one in that set.
Participants were asked whether the line on the right was the same as
line A, B, or C on the left.

A B C

Participants were in a room with several other people, and
each was asked to give an answer out loud. Unbeknownst to the
participants, the other people in the room were working with the

researcher, and all gave a wrong answer. Instead of saying that the line on the right matched the middle one in the set on the left, line B, they picked one of the other lines.

The real participant would be asked to give their response after repeatedly hearing the wrong answers from people who were presented the same task. Video recordings of the experimental sessions show that participants were uncomfortable—tense, anxious, troubled. Everyone seemed to agree on an answer that clearly contradicted what the participants saw. They looked around and squirmed, as if saying, *What are they talking about? Or Do they know something I don't? Or Did I misunderstand the question?* The result: about 75 percent of participants went along with the wrong answer; they conformed with the group. This is the power of social pressure in action. Even when nothing tangible was at stake and when the correct answer was unequivocal, three-quarters of the participants succumbed to social pressure.

So, what happens when there are *many* possible answers, which is by definition the case with creativity? In one experiment, researchers gave people a common creative thinking task—come up with different ways a tin can could be used. Participants were tested in a large room that could seat over 500 people. Not all the seats were filled, making it possible for people to be in the presence of others but also to sit apart from them. Some were told to work silently, and others were asked to think aloud as they listed different ideas. The results showed that thinking silently helped people to come up with more original ideas. Researchers thought that the mere act of thinking aloud created a spotlight effect, a psychological sense of being observed and judged by others.

In these experiments, participants felt a push to self-censor their more unusual ideas even though they did not know the other people in the room and nothing that happened in the experiment could affect their lives. They could not gain anything by impressing the experimenters; nor could they lose anything because of what they said or did.

But if we are in a work meeting pitching new ideas, we do have to consider how we will be perceived and whether voicing our more unconventional ideas will impact our standing on a team. Could we be perceived as not being a team player? Could this jeopardize our future opportunities? The social pressures are much stronger "in real life" than in a one-time experiment with no bearing on our lives. If people subjectively experience such pressure that they end up giving conforming answers in a laboratory study, how much greater is that experienced pressure when the stakes are high? Risking our social reputation becomes possible only if we make a purposeful decision to do so.

The Internal Risk Monologue

In my lab at Yale, we studied what goes on in people's minds when making decisions about whether to share their creative ideas or not. We started studying students in high school because that is where we learn habits and attitudes about creativity that tend to stay with us.

The first concern we discovered is about how one's ideas would be received. This is a worry that looks outside ourselves and wonders about any potential negative social consequences of sharing ideas. Will others think our ideas are silly? Laugh at them? Could they judge our ideas as challenging their authority or being disrespectful? Could our ideas anger them?

Another consideration is about how we feel when we face the decision whether to share ideas. If we feel overwhelmingly self-conscious and anxious at the mere thought of presenting something unconventional, we are more likely to decide that it is better to be safe than original. Teachers and university professors are only too familiar with students asking what they need to do and what exact steps they need to follow for an assignment. Teachers and professors want students to think deeply, make connections, and be creative, but students are anxious about their grades and would like to reduce their concern by sticking to a well-defined formula. This happens at work too, when employees ask for very precise directions about what their tasks are and how they should perform them. Supervisors and leaders, especially those who strive for creativity and innovation, want to see initiative, independence, and original thinking, which cannot be expressed by following a to-do list or a set of predetermined steps.

Finally, the third consideration is crucial for daring to be creative. It is an attitude that says creativity is meaningful and valuable—so much so that it is important for one's identity. Once we believe that creative work is central to who we are as a person, we become willing to accept and cope with a certain level of discomfort and anxiety about potential social disapproval. If it matters that much, we are willing to deal with some tension and stress.

It is easy to see how we take this internal negotiation with ourselves into the world of work. We have ideas—but how will our colleagues react to them? What will our supervisors and leaders think? Will they think our ideas challenge their approaches? Are our ideas going to be welcomed or criticized and shut down? Perhaps there could even be longer-term consequences for our reputation, such as when our colleagues or bosses deem our speaking up as too strong or as inappropriate for our role. If we voice ideas that are unwelcome, we might not be included in conversations we need or want to be a part of. Or we might miss out on desirable projects. Considering these risks, wanting to avoid embarrassment or exclusion can be quite rational.

Avoid the Reasonableness Trap

Research shows that decision-makers in organizations are especially susceptible to wanting to avoid reputational risks. In one study, researchers asked decision-makers in a company with more than $10 billion in annual revenue to judge an idea for a new product. This included the CEO and senior executives, as well as managers in different technical and administrative positions across company divisions. Everyone judged the same idea presented in the format used by the

Kickstarter crowdfunding platform. However, researchers told some people that the idea had high social approval (268 backers, 94 percent funded by supporters), and they told others that the idea had low social approval (12 backers, 22 percent funded). Knowing that others approve of a project signals that we do not have to worry about standing out for championing the idea—there is less chance of reputational risk.

The study showed that those who spent more time making decisions in their work roles were more likely to adopt what scientists call an *economic mindset*—a concern about being rational and reasonable, focusing on specific and accurate metrics, and making "correct" decisions (whatever that meant in their opinion). And this mindset had consequences for how they evaluated ideas. Decision-makers rated ideas with high and low social approval as equally useful. But when they thought the idea was not very popular (low social approval), they rated it as less creative. It seems that discounting the creativity of the idea allowed decision-makers to justify to themselves why they were not supporting it. Looking for reasons that seem rational and data-driven becomes a form of self-defense.

More than 100 years ago, Sigmund Freud talked about defense mechanisms as unconsciously motivated thoughts or actions intended to protect us from psychological threats. Rationalization is a defense mechanism by which we offer seemingly rational reasons for decisions and actions, but in reality they are just excuses. When decision-makers say to themselves, *This is not that creative anyway*, they can discard ideas and continue seeing themselves as valuing creativity. If we explain our reasons as rational and logical, others are likely to perceive them as such too (after all, they are based on focus group discussions or hard metrics!), and we are unlikely to be criticized or blamed. By relying on them, we shield ourselves from criticism and potential failure. However, in preventing what perhaps could tarnish our reputation, we are also precluding what could build it. We stagnate.

If you are a leader in business, a mentor, or a teacher who aspires to creativity, you need to work backward from the questions that people ask themselves. First, you need to ask whether you are showing that you value creativity in your decisions and actions (and not just words). When it is clear you value creativity, those around you will be more likely to value it too. Next, you need to consider how you react when people share their ideas. Chances are you are not saying unconventional ideas are silly. But you need to reflect on whether you are inadvertently shutting ideas down prematurely in other, less explicit ways. Are you jumping to think of what is reasonable and readily possible in the short term (and therefore not very original) before considering what might become possible (and what could be built into a significant creative contribution)? Finally, are you encouraging people to express their thoughts and opinions even when they are uncertain and hesitant to do so?

HOW TO TAKE CREATIVE RISKS

Psychological risks make it difficult to share and engage with creative ideas. Some people find it easier to tolerate these risks than others. But we can all learn to accept some risk.

Recognize the Bias Against Creativity

The first step in choosing creative ideas is knowing that experiencing uncertainty and any kind of risk biases us against creativity.

In one study, researchers divided people into two groups, one designed to experience uncertainty and one not. To make participants feel uncertain, researchers told one group that they might receive an extra payment for taking part in the study but would be paid based on a random lottery; that is, they might or might not get this additional money. Participants in the other group were not told anything about the extra payment.

Then, both groups took a test of implicit associations about creativity. This test measured how quickly people associate the term "creative" as good or bad and how quickly they associate the term "practical" as good or bad. Participants were also directly asked how positive (versus negative) they considered words related to being creative ("inventive," "original," "novel") and words related to being practical ("functional," "constructive," "useful"). The first test measures unconscious beliefs, and the second set of questions assess conscious beliefs.

The results showed that when asked directly, people said they valued creativity and practicality very similarly; they consciously thought of them both as positive and desirable, whether they were in an uncertain situation or not. But when they had to react quickly, without having time to deliberately consider their responses, it turned out that those who were exposed to uncertainty valued creativity less than practicality. The experiment revealed an unconscious bias.

This bias against creativity when we feel uncertain does not happen only in laboratories. Decision-makers at all levels in organizations show this bias. And it is understandable how it happens. Managers and leaders who have the responsibility for allocating resources for ideas are key to organizational performance. They are the ones who decide whether to engage with creative ideas and start the process of developing them into products and services. In making these decisions, they face a dilemma of choosing a safe path by adopting a tried-and-true course of action or following a novel but uncertain one. The risk of the decision to choose a familiar approach is that the results will not bring about exceptional growth. However, choosing the tried and true has known benefits—decision-makers are reducing the chance of loss if the idea does not work out.

Social psychologists have widely experimented with unconscious influences on behavior and found that simply understanding that biases exist reduces their effects. Once you know that a certain level of risk is necessary for creativity, in terms of both challenging ourselves (intellectual risks) and accepting uncertainty about others' reactions (social or reputational risks), you can intentionally decide to override the unconscious pull toward less original ideas.

Make a (Mental) Risk Balance Sheet

If we prevent the bias against creativity, we still have to balance the risks inherent in choosing creativity with its potential benefits. Psychologists Robert Sternberg and Todd Lubart borrowed the marketplace metaphor to describe how to maximize successful creativity. If we imagine a marketplace of ideas, creativity will be optimal when buying low and selling high. That means creating a new and untested product that meets an unknown need in the hopes that demand will skyrocket once people realize its value. If people are not aware of the need and opportunity for alternative forms of lodging, shoes with minimal padding, or affordable but stylish eyeglasses, the market will not be crowded with anything similar, and those who take the risks can build such creative products as Airbnb, Xero Shoes, or Warby Parker eyewear. This sounds very sensible—perhaps even obvious. Yet, research shows that decision-makers too often tend to go for ideas that are already popular in the marketplace of ideas.

Max Miller had an idea that was not popular at the time. There were no other prominent YouTube channels dedicated to recreating historical recipes and the stories of their eras. There were certainly food and cooking channels that occasionally mentioned history and history shows with an occasional food-related episode. But Max put these two together. Even *The Great British Bake Off* had stopped doing its food-history segments by the time he launched his channel. In retrospect, we know he "sold it high." Just a few months after it was launched, the *Tasting History* channel had a viral video (about *garum*, a fish sauce essential to the cuisine of ancient Rome), and it has continued growing steadily since. Now other channels are trying to replicate Max's success. Even a well-established outlet like TV's History Channel now has re-creations of historical recipes.

Of course, buying low could mean finding valuable opportunities previously not considered by others, but it could also mean that an idea is not good. An idea might be original but not effective, or it might be so ahead of its time that it cannot achieve wide acceptance.

Steve Jobs, founder and longtime CEO of Apple, was a master of buying low and selling high in the marketplace of ideas. He described his approach by saying, "We have a lot of customers, and we have a lot of research into our installed base. We also watch industry trends pretty carefully. But in the end, for something this complicated, it's really hard to design products by focus groups. A lot of times, people don't know what they want until you show it to them." This comment is not meant to insult customers. Rather, it points out that it is hard for people to imagine innovative products and how they could be used. When focus groups discuss a product, they stay close to something with which they are familiar, and they can only envision and suggest small and incremental changes to well-known products. Products that become game changers are more difficult to imagine and often have a harder time gaining acceptance, even from experts. This is the case regardless of the product, from impressionist art, which was not immediately embraced by the art world, to the first Harry Potter book, which was rejected by nine publishers.

Jobs did not rely on focus groups or already existing data and metrics as a crutch. He invested in getting that information, respected it and took it into account, but did not allow it to dictate his decisions. He profoundly understood what it takes to choose creativity. This is clear from the success of the products he championed, from the original Macintosh personal computer to the iPod, iPhone, and iPad.

Focus groups can agree about their liking of movies in the Marvel universe but will be less consistent about original character-driven movies. That has been the critique of the emphasis on blockbuster movies in recent years by directors who have helped create classics that appear on every list of best movies of all time, such as Francis Ford Coppola and Martin Scorsese. Studio decision-makers rely on superhero stories, sequels, and remakes (e.g., Disney's live-action versions of their animated hits) instead of riskier, original stories.

Crucially, even the best judges will on occasion make a wrong choice. Steve Jobs considered Dean Kamen's idea for a two-wheeled motorized personal vehicle, the Segway, "as significant as the personal computer." Despite this praise, the invention did not live up to that description. Two decades since its launch, the Segway exists, but its users are relatively few. It certainly did not change the way we all get around in the way that the iPhone changed how we communicate. Although Jobs had issues with the design of the device and the way it was launched, we can consider his initial enthusiasm for it a misjudgment. Some original ideas are not effective, for one reason or another, and do not end up making a mark on our lives and society.

We could argue that the Segway was not a risk worth taking. However, if you are not willing to occasionally miss, you will end up in a situation where you do not try at all or invest only in surefire ideas for which there is widespread agreement and support (and you will not be buying low because everyone under the sun wants to jump on the bandwagon). The problem with such ideas is that they tend to reach saturation, like the Marvel movie franchise.

The alternative is to deliberately choose projects that involve some risk. The National Science Foundation in the United States supports fundamental research in science and engineering by providing funding for proposals judged on intellectual merit and the potential for broader impacts. Program managers are explicitly encouraged to recommend projects considered high risk by external reviewers. Each proposal is evaluated for creativity, originality, and transformative potential, and specific programs provide funding tailored for exploratory research in early stages of development on untested concepts. Whether in science, entrepreneurship, or organizational contexts, the temptation is too great to choose only safe, and therefore rather conventional, ideas. As the National Science Foundation formally does in supporting early-stage research, you will need to fight this temptation by purposefully tolerating measured risks.

Manage Uncomfortable Uncertainty

One analysis estimated that on average, one commercial success emerges from more than 3,000 ideas and decisions about them. At each decision point along the road of creative work, you will have to choose between more comfortable, safer options and more uncertain, original ones. Part of how we manage uncomfortable uncertainty is by putting great attention on the quality of the ideas and how they are implemented, and part is by learning to accept ambiguity as inevitable in the creative process.

Organizational psychologists at the University of Nebraska in Omaha conducted studies to examine how attributes of products influenced decisions to allocate funds. They created video pitches for a new dating app that differed on originality, product quality, and pitch quality. The original app was presented as having a new way to connect users with potential matches. Instead of having users scroll through lists of other users, as is common on currently popular apps, the product matched users based on their biological (e.g., age, height) and psychological (e.g., personality traits) profiles. High-quality products were described as clear and intuitive to use, providing a detailed description of potential dating matches, and showing criteria on which the match was based (contrasted with low-quality products that presented irrelevant information and had a limited user interface). Finally, high-quality pitches had good video and sound quality (contrasted with low-quality pitches in which narrators stumbled and had shaky camera work). Researchers showed different pitches to judges and asked them how uncertain they were about the product pitched—whether they had doubts about it and whether they were unclear how things would go with the product.

Results showed that original products created feelings of uncertainty—it is hard to predict how something that is fundamentally different from existing products will do. However, this sense of uncertainty was lessened when presentations included more technical details for products, when the design was user-friendly, and when pitch presentations were smooth and sophisticated. Put simply, when you want to sell a creative product, high-quality execution is essential to relieve doubts and the discomfort of venturing into something that departs from the familiar.

However, the quality of the products and how they are pitched do not fully remove the experience of uncertainty and doubt about whether to choose creative ideas. Some ambiguity is left. When we accept that uncertainty and risk are inescapable in creative work, we make a decision to tolerate them in spite of their unpleasantness. To tolerate ambiguity, we do not have to be attracted to it or enjoy it; rather, we have to be willing to experience some amount of discomfort for the sake of our creative work.

By contrast, those who do not tolerate ambiguity experience uncertain and unclear situations as psychologically threatening. They are thrown off their balance, experience anxiety beyond their ability to cope, and can get overwhelmed. Instead of staying with the discomfort to explore problems and their potential solutions, those who are not able to tolerate ambiguity find ways to grasp for something familiar and act in ways previously tried-and-true. Result: conventional work.

Studies of creators in different domains and industries show this vividly. Architecture students describe states of ambiguity and uncertainty as unavoidable. Although these experiences happen throughout the process of creation, they are most intense at the beginning. Those who are intolerant of ambiguity are not able to cope with feelings ranging from anxiety and frustration to despair. As one architecture student who took part in a research study put it, "Because of these feelings, I do not want to keep thinking for a long time. . . . I always hope to have ideas as soon as possible." Because our minds start the thinking process with what is familiar, this desire to settle on an idea quickly usually results in something rather commonplace. For an architect, this can be a design that meets client specifications or requirements but without being really creative. They might still be able to do and keep their job, but they will not leave a significant mark with their work.

On the other hand, those who are tolerant of ambiguity do not settle on their first ideas. When they reflect on it, the architecture students realize the importance of accepting and even prolonging the period of uncertainty. "I believe that if everything goes smoothly, easily, and without stumbling, there will be definitely something wrong," another participant in the study said. "I think that in order to achieve novelty, you must suffer." Not everyone experiences this discomfort in the face of ambiguous tasks as suffering, but it is common to feel stress, tension, and doubt. The experience in itself is not a sign that we are stuck. The key is how we respond to this stress.

Or consider the engineering design process. In a Pennsylvania State University study, scientists analyzed each stage in the creative process, from generating ideas to building product prototypes. Participants worked to design a new and innovative product to quickly froth milk. They were instructed to focus on both form and function and design a product that was intuitive to use.

After generating their own ideas, researchers asked participants to review ideas generated by others using a process that is similar to the rapid filtering selection in industrial design. They placed each design idea in one of two categories: "consider" and "do not consider." Designs could be classified as worthy of consideration if the entire concept could be developed or included specific elements that could be valuable for further testing or prototyping.

Teams did not have any trouble generating ideas. On average, each team came up with twenty-two distinct ideas, and they selected eight of their peers' designs for further development. However, many teams did not end up choosing original ideas for continued development and prototyping.

Those who tended to select creative ideas for further consideration were not averse to ambiguity. The lesson is simple: tolerate the ambiguity and risk in creative work. As you accept the risks, you will become able to better discern truly original ideas and choose the ones worthy of consideration, development, and implementation.

Of course, we can try to reduce ambiguity by seeking to learn more, such as when creators look to focus groups or success metrics for previous work. Sometimes these approaches provide valuable information. But as Steve Jobs knew very well, sometimes they make us feel we know more, when in reality their utility is limited.

Max Miller tries to pay attention to metrics showing which videos do well, but also realizes that this is at best an imprecise affair. He described his thought process: "For a while it was like, *Oh, if it's ancient Roman, it's going to do amazingly well*. And then I've had a few that are ancient Roman which haven't done well. Then I thought, *If it's about a specific character in history, it's going to do very well*. But then I made a Marie Antoinette episode and it flopped. Similarly, I predicted the more ancient it is, the better. Turns out, not always true. Or, if it has to do with World War I or II, that's going to do great. Not necessarily." He discovered that there is uncertainty in the other direction too—expecting that a topic will not be a big hit and being pleasantly surprised. "I did a video about the molasses flood of Boston," he said. "I thought that video was going to do just okay. But it has become one of the most popular videos I've ever done." He continues to pay attention to metrics but now understands their limits. "What we have found is that we really don't know," he concluded. And he accepts this as a part of the creative process.

We have two main ways to respond to uncertainty: avoid it or accept it. When our goal is to avoid uncertainty, we can distract ourselves and make ourselves feel better by doing something familiar and comfortable. Max could have continued his job at Disney and enjoyed baking for his coworkers and telling them tidbits of history. This choice would not have been without merit or creativity. But it would have foreclosed opportunities. Avoiding uncertainty means we are failing to embrace that which might be possible.

Yes, You Can

Elisabeth O'Bryon is an accidental serial entrepreneur. She was a very good student and always had a plan. She went to college and then graduate school. Growing up with a brother who struggled with a learning disability, she saw firsthand how sometimes students are not served by the existing educational system. And she wanted to help those students. Elisabeth received a doctorate in school psychology and started her career at a research institute, adapting educational programs for Spanish-speaking preschool students and their families. Being a researcher could have been her career.

Chance intervened. Elisabeth took a weekend trip with two best friends from high school. As they chatted and enjoyed each other's company, they ended up wondering, in a "wouldn't it be cool" way, about friendship apps. They imagined an app used by a group of friends that would ask fun questions, with everyone in the group trying to predict each friend's answer.

It was just a conversation over drinks. Elisabeth certainly did not think of herself as someone who could develop an app. And she definitely did not think of herself as a risk taker.

But as the weekend came to an end, the friends returned to the idea. What if they actually made the app? None of them worked in technology fields, but they believed in the idea. They loved it and thought others would too.

They were aware of the risks. None of them had started a business before, but they were willing to take the intellectual leap of doing what they did not yet know how to do. They did not know how their idea would be perceived by others, but decided to try anyway. The question was about the first action to take.

Although they had a good idea, the founders did not have the expertise to build the app themselves. So, they started with step one: hiring an engineer who would be able to make their idea into reality. Pulling from personal savings, they could afford to hire an overseas engineer. Step one turned into step two: creating a set of features to be included in the app. One solved problem turned into another. What started as a generalized "I am not a tech person or an entrepreneur," step by step changed into "Well, I can solve one problem and then go to another one," and it eventually turned into "Well, yes, I can build an app." And the *Know Your Crew* app was born.

Although the app did not become wildly popular, the experience expanded Elisabeth's sense of what she could do. And it opened new opportunities. Her tech experience helped her get a job at the national nonprofit organization Great Schools to develop a platform for school-to-home text messaging. The pilot project did not end up becoming a priority at Great Schools, but the CEO believed in it and encouraged Elisabeth to spin it into a stand-alone organization. The two of them cofounded Family Engagement Lab, a national nonprofit that bridges classroom learning and learning at home. The organization builds technology-enabled tools that make it easy for teachers to share information and families to help children learn.

Elisabeth built a successful organization from an idea and a small pot of seed funding. And, very importantly, she built it because she thought she could. She had the belief in herself that psychologists call *creative self-efficacy*. Many tales of successful entrepreneurs are built around the familiar theme of the need to believe in yourself; indeed, it has become a bit of a cliché in any story of success, from business to technology to the arts.

Not obvious, however, is that you do not have to *start* with a belief in yourself. Instead, you need a growth mindset that says that creativity can be built and learned. That said, I won't be preaching self-help-y limitless potential—at 5' 1", I am not going to be a successful and creative basketball player like Caitlin Clark or Toni Kukoč no matter how much I believe in myself. But I will share science-backed strategies about how to build creative self-efficacy in your work, both for yourself and others, if you begin with the foundation of a growth mindset.

CREATIVITY CAN BE LEARNED

Elisabeth did not start out believing that she could develop a smartphone app or build a national nonprofit. But she did believe that she could learn. She did not dismiss her ideas or give up on a cause she was passionate about because she did not see herself as an entrepreneur. And she did not believe being an entrepreneur was an either/or scenario—either you are born that way or you are not. Her belief that any of these things were possible came from a *growth mindset,* or the conviction that abilities can be cultivated and enhanced by effort and practice. (Contrast this with a *fixed mindset,* which says that whatever you were born with is what you've got, and it cannot be changed.) When it comes to creativity, the conviction that you have the skills necessary to follow through on your ideas and that they can be developed is what psychologists call a *growth mindset.*

Professor Maciej Karwowski and his colleagues at the University of Wrocław studied the consequences of how we talk and think about creativity. To one group of people, they described creativity as being evident in great discoveries or inventions, in products that change how we live, or in great works of art, music, and literature. Creators who fit this description include the likes of Marie Curie, Steve Jobs, and Claude Monet—eminent, Big-C creative individuals whose names we know and celebrate.

To another group of people, they described creativity as recognizable in the original or imaginative ideas and behavior of those around us. Examples of such creativity include coming up with new solutions to problems at work, improvisation in the kitchen, amateur photography, and so on. Creators who fit this description are not famous. Instead of in the media and history books, we find these creators among our coworkers, friends, and family members. Put another way, they are little-c creative individuals.

After reading these different descriptions of creativity, participants in the study were asked about their creativity mindsets. Having a growth mindset meant agreeing that anyone can develop their creative abilities and that it is always possible to grow one's creativity, regardless of how creative one is at any time. By contrast, having a fixed mindset meant agreeing that people are either creative or not and cannot change their creativity much, no matter how hard they try. In this view, creativity is just an innate trait, and we either have it or we don't.

When people were presented with descriptions of creativity as something that radically changes culture (genius, Big-C creativity), they were more likely to agree with the fixed creativity mindset and see creativity as immutable.

It makes sense. Creative geniuses who readily come to mind seem different from the rest of us, and their accomplishments seem unreachable. It must be that they were born with extraordinary talent that the rest of us were not gifted with. We were simply not fortunate enough.

On the other hand, when made to think of creativity in terms of original and effective behavior in our everyday actions and work, people were more likely to agree with the growth mindset and see creativity as a skill that can be built with experimentation and tinkering, effort and practice. They saw creativity as attainable.

These mindsets about creativity matter. A growth mindset builds our belief that we can be creative—regardless of how much talent or ability we were born with. This "yes, I can learn to be more creative in doing this" is the basis for creative self-efficacy that Elisabeth started with. In turn, greater creative self-efficacy makes choosing creativity easier, enhances creative thinking, and ultimately helps translate creative work into real achievements.

This research has great practical importance. Educators tell stories of eminent creators when they want to inspire students. Professional conferences and corporate events alike advertise eminent keynote speakers who seem to be preternaturally gifted. The origin stories of major consumer products are shrouded in myths that portray creators as geniuses who came up with ideas and products out of thin air, through sheer force of their God-given talent. It is then not surprising that too many people doubt their ability to be creative themselves. Very few wouldn't look at those models and conclude they'd never measure up. We must be careful. Aiming to inspire, we can inadvertently discourage creative action.

"YES, I CAN" BELIEFS

Creative self-efficacy means trusting that we have the power to be creative on specific tasks in specific contexts. It is a combination of knowing ourselves and what we are capable of and having confidence in our ability to execute successfully. Importantly, these are not general beliefs, like thinking we can be creative regardless of what we are doing. I do not believe that I can be artistically creative and illustrate this book to give its lessons a visual form. But I believe I can effectively communicate what it takes to get started in creative work, persist in the process, and navigate the social side of creativity. Similarly, we can believe in our ability to be creative on one project but not another. And crucially, creative self-efficacy is not an all-or-nothing proposition. People differ in the extent to which they believe in their ability to be creative and trust it more or less at different times. Most hearteningly, it is possible to build creative self-efficacy through experience, sometimes in dramatic ways, from a generalized belief that some creative feats are beyond our capabilities (such as Elisabeth's "I am not an entrepreneur"), to gradual and limited increases in confidence ("I can do this particular creative task"), to a change in how we see ourselves ("I am an entrepreneur after all").

Organizational behavior scholars Pamela Tierney and Steven Farmer studied creative self-efficacy and how it matters for Pro-c creativity across industries and in a broad range of jobs, from machinists, tool makers, and technicians to program managers, buyers, and business analysts. They measured people's creative self-efficacy beliefs by asking them to rate how much they trusted their creative abilities, the extent to which they expected they could think in creative ways, and how confident they were in their ability to solve problems creatively at work. In addition, Tierney and Farmer asked about general job self-efficacy (how well people thought they could do their jobs overall), and they recorded the level of complexity of different jobs based on objective features of specific roles. Finally, they asked supervisors to rate each person's creativity at work. Researchers asked multiple questions to assess a range of ways creativity could be demonstrated in the workplace—how often people identified opportunities for new products or processes, came up with novel but operable ideas, tried out new ideas and approaches to problems, solved problems that eluded their colleagues, and found new uses for existing methods or equipment.

There were several key findings. First, people differ in how strongly they trust their ability to be creative at work, some being more confident than others. Second, creative self-efficacy is not the same as overall job efficacy. That is to say, even if people have a great deal of confidence in their capacity to do their job well, they might not be as confident in their ability to respond to work challenges or opportunities creatively. Third, people who had stronger creative self-efficacy tended to work in more complex jobs. These jobs are more likely to provide opportunities for creativity, whether in relation to working with data (analyzing and synthesizing), with people (negotiating or mentoring), or with things (precision work or setting up). Most importantly, the level of people's creative self-efficacy predicted supervisors' judgments of employee creativity. This is impressive when we take into account that creative self-efficacy beliefs tend to be private. Supervisors are not likely to know directly what people think of their own abilities. Rather, they are evaluating what people do and what they demonstrate in their jobs. These findings show that people's trust in their creative abilities helps them engage with work in novel ways, making creative self-efficacy visible in their actions and achievements.

Studies repeatedly show the importance of creative self-efficacy for creative action. These studies have been conducted on diverse samples, ranging from elementary school children and university students to workers across various industries—nonprofit employees, scientists in research and development, and operations and project managers, as well as inventors and entrepreneurs. And the guiding role of creative self-efficacy in creative action is clear in countries that differ in many cultural characteristics—South Korea and China, the United States and Australia, Norway and Israel, Poland and Pakistan. When scientists conducted analyses to review research across all existing studies, the relationship between creative self-efficacy and the creation of original products proved to be significant and robust.

Creative self-efficacy not only differs depending on what we might do—writing versus illustrating a book—but also fluctuates over time, even on a single project or task. At times we trust our ability to be creative, and at other times we have doubts. These fluctuations are not signs of weakness or a lack of potential and capacity to create. Rather, these variations are an integral part of the creative process.

When creativity scholars assessed participants' creative self-efficacy before the start, in the middle, and at the end of a creative project, they found a distinct pattern in how people thought about their own creativity. Creative self-efficacy was at its lowest at the beginning of the project. The fact that this is a common experience will be good news for anyone who is beset by doubts before the work has even begun. As people start a new project, they realize how challenging it will be and feel uncertain about how well they'll be able to do. Uncertainty always brings about doubt.

But there is even better news: as people begin working on the project, their creative self-efficacy grows, and it is highest at the end of the process. At that point, people can observe the fruits of their labors and assess how they performed. Having a finished project also makes it easier to trust in their creative abilities for the future. *I've done this once*, they may think, *which shows I can do it again.*

What's more, these fluctuations in how people view their creative self-efficacy throughout the creative process parallel how they experience their work emotionally. As they first approach the work, they describe primarily negative emotions, such as anxiety, anger, boredom, or shame. The opposite is true at the end of the work—people report mostly positive emotions such as enthusiasm, satisfaction, or comfort.

How much the sense of creative self-efficacy changes during a course of creative work can be rather dramatic. In a talk at the Massachusetts Institute of Technology, F. Richard Myers, NASA's James Webb Space Telescope ground segment and operations lead for Northrop Grumman, summarized the work process on the telescope and the team's collective sense of efficacy in this way:

1995–2002: We should do THIS

2003–2009: Can we do THIS?

2009: I'm ready to help do THIS

2010–2011: Hey, you can't do THIS

2012–2016: We can do THIS

2017–2018: THIS is *really* hard

2019: We got THIS

2020: YOU'VE GOT TO BE KIDDING ME

2021: We are doing THIS!

December 25, 2021: THIS is happening!

2022: We did THAT

2023–???: THIS is all yours

Knowing that creative self-efficacy ebbs and flows can be empowering. I recently spoke to a room full of creative professionals—product and event designers, creative directors, brand directors, and creative strategists. Creativity is at the core of what they do, and intuitively they are aware that confidence rises and falls. But stating explicitly that creative self-efficacy rises and falls and that doubts are inescapable reduces the stress of these fluctuations. After my talk, multiple people approached me to say how much they appreciated learning that doubts are not unusual and that we should not be surprised when we have them.

As you face creative work and especially as you embark on new projects, remember that you can build your creative self-efficacy. But you can't eliminate all the insecurities associated with creative work. Even those with very strong creative self-efficacy still occasionally experience doubts, misgivings, and apprehension. These experiences are normal and do not signal the decline of your creative abilities or put in question the future success of your work. Carry on despite these feelings, knowing that the closer you come to completing your project, the higher your creative self-efficacy will climb.

YOU CAN BUILD CREATIVE SELF-EFFICACY

For some people, creative self-efficacy comes easily. Those who favorably compare their creativity to that of others or express confidence in their creative abilities share some personality traits. They tend to be more open to new experiences; they are curious and imaginative, describe themselves as complex, and are interested in art and intellectual matters. More conscientious individuals (goal oriented, self-disciplined, ambitious) are likely to build their creative self-efficacy beliefs as they diligently immerse themselves in their work and persist in difficult goals.

Because extroverts tend to be generally more self-assured and optimistic, they are also more likely to have high creative self-efficacy. Introverts can certainly believe in their own creativity, but being more reserved and less naturally exuberant, they can be a bit subdued in their creative self-efficacy as well. Similarly, those who are more emotionally sensitive—self-conscious, timid, or tense—tend to doubt their creative potential more.

Personality is not set in stone, and it can be influenced by life experiences, such as attending university or living abroad. However, because we tend to choose where we live, what we study, and what we do, and these choices are in part based on how different options fit our personality, there is great stability in our traits by the time we reach adulthood. Psychologists tell us that personality traits create thresholds for how we think, feel, and tend to act. In other words, for people who have a pronounced trait, believing they can think and act in certain ways takes less effort. For example, those who are open to experiences tend to more easily believe that they can be original, clever, inventive, and creative; those who are more conscientious think they can master challenges that take work, dedication, and effort; those who are extroverted tend to think more positively overall; and those who tend to be nervous and anxious are less self-assured and more likely to be troubled by challenges that come their way. Each of these traits makes creative self-efficacy more or less likely.

But we are not born with or without creative self-efficacy. This is something we learn.

Often, we learn without even knowing it consciously. *The Little Engine That Could* is a children's book based on an American folktale and popularized by the 1930 retelling by Watty Piper (the pen name of Arnold Munk, who was the owner of the Platt & Munk publishing house). The book tells the story of a little train engine that takes on a challenging task of bringing toys and food to children over a mountain. The train carrying precious cargo for children breaks down, and the toys approach a series of trains in a yard for help. All with no success.

Finally, they come to a very little blue engine, which is used for switching trains. It has never done anything like carrying a load over the mountain. After some reluctance, the engine successfully makes it to the destination before the children wake.

The book is often interpreted as teaching the power of confidence and belief in oneself. But on a closer look, its lesson is much subtler. The engine does not say it *can* do the job. It is not glowingly positive, like all the messages about the power of confidence and optimism would make us think. Rather, the engine keeps telling itself, "I think I can—I think I can—I think I can." This phrase does not show certainty and a feeling of positivity or unwavering self-assurance. Instead, it shows a desire for growth. The little train is trying to prove to itself that it is able. It starts from a lack of conviction, begins trying, and finally comes to realize it is able, after successfully accomplishing something new and difficult. Even at the end, it does not exclaim with certitude and triumph in an "I knew I could" way but reflects with "I thought I could." The little engine was encouraged by the toys, started out unsure, and learned that it could, after all, by trying.

How can we take a cue from the little engine that could and build our creative self-efficacy? Social psychologists have identified four specific ways to do so: we learn that we can be creative by (1) observing what others do, (2) learning from our own experience, (3) noticing how we feel, and (4) receiving encouragement from others.

Observe What Others Do

Before we even start considering whether we can do something—writing a book or building a prototype for a new product design—we envision that someone like ourselves has the ability. And imagination is informed by experience. Moreover, the experience does not need to be our own.

We can build creative self-efficacy by observing the world and those around us. We learn from the experience of others in our immediate environment, like colleagues and coworkers or even fictional characters from books and movies. These others become role models—examples of who we could be and of what we could be capable of.

Consider entrepreneurship. It is creative by definition. Ideas for business products or services have to be conceived, developed, built, and sold to users. Growing up in the 1980s in Eastern Europe, I could not see this process of business creation around me, either as valued on a societal level or in my immediate environment. My parents were engineers and proud to work at and contribute to a very large corporation that designed and produced everything from toys to auto parts to clothing. They were certainly creative—my dad designed and built a leisure boat from scratch, and they both developed innovative products using synthetic polymers for industrial applications at work—but they were not attracted to striking out on their own or willing to take the risks this would require. I had models of professional creativity in organizations but not of entrepreneurial creativity. It never occurred to me growing up that I could be an entrepreneur.

A large study in Sweden shows just how important having close role models for entrepreneurship is. Researchers drew a random sample from Sweden's Multigenerational Register, which lists everyone born from 1932 onward, and identified individuals who were adopted. An unusual feature of the Swedish data is that children's records aim to identify both biological parents, which made it possible for researchers to analyze data about the birth parents of approximately 4,000 adopted children, as well as a comparison group of more than 400,000 nonadopted children. Finally, researchers used governmental records to determine the income, education, industry, and residence of each child, now grown up.

Analyses showed that parents had a great influence on whether children became entrepreneurs themselves. Having one entrepreneur parent raised the chance of children being entrepreneurs by an astonishing 61 percent. The findings for the adoptive children point to some influence of genetic factors; having biological parents who were entrepreneurs increased the chance of children becoming entrepreneurs by 20 percent. However, the influence of parents with whom children grew up was much stronger. With entrepreneurial adoptive parents, children's chances of being entrepreneurs increased by 45 percent.

Importantly, these results could not be explained by how researchers defined whether someone qualifies as an entrepreneur; they examined four different ways of defining entrepreneurship, and results were similar across all of them. Neither could the results be explained by children inheriting their parents' businesses, their access to capital and wealth, or whether they worked in the same industry as their parents. The only explanation for the intergenerational transmission of entrepreneurship was parental role models.

Furthermore, the data showed that we are more likely to learn from role models who are similar to us, exemplified by the fact that daughters benefited most from their mothers' entrepreneurship and sons from their fathers' entrepreneurship.

Similarities that we see between ourselves and others make them more persuasive as models. We become able to identify with them and see their successes as potentially our own. And this is not the case just in entrepreneurship. Not only did Pierre and Marie Curie's daughter Irène also become a scientist, but just like her famous parents, she won a Nobel Prize (the elder Curies got the prize in physics and their daughter received the award, along with her husband, in chemistry). Dan Brown, author of thriller novels that have sold more than 200 million copies worldwide, tells a story of how he read *The Doomsday Conspiracy* by Sidney Sheldon on a beach vacation to Tahiti and thought, "Life seemed to be trying to tell me something. I began to suspect that maybe I could write a 'thriller' of this type one day." An even more striking example is actress Whoopi Goldberg, who ran to her mother in excitement when she first saw Nichelle Nichols as Nyota Uhura on the original *Star Trek* show in the 1960s. This was the first time she encountered someone who looked like her in an important role on TV. She recognized herself, and she started to wonder whether she could do it too. Entire books could be filled with such stories, in which someone becomes convinced of their own potential by seeing role models with whom they can personally identify. When a culture provides a broad range of potential role models, it will be able to inspire the maximum number of people to believe that creativity is something they can do too.

At work, we have a ready group of potential role models. We are surrounded by colleagues, supervisors, and leaders who have things in common with us. At the minimum, we work in the same industry and at the same organization, we work on similar tasks, and we likely have some common interests.

Leaders in particular can influence the creative self-efficacy of entire teams. To study how this happens, organizational behavior researchers asked leaders how they empowered their people and studied how these behaviors translated to creative self-efficacy on individual and team levels.

The results showed that leaders' empowering actions predicted higher team creative self-efficacy. Leaders served as role models by making their own work visible and providing an example of high-level performance. At the same time, leaders supported employee initiative and showed concern for how workers would reach their goals and, in this way, demonstrated their trust in people's abilities.

Leaders' behavior did not just affect individual workers. Rather, employees tended to describe their teams as having confidence in their ability to generate novel ideas and solve problems creatively, especially when teams had to work together to achieve their goals. And higher creative self-efficacy had important consequences. Leaders who boosted team creative self-efficacy were rewarded by greater team creative performance.

Once we see others who make it clear that being creative is possible, we are more likely to start believing we can do it ourselves. When you start a new project or endeavor and are less than sure of your creative abilities (you are starting something new, after all), look around. Find your "If they can do it, so can I" person. For me, as I was growing up, this was Luida, a friend and neighbor a year older than I. I saw her successfully go through the milestones of high school and university entrances. Her example convinced me that I could do it too. And in my professional career, these role models are colleagues who often become collaborators.

The models of those already doing what we currently only aspire to do light our imagination of what we can do. Often, you will find those people around you.

Learn from Your Own Experience

The most powerful way to build creative self-efficacy is through personal experience. We learn we can be creative in the future when we realize we have already done something creative. In one study, researchers asked a large group of people about their creative achievements in different domains, as well as how much they trusted their creative abilities in general. Then, participants were given two standard creative thinking tasks: coming up with ideas for unusual uses for a brick and a tin can. Before starting the task, people indicated to what extent they believed they could generate creative solutions to the specific problems in front of them and how strongly they believed they could come up with more original ideas than others. Researchers recorded how many ideas people actually generated and, after the task, asked participants again about their creative self-efficacy for those tasks.

Researchers found that people who had more creative achievements—those who had published or sold their work, received patents, raised money to pursue their work, or been nationally recognized for their work—were more likely to have high creative self-efficacy, both in their everyday lives and in the assigned tasks in the study. Moreover, those who had greater task-specific creative self-efficacy ended up generating more ideas, and having more ideas in turn further strengthened creative self-efficacy after the task. This means that people's beliefs came from what they did on a larger scale, such as their professional achievements, as well as what they did on the smaller scale of specific tasks.

As we observe our own actions, we build a creative identity. Researchers studied this process in detail in the workplace. People who describe their work as finding new solutions to obstacles, offering fresh perspectives on old problems, and helping others develop and implement new ideas tend to adopt a creative worker identity. This means that they often think about being creative, and they see being creative as a large part of their professional identity.

Our identity becomes a self-fulfilling prophecy: we see ourselves as creative, which convinces us we can be creative on important projects or goals, which makes it easier to approach those projects, get started, and take actions to move us from ideas to achievements.

Organizational psychologists confirm what individual experience shows. When people are repeatedly surveyed, as their creative personal identity strengthens, their trust in their abilities to be creative in their jobs grows. And these are not just opinions and feelings. With greater creative self-efficacy, creative behavior at work increases, and it shows in their results.

Before Elisabeth O'Bryon saw herself as an entrepreneur who could build a successful national nonprofit organization, she started on a side project developing an app with her friends. As they made progress and attracted their first investors, Elisabeth started seeing herself not just as a creative researcher but also as someone who could create an organization that addressed the problems she was passionate about.

If you aspire to a great creative feat—striking out on your own or building a business that solves an important problem—you can build creative self-efficacy each step of the way. One step will show you that you might be able to do it; the next one and the one after that will strengthen this conviction. As creativity becomes part of who you are as an individual and you learn from progress and success, you will no longer base creative self-efficacy on each individual creative victory. It will become a part of your creative identity.

Notice How You Feel

The third way we can build our creative self-efficacy is by noticing how we feel about our creative work. When we hit a roadblock and feel frustrated and stuck, our confidence wavers. Even our daily rhythm affects our beliefs, so that people who feel more alert and energetic in the morning also think of themselves as better able to be creative in the mornings. What you need to focus on instead is the bigger picture of the changes in how you feel in the course of a creative project.

Professors Rogelio Puente-Diaz and Judith Cavazos-Arroyo conducted a series of studies to examine the role of feelings about creative work for creative self-efficacy. They asked business students to work on a creative marketing problem. The task described how Apple was about to launch the Apple TV+ streaming service, and although the organization had confidence in this new product, it also knew there were important competitors in the market, such as Netflix and Amazon Prime. The challenge for business students was to develop novel and useful marketing strategies that could be recommended to Apple.

Before participants started to work on this problem, they were asked to rate their confidence that they would create original and effective strategies. After they completed the task, participants were asked about how satisfied they were with how they did, and they rated each of their ideas from 0 (not creative at all) to 100 (very creative). Finally, participants were again asked about their creative self-efficacy. This time, however, they did not look forward and project their beliefs into the future; they looked backward and indicated how much they believed they generated good ideas to help Apple, how confident they were that their strategies would be evaluated positively, and whether they generated strategies to the best of their ability.

The researchers found that creative self-efficacy after completing creative work was based in part on people's beliefs before starting the project. Greater self-efficacy before starting work on a new project helps people feel more satisfied as they work, and these feelings in turn boost creative self-efficacy after the work is done.

Feeling more positively about one's performance also helps people see what is valuable in each of their ideas. These feelings serve as information to judge our ability to work creatively. The reasoning goes "If I am happy with what I did, I must be able to work creatively."

What we can take from this study is to be mindful of how we approach our work. Remind yourself before starting a project that creativity grows with experience. Embracing this growth mindset will boost your initial creative self-efficacy. The beginning is the point in the creative process where uncertainty tends to be the highest. Can you do it? You hope so, but this is novel territory, and you can't be sure. But perhaps you have observed someone else succeeding in similar work. Now you have a role model, and their example strengthens your belief that you can do it too. Or perhaps you can recall a time when you persisted despite your initial uncertainties, learned about what you could do by actually doing it, and felt satisfied with and proud of the results. Approaching a creative task or project with creative self-efficacy (even if you are not free of doubts), triggers a virtuous cycle of confidence, good work, and satisfaction with your results. And once this happens, you will trust that you can be creative in the future too.

Learn from What People Expect of You

In addition to observing others, learning from personal experience, and noticing how we are feeling about creative work, our creative self-efficacy is powerfully shaped by others' expectations. People's expectations influence how they act toward us, and that in turn affects how we see ourselves and what we do. In particular, those who are higher in status or to whom we look up—parents, mentors, leaders—have the strongest influence on us.

In our professional lives, supervisor and leader support boosts our belief that we can be creative at work. Supportive supervisors encourage people to set creativity and innovation goals, acknowledge and praise creative work, and express their confidence in employees' creative potential. When supervisors have such expectations, workers notice, and their own creative self-efficacy is strengthened.

We are even sensitive to changes in expectations. When researchers followed workers over six months, they found that when supervisors' expectations of employee creativity increased, employee creative self-efficacy grew too. Moreover, these changes in creative self-efficacy were related to greater creative performance at work.

People reason that there must be a basis for supervisors' and leaders' expectations. If supervisors expect them to show creativity at work, they are probably seeing them as having potential for creativity. Therefore people conclude that they should be able to rise to the occasion, solve problems creatively, and be creative in their jobs. Supervisors' creativity expectations are a form of persuasion and actively shape our own beliefs.

As you build the strong foundation of personal mindsets and beliefs to get you started on ... writing that novel, building a newsletter that informs and delights, starting a company ... or whatever your creative work and goals are, look around you. Learn from the models of people at work and in your community. If they can do it, why not you? Learn from personal experience. Of course you can do it. After all, you have done some of it already. It felt good, didn't it? And trust what people tell you when they believe in your creative potential. Their trust in you and their expectations of you are not groundless. Even if at times you do not see it yourself, chances are they see the bigger picture.

Creative self-efficacy is important in getting us started on the route of creative action. However, it is just a start. Believing in your ability to be creative is the first step, but belief alone does not guarantee creative achievement. Rather, once we get started and engage in creative action, it is crucial that we have strategies that keep us engaged in the creative process from start to finish. The second part of the book is about just that: strategies that will take us from our first steps of formulating a tentative idea all the way to accomplishing original creative feats.

PART TWO

Making Creativity Happen

4

Driven to Create: Between Interest and Constraint

Shaminda Amarakoon is the chair of technical design production at the Yale School of Drama and has a number of Broadway and off-Broadway credits to his name. The son of an engineer father and a piano teacher mother, he developed interests in both science and art at an early age. When it came time to choose a course of study for college, Shaminda's family urged him to pursue science, and he began studying biochemical engineering. It turned out this was not for him. He got into theater by way of working backstage—putting things together, learning about the properties of materials and the science of how structures had to be made—and developed a passion for the technical work of theater. This was an opportunity to bring together his interests in the sciences and engineering and his love of art.

Now Shaminda works behind the scenes on things like light design, scene design, and costuming. Often, people consider these aspects of theater purely technical, in contrast to the "creative" side of theater. But this is a narrow notion. Working within the strictures of multiple constraints, from the laws of physics to safety requirements to budgetary limits, Shaminda and his technical design team manage to bridge fantasy and reality. They do no less than bring abstract visions to life. All of which requires abundant creativity.

Shaminda's creative work is driven by two kinds of forces. First is the sense of challenge and the enjoyment he derives from devising and building the physical structures and elements required for theatrical shows—all the things we as audiences see that help create the magic of theater. And second, when it comes to specific things he and his team build, he is driven by the demands of the show's creators (their artistic vision for a particular play or musical) and the constraints of what is feasible (i.e., he must work with the materials, crew, and budget that are available to him). When he was creating the scenography for the Broadway revival of *The King and I*, for example, he had to bring to life the art designer's vision of a scene in which flowers would flow down from the ceiling. Artist sketches portrayed a whimsical tableau, as if the blooms were suspended in midair. That was one constraint, and a very challenging one. Another constraint was that anything Shaminda and his team came up with had to be hardy enough to be used eight times per week and able to withstand maintenance and repair. The creative challenge was, in Shaminda's words, to devise a marriage of the "organic" with the "technical."

Creativity scholars call these two aspects of the creative drive *motivation* and *attention* (or sometimes *focus*). Motivation is about how and why we are driven. Are we, like Shaminda, motivated by the excitement, joy, and sheer challenge of creation? Or perhaps by a desire to gain recognition, help others, or simply do what we are required to do? Attention, meanwhile, is the cognitive aspect of the creative drive. It directs us toward a specific creative goal, focusing and shaping our work. Both how we are driven and what directs our attention have important consequences for our creative work and achievement.

WHY DO WE WANT TO BE CREATIVE?

Motivation is the force that propels us toward a creative target, the reason we pursue it. Professor Teresa Amabile makes a fundamental distinction between intrinsic and extrinsic motivation in work. Those who are intrinsically motivated engage in work for two main reasons: (1) enjoyment—they love getting absorbed in what they do and relish tackling new problems; and (2) challenge—they are drawn to difficult or thought-provoking questions or problems and want to figure things out for themselves. By contrast, those who are extrinsically motivated engage in work because of the rewards and recognitions it can provide or because they want to compete and do better than others.

Creative work thrives on intrinsic motivation. However, both intrinsic and extrinsic motivation have a role to play—when deployed at the right time.

Regardless of what people do, those who achieve something original and effective tend to find their work inherently fascinating and its challenges energizing. Amabile and her colleagues studied close to 2,500 participants and asked them questions that assessed both intrinsic and extrinsic motivations, as well as their creativity at work. To hear from a wide range of people, the researchers recruited university students in a variety of majors, as well as professionals in diverse jobs, from administrative assistants to senior leaders, and in diverse industries (a national camera company, an advertising firm, a fabric mill, and a paper and printing company, among others).

They found that for students and adults alike, those who were more intrinsically motivated ended up being more creative. Intrinsically motivated art students, for example, spent more hours creating art and completed more artworks. Their instructors described them as committed to their art and as having higher potential as artists than their less intrinsically motivated peers. Amabile and her team also found that intrinsically motivated employees had more creative ideas and made greater creative contributions in their jobs than those who were not intrinsically motivated.

Part of the reason intrinsic motivation helps creative work is that it sets a virtuous chain of events in motion. The experience of enjoyment, curiosity, and challenge helps broaden people's thinking and enables them to tackle creative tasks and problems from different angles. As people make progress, their motivation is further strengthened because advancing toward our goals in itself is motivating.

Although we are pretty clear that intrinsic motivation drives and helps creativity, this does not mean that to be creative, people cannot be interested in recognition or money as well. People can love what they do, thrive on challenge, and *also* appreciate being well compensated and acknowledged for their work. Intrinsic and extrinsic motivation can have a synergistic effect on creativity. They can act together and boost each other.

Extrinsic rewards work best to drive creativity when they acknowledge the value of one's creative work. For example, we might strive for high performance reviews at work or for merit pay. When positive performance reviews explicitly praise creative accomplishments, or when merit pay is tied to creative performance, we realize that our organization values creativity. And as a result, we become more motivated to turn in creative work.

However, performance reviews that don't mention creativity and merit raises that aren't tied to creativity will not motivate people to work more creatively. If employees believe, correctly or not, that these rewards are only based on the *amount* of work they do, they are going to focus on conventional work (responding to emails quickly!) rather than engaging in creative work. If workers have doubts about whether their leaders or workplaces value creativity, they will likely decide that the risk of pursuing creative work outweighs its benefits.

Extrinsic rewards will also be more helpful during certain phases of a creative project than others. Creative work includes times that might not be fun and can even approach drudgery—dealing with administrative requirements in the process of developing new medications, going through endless revisions when writing a book, painting over a corner of a canvas until you get it just right, jumping through approval hoops when developing a new consumer product. You have to get through these times somehow. My strategy is to set up little rewards. I promise myself to celebrate with some ice cream (or cheesecake perhaps) if I complete a dreaded task without procrastination.

Develop Your Passion

If we dig beyond intrinsic and extrinsic motivation, we discover that the drive to create can have different origins. People who see work as utilitarian—as a means to an end, such as supporting a lifestyle or a family—can pursue creative work if the tasks calling for creativity are explicitly assigned to them. Those who value relationships at work and see work as a place of togetherness will be creative as a way to support others. For example, an administrative assistant who is motivated to take care of her colleagues—her work family—can come up with original ways to foster community by making personalized birthday cards and a space for team member shout-outs. These are acts of little-c, or everyday, creativity.

When craftsmanship drives creativity, people want to constantly improve and attain exceptional quality in what they do. Making exquisitely elaborate Japanese textiles has been a tradition for more than 1,000 years. Masters of this craft, like textile designer Kondaya Genbei, spend decades learning how to design and produce fabrics, starting with making the thread from precious materials like silver foil, mother-of-pearl, or lapis lazuli, to weaving the threads into intricate designs on historical looms. Each step of the process calls for immense skill. The resulting products inspire awe through the beauty, quality, and care that they exude.

Although different approaches to work can lead to creativity, some ways of approaching work—namely, drive for a cause and pursuit of a passion—are particularly likely to result in it. When creative work is driven by passion, people have a burning desire to pursue this work and are deeply committed to it. And people can be passionate about their work regardless of what they do—from forest management, to preparing the most comforting comfort food, to manufacturing sustainable footwear; from developing new medical treatments to delivering high-quality healthcare; from designing entertainment experiences to running museums; from founding companies to developing processes that make work or consumer products safer. Moreover, passionate individuals see their work not simply as something they do but as a part of who they are. For example, those who are passionate about writing do not just see themselves as people who write for a living; they see themselves as writers. Passionate business owners do not just happen to start businesses; they see themselves as entrepreneurs. Objects of passion become central to people's identity. And because our identity tends to have a great influence on our actions over time, passionate people tend to set goals and do what they love (e.g., *I will write a book* or *I will take this company public*), and they persevere in the face of obstacles.

Passion fuels the creative drive, and it has tangible consequences. Entrepreneurs who are passionate about what they do and have high creative self-efficacy are able to continue working on hard projects even when others oppose them. They do not give up, regardless of how challenging the work becomes. Some entrepreneurs are particularly passionate about inventing products or services; they love the search for new ideas and scanning the environment for new opportunities. Others are passionate about starting companies; they feel most excited about establishing new organizations and draw energy from being a company owner. In either case, these passions drive them to work through challenges and motivate them not to quit when many others would.

The flame of passion becomes obvious to those who work closely with passionate people. When employees notice founders' passion, they themselves are more enthusiastic and energized at work and have greater clarity about their responsibilities and goals. And this passion pays. Founders who are passionate about developing organizations—who are excited about finding the right people to work for a business, persuading investors, and pushing employees and themselves to grow and improve the company—become more committed to their goals, and this in turn boosts venture performance measured in terms of employee and sales growth.

Passion invigorates us and gives us an extra boost of energy when the going gets tough on creative work. This fact is often translated into advice (or a directive!) to find your passion. Such advice seems reasonable; if we aspire to creativity, and passion helps it, then we have to find and follow our passion. Right?

The problem is that the idea of finding our passion implies that it is already there, part of us, although perhaps dormant so that we are not aware of what exactly it might be. Passion is assumed to be akin to a fixed trait. When we aim to discover our passion, we are made to think that this trait will get awakened.

How we think about passion matters, and this view of passion as a trait has rather unhelpful consequences. Researchers at Stanford University found that thinking of passion as something dormant to be found within us tends to narrow our interests. Those who viewed passion as a trait and were passionate about technology and science were not interested in learning about topics in humanities and the arts and thought there were few connections between the two. The same was true of those who viewed passion as a trait and were passionate about the arts and humanities; they were less interested in learning about technology and science and saw them as unrelated to their own interests.

But creativity benefits from broad interests. Indeed, Nobel Prize laureates in the sciences are almost three times as likely as members of the general public to have arts and crafts hobbies, such as visual arts, music, woodworking, glassblowing, or performing arts. The narrowing of interests in those who see passion as a fixed trait ends up limiting creativity.

Those who view passion as a trait also tend to expect they will have unfaltering and boundless motivation for their work. They do not realize that pursuing a passion is not always fun or smooth. Relatedly, when they experience difficulty, their interest is likely to diminish.

Rather than urging people to *discover* their passion, we should inspire them to *develop* a passion. Shaminda was not always passionate about technical design in theater. He had interests in both the arts and the sciences. By exploring the backstage side of theater, he developed a new passion that led him to much creative success. I started my career as a creativity scholar passionate about basic scientific research. Only after I received a grant to create programs that teach creativity and emotion skills and saw their impact did I develop a passion for using the lessons of creativity science to develop people's capacities to make creativity happen.

Steve Jobs was already passionate about electronics when he dropped out of Reed College after his first semester. Curious after seeing an ad on campus, he decided to take a calligraphy class. He learned about typefaces and about spacing between different combinations of letters. And he became passionate about the historical and aesthetic subtlety he learned. In his 2005 commencement speech at Stanford University, he recalled that at the time he did not foresee any application of this knowledge. Yet, when he and Steve Wozniak started Apple, he poured what he learned into the personal computers they designed. And we have to thank Jobs's openness to developing new passions for the wealth of fonts available on our computers today.

What this research means is that you do not have to put pressure on yourself, on those you supervise, or on your children to find a passion. Rather, we can develop passions by following our interests and seeing where they lead. Approach them with a "Why not?" attitude.

Curious about AI prompt engineering? Take that webinar. A relative has invited you to go bird watching? Even if you have never thought of doing such a thing before, try it. You are not limited to a single passion in life, and inspiration can come from the most unexpected of places. Unlike what all that "find your passion" advice implies, you can develop various passions at different times in your life. Or you can develop multiple passions simultaneously, as is the case with creative polymaths from Leonardo da Vinci (painter and draughtsman, scientist and engineer) to Benjamin Franklin (diplomat and statesman, writer and printer, scientist and inventor), from Brian May (Queen guitarist and accomplished astrophysicist) to Jaylen Brown (creative basketball player for the Boston Celtics, social justice leader, and education advocate). If you do so, you are not diminishing any particular passion but enriching them all, just as Steve Jobs did in bringing his love of typefaces to Apple.

One final cautionary note about passion: It might seem counterintuitive, but it *is* possible to have too much passion. Robert Vallerand at the University of Quebec showed that passion can turn into obsession. Such obsessive passion means that the urge for an activity is so strong that people cannot help themselves from doing it, they have difficulty imagining life without the activity, they are emotionally dependent on it, and their mood is based on their ability to do it.

When you become obsessively passionate about something, you can still perform at a high level. But it comes at a price to physical and mental health. The nonstop activity fueled by obsessive passion—after hours, on weekends, during vacations—can lead to greater conflict and burnout, which in the long run hurts the creative performance that it once fueled. There might be times that require a certain level of obsession in creative work, such as when you're about to launch a product or finish a book or get a project over the finish line. To prevent the dark side of passion from taking over, you will have to balance these times of furious activity with calmer times. Downtime refills the creative well.

Pursue a Cause

Creative work can be driven by a cause—the desire to help address social problems, small and big, serve underserved or neglected groups, and contribute to making a better and more just world. Social entrepreneurs start for-profit companies or nonprofit organizations with the mission to advance the common good and ameliorate social ills. They are not disinterested in company earnings, but they also, or primarily, want to contribute to solving problems such as ending hunger, providing equitable access to quality education, preventing disease and increasing availability of medical care, or addressing environmental issues.

When Blake Mycoskie visited Argentina in 2006, he witnessed profound poverty just outside the capital. As a serial entrepreneur, he directed his desire to help into founding a start-up. Having seen the pain of poor children who ended up barefoot and suffering from blisters, sores, and infections, he wanted to help provide shoes for as many children as he could. He founded Shoes for Better Tomorrows, later shortened to TOMS, with an innovative business model—for every pair sold, one pair would be donated to those in need. The first shoes were based on a design traditionally worn by rural workers in Argentina and manufactured locally. Since then, production has expanded into Ethiopia, Kenya, India, China, and Haiti. More than 100 million shoes had been donated by 2020, and TOMS inspired other companies, such as Warby Parker eyeglasses and Better World Books, to adopt the "buy one to donate one" model.

Starting companies is not the only way to help others or address social issues. Psychology professor Marie Forgeard studied professional artists and scientists and found that they often described being motivated to help people understand others' perspectives, worked to provide a more accurate and richer understanding of reality to benefit society at large, and hoped their work would have positive effects on the lives of others.

We just have to look at prominent artists and scientists for examples. Jacob Lawrence wanted to depict the lived experiences of African American workers during the Great Migration from the (largely) rural South to the industrial North and Midwest in the first half of the twentieth century. He painted sixty panels that documented the realities of the migration, from its origins to its consequences: from the difficult conditions people were leaving, such as hunger brought by price increases during World War I and the boll weevil's devastation of cotton crops, to the act of leaving on crowded trains, to the overcrowded housing and race riots in migrants' new home cities. He created great art and documented the realities of the migration. Or consider Albert Chi, a trauma surgeon, professor of medicine, and biomedical engineer, who is driven by the desire to improve the lives of people with traumatic injuries. In his TEDx talk, he related that one of his personal career goals is to create advanced prosthetic technology that is affordable and accessible to all who need it.

Finding your cause does not require you to single-handedly solve major world problems. Working to improve the everyday lives of those around you fits the bill too. I noticed that the science of creativity is not translated into forms digestible by people who are interested in how to build their own and others' creativity but lack the technical background to read research reports and articles. And this motivated me to share the scientific insights and help you learn what you need to know to be more creative. You might notice your employees' frustrations with the existing workflow and be motivated to redesign it. Or you could work to develop products that will make people's lives a little more pleasant or efficient. When you find your cause, it will sustain you through the long road of creative work.

FIND CREATIVE FOCUS

To start and sustain creative work, motivation is necessary but not sufficient. The energy of motivation needs to be directed and focused in original and effective ways. This direction and focus are challenging and not obvious in creative work. We start with a blank canvas or a block of marble, a clean white board or a new computer document. As much as the slogan "possibilities are endless" sounds appealing in the abstract, attempting to start work with endless possibilities can be paralyzing.

Research shows that when we face a completely open-ended task, we start with what is familiar. The trouble is that this is not a way to creativity. We need to direct our thinking and actions toward a more original path. One of the seeming paradoxes of creative work is that we do better when we are directly asked and expected to be creative and when we focus our thinking by constraining it.

Expect Creativity

When creativity is *expected*—when we expect it from ourselves or others expect it from us—it can make our jobs as creators a little easier. An explicit requirement to be creative moves our thinking about creativity from an optional "nice to have if possible" to a goal we purposefully pursue. And rather than feel like a burdensome "should," required creativity has a way of giving us permission to create—to devote time and energy to creative work and the exploration of new possibilities. Knowing that creativity is expected can also help quiet the internal monologue that wonders whether others—peers, coworkers, team members, leaders—will react negatively to our original ideas and solutions or our decision to pursue them.

In the workplace, creativity is often expected. A project manager asks a designer to create a product with a particular purpose (an ergonomic car entertainment system, perhaps?). A specialist at a marketing agency is assigned the task of naming a particular product. A senior leader who joins an established company inherits challenges and problems and must devise novel solutions for each of them. As the head of technical production design, Shaminda has a mandate to create scenography for various productions, which requires him to direct his attention to the demands of each specific play and the particular vision of each artist.

When explicitly asked to focus on being creative on a particular task, people rise to the occasion. In one experiment, creativity scholars at the University of North Carolina wanted to see how people performed on creative thinking tests when asked to focus on the quantity (as is common in brainstorming sessions) versus the creativity of their ideas. Participants were asked to think of possible uses for two common objects, a rope and a box. Researchers told subjects, "The goal is to come up with creative ideas, which are ideas that strike people as clever, unusual, interesting, uncommon, humorous, innovative, or different" and that "it is more important to come up with creative ideas than a lot of ideas." Others were told simply that the goal was to devise "as many uses as possible." All responses were then evaluated for creativity by independent judges.

The results showed that what people were required to do made a significant difference. When directly asked to be creative, they ended up thinking more creatively. Having the explicit instruction to focus on creativity meant that people could be intentional and purposefully direct their attention toward uncommon and clever answers. What's more, there was an added benefit for emotionally sensitive and self-conscious individuals: being explicitly asked to be creative alleviated their worry about what good answers to open-ended questions might be and removed ambiguity from the task.

This might seem surprising. Facilitated brainstorming sessions often instruct participants to focus not on the quality of ideas but on the quantity. Quality, we are told, will come as a by-product of quantity. But creativity science tells us this is not necessarily the case. We will be more creative if we expect and aim for creativity. We can place these expectations on ourselves. At work, they are often placed on us, but the result is the same: we will be more creative if we are expected to be creative. And if you are a leader, those you work with will be more creative if you ask them to aim to be so.

In addition to aiming for creativity, we should expect that creative endeavors will take time. If we spend more time and effort on a creation, more original ideas will arise. The trouble is that people tend to believe that their first ideas are the most creative ones.

Professors of organizational behavior Brian Lucas and Loran Nordgren conducted a series of studies in which participants were given a problem requiring creative thinking and asked to come up with multiple solutions. Lucas and Nordgren asked some participants to predict whether their early or later ideas would be more creative, and they asked others to look back at their ideas after they'd completed the creative thinking task. Regardless of how they set up the experiments, the results were the same. People thought their most creative ideas came early on, but outside observers consistently rated the ones that came later as the most creative.

The implication of this research is that we systematically underestimate the importance of effort, time, and persistence in creative work. We've all likely taken part in work meetings in which we were asked for quick creative ideas, and some of the ideas that emerged might seem good. But we should also recognize that if we do not allow for more time, those ideas will not be as creative as they could be. The most difficult advice of this book is probably that you should find the time for creative work, despite the time pressures we are all under.

Constrain Your Work

The most powerful way to focus our creative drive is by imposing constraints on what we do. This seems counterintuitive. We tend to believe that creativity requires unbridled freedom. In a study conducted in six countries, 70 percent of participants said that people are most creative when they have full freedom in their actions. But it turns out this isn't the case.

We may chafe against the notion of constraints. They impose conditions or restrictions on our thought or behavior, either by prohibiting something or putting stipulations on what we can do. Designers have to incorporate into their work specific requirements given by clients. Journalists follow assignments and are limited by the form and style of media for which they work. Software and product engineers need to include features that users have come to expect or enjoy. Even artists are often constrained by the audience for their work, be it an individual who commissions a particular piece or a gallery owner who looks for specific kinds of pieces. Perhaps the most famous work of art of all time, Leonardo da Vinci's *Mona Lisa*, is believed to have been a commissioned portrait of the Italian noblewoman Lisa del Giocondo. And Pablo Picasso's *Guernica*, the most celebrated antiwar work of art in history, was commissioned by the Spanish Republican government. Da Vinci was constrained in his choice of subject matter. We do not know whether, if given the choice, he would have painted a portrait at all or would have painted Lisa del Giocondo specifically. And although Picasso was not limited in the particular subject, he was constrained in having to portray the horror of war.

Constraints also direct creative work by pushing us to consider ideas or approaches that we otherwise would not. Because when people are left to their own devices, they tend to look for what is easy, "unrestrained" work is less likely to be original. If something is easy and can be devised quickly, it will be obvious to many and therefore not surprising or unique.

Imagine setting out to design a toy that children ages five to eleven would enjoy. Researchers assigned this task to designers to see who would develop the most creative toys, the people who had greater creative freedom or those who had to work within constraints.

All designers were given twenty shapes that they could incorporate into the new toy. Then, some were asked to choose five shapes from this set; others were asked to roll a twenty-sided die and had to use a random set of five shapes determined by the roll. Some people in each group were told that they should use all five shapes in their design, and others were told that they could use either some or all of the shapes. After the participants completed their designs, a panel of experienced judges evaluated the creativity of each new toy.

The results contradicted what we intuitively think we want and what we think works best. The designers who had the freedom to choose the shapes they would use created the least creative toys. Those who had to use randomly selected shapes but could pick whether to use some or all of them fared a bit better. But the designers who had no choice in what shapes to use and had to use all those they were given ended up producing the most creative toys.

Research shows that having constraints results in more creative products, no matter what kind of creative work one is pursuing. When constraints introduce something unexpected (for example, to write a few lines for a birthday card containing the word "carrot"), they push us toward original ideas because obvious ideas do not fit the bill.

When we create without constraints, on the other hand, it turns out that our tendency is to rely on what is familiar. If we are drawing an alien, for example, most of us automatically think of creatures with arms, legs, trunks, and heads. Perhaps their eyes are bigger, or they do not have five fingers, but they tend to be rather humanlike. Now imagine being asked to draw an alien with no bodily means of locomotion. Some of us would come up with a creature who floats through their environment, some would create a technology-enabled form of transportation for our alien, and still others would come up with an entirely novel and unexpected conception of alien life. A constraint that forces us into unfamiliar territory unlocks greater creativity.

The practical implication of all this research is clear. You can purposefully leverage the power of constraints. This is what the composer Igor Stravinsky referred to when he said, "The more constraints one imposes, the more one frees oneself. And the arbitrariness of the constraint serves only to obtain precision of execution." What artists and other creators who impose constraints on themselves have discovered is a method for focusing their attention away from limitless possibilities, which we can experience as overwhelming and which can lead us to opt for easily imaginable solutions.

In imposing limits, you need to be careful that they help focus you and challenge you to direct attention in new and unexpected directions. Not all constraints are created equal. Sometimes that means questioning existing constraints and imposing new ones. When nineteenth-century artists limited their work to representing reality, they limited how original they could be. Only when Hilma af Klint and Vassily Kandinsky decided to remove the constraint of having to depict real objects, places, or people did something dramatically new emerge—and abstract art was born. Even if you do not start a new art movement, constraints will help you move beyond the customary and predictable and venture into original territory.

Of course, you don't want too much of a good thing—too much constraint becomes overly frustrating. You have to find that sweet spot between beneficial and, yes, liberating constraints and those that crush your creative drive. The problem is that where this spot lies isn't always obvious. You will discover that finding it is largely a matter of trial and error. I will not sugarcoat it. There will be times when you get frustrated and possibly feel discouraged. Along the long road to creative success, you will need skills to manage these feelings so that you can take the edge off and they do not control you.

Make Plans, but Watch Out That They Do Not Control You

Creative drive needs plans to focus and give direction to our work. When we make plans, we are approaching work with a notion of how to reach a target. The act of formulating a plan puts us in a doing mindset—we turn the creative drive into driving to a goal. The goal is no longer an abstraction, an idea that we want to work on, but something we can achieve if we put in the necessary work.

Creative plans, though, aren't roadmaps. This becomes clear when we contrast them with plans for accomplishing other kinds of goals. Consider a goal to take up running for exercise. Some years ago, I enrolled in a "couch potato to 5K" program at a local running store. It was a structured program of running three days a week in slowly increasing increments. At first, we ran ten one-minute intervals broken by one-minute walking periods, and by the end of the program we built stamina for thirty minutes of uninterrupted running. The plan for how to get from a decision to run a 5K race to actually doing it was very precise. People only had to show up and stick with it. Grit in action. As the famous Nike slogan says, *Just Do It.* "Just" does not mean that it is easy, though. There is a lot of inertia in human behavior. It is rarely convenient to show up, and April in New England, where I live, does not exactly have the most pleasant weather.

Unlike my decision to take up running, which involved a clear plan and following a set of predefined steps, creative work tends to be ill-defined. That does not mean that the desired end is not clear—complete a book, develop a new mobile phone app, design a new kind of museum. Rather, this means that there is no clear path or set of steps that can be mapped up front and followed from start to finish with no deviation. It is not obvious where to start or in which direction to go. There is no off-the-shelf template to follow. You, as a creator, will have to draw out and develop the specific directions for your own path.

It would be nice if a guide could give us turn-by-turn instructions on how to navigate our way from idea to finished product, but in the case of creative work, such directions would not be effective. The route to a creative end will always have unexpected closures that require detours, unforeseen obstacles and traffic jams, and plenty of ambiguous road signs. Our turn-by-turn instructions might get us started, but we will inevitably get lost and delayed somewhere along the way.

The key to planning for creative work is to balance finding focus and maintaining openness. We start creative work with an idea, but in the course of working on it, new ideas tend to emerge, perhaps based on feedback or on learning something unexpected. Our plan has to enable a way to give such ideas a chance. Throughout the project, we need to be able to explore or test ideas before fully committing to them. In a study of education leaders I conducted to examine this process, one innovator described it best: "I love to create outlines toward reaching goals. Yet, I stay general and avoid rigid tasks." Flexibility in planning and managing our progress toward goals contributes to more creative action and to the greater creativity of our eventual products.

Psychologists have studied what kinds of plans are the best tools for creative work. Studies of college students showed that the writing they produced after being instructed to create outlines was of higher quality than their writing without outlines. Importantly, just having a mental outline is sufficient; having a formal written outline is not necessary. Outlines free our mental resources from having to consider what to do and how, while also leaving a door open for changing and evolving ideas. They offer that perfect balance between structure and flexibility that benefits creativity.

Another study compared the effect of specific kinds of plans on creative problem-solving. Researchers asked different groups of people to (1) create a chart and timeline listing detailed steps to be taken, (2) base their plans on recalling and applying personal experiences that fit the problem, or (3) anticipate derailing events. Each of these approaches to planning how to make progress on a goal was compared to others and to a condition of not making explicit plans.

The results showed that relying on past experiences and creating detailed task lists did *not* lead to original and high-quality solutions. What proved most helpful was focusing on potential obstacles that could threaten progress toward goals.

As you make plans, remember to make them flexible. Creativity cannot be reduced to a neat set of steps, and attempting to do so will be trying to fit a square peg into a round hole. You might force it, but your original goal of creativity will not be fulfilled. Instead, try to anticipate what might go wrong and where. You might not foresee all challenges, but you will build in sufficient flexibility to help your creative work.

MANAGING THE CREATIVE DRIVE

The creative drive that takes us to successful creative performances and products follows the Goldilocks principle. Scientists borrowed the folktale about a curious little girl, Goldilocks, who strays deep into the forest and comes across a hut just as she gets tired and hungry. The hut is empty but has three settings at the table. In one, the food is too hot, in another it's too cold, and in the third, it's just right. After she eats from the just-right bowl, she finds the bedroom. One of the beds is too small, and one is too big, but the third is just right for a nap. The Goldilocks principle asks us to examine what is too cold or hot, too small or too big in our creative drive. Creativity will be most likely to flourish when we do not aspire to too small or too big, when we do not go for something that is so simple as to be commonplace or so difficult as to be unmanageable.

The most successful creative drive unites the challenge of striving for an original achievement with the skills to match the challenge. The magic of this match is that it makes people more likely to experience flow—a psychological state in which we lose a sense of self-consciousness, time seems to fly, and our actions appear to cascade one after another. When we are in flow, we are fully absorbed in what we are doing.

Psychologist Mihalyi Csikszentmihalyi, who first described the flow experience and pioneered the study of this state, interviewed more than ninety highly creative individuals, from innovators to artists to scientists who changed how we understand the world (including fourteen Nobel Prize winners), and found that they often experienced flow in their work. Not only did flow help them bring ideas to life, but the experience was also rewarding in itself. These exceptionally creative individuals pursued the flow state over and over, and they experienced it routinely. Flow both puts us in a psychological state of ideal focus and boosts our motivation for future creative work.

Creative drive that leads to more flow in Big-C creators also boosts daily creativity in Pro-c creators. Pushing yourself to the outer edges of challenges you can meet will be especially helpful when you are implementing ideas and need intense focus paired with a sense of clarity and control. At those times, you will benefit from creating long chunks of time for uninterrupted work.

The challenge of the creative drive is to strike a balance. The line between optimal and overwhelming constraints and challenges is not clear. Developing passions but not allowing them to take over our lives is an added difficulty, and we need to manage our creative drive so that it stays in the Goldilocks zone. The upcoming chapters of this book examine the emotional side of creative work and provide insights into how to harness and how to manage the emotional roller coaster of creative work.

Problem Finding:
From Inspiration to Exploration

When we learn of new inventions, reflect on the products we enjoy or that impact our lives, or wonder about how unimaginably complex systems are created (*How do tens of thousands of daily flights around the world get scheduled?*), the question we usually ask is, "How did they think of that?" We want to know who came up with these incredible ideas and how.

However, creators and scientists who study creativity agree that asking about idea generation is not the most relevant question for understanding successful creativity. Rather, the key to creativity is what scientists call *problem finding*—the process of asking questions, identifying opportunities for creation or examination, and framing and reframing questions in ways that interrogate existing ways of doing something and exploring new ones. "Problem" in the context of creativity is not a nuisance or an obstacle, the way we use that word in everyday discourse. Rather, a problem is something that gets us going, a question that drives our work. It is a particular approach to a topic. The "finding" means that there are multiple ways to pose a problem. Problems come in different levels of generality. The most general problems are not too helpful because they do not direct the search for solutions, and we have to find a more fruitful route.

Albert Einstein and Leopold Infeld wrote, "The formulation of a problem is often more essential than its solution, which may be merely a matter of mathematical or experimental skill. To raise new questions, new possibilities, to regard old questions from a new angle, requires creative imagination and marks real advance in science." What these giants in the world of physics were describing regarding the nature of scientific inquiry applies to other fields too, from fashion design to the development of new technologies, from art to business innovation.

The term "problem finding" can seem counterintuitive. We think of problems as something given to us, and we react to them by generating ideas and potential solutions. It makes sense that we would think this way, because school and work—the contexts in which we spend the majority of our time—operate by assigning us problems to solve. At school, we are asked to solve problems in math, answer specific questions when discussing literature (remember those book reports?), and demonstrate different scientific phenomena. At work, we are often assigned projects that will solve a problem for our bosses, customers, or clients. Even when psychologists first started developing tests of creative thinking, they took a similar approach of presenting problems to people and observing how they solved them.

But even with presented problems, we have to find an angle or a perspective to take. This is because creative problems usually start out broad. Imagine being tasked with creating digital training that was previously only delivered in person to build in-demand work skills or with developing a new algorithm to recommend podcasts to users. Such problems are very much like what Whitney Wolfe Herd had to contend with when she set out to create a new kind of dating app. A very broad problem. The creativity behind the Bumble app, which she founded, came from a particular framing of that initial goal: *What if an app was designed around the experience of women?* Other ways of framing the problem could also be imagined, such as tailoring an app to a specific group of potential users or devising a new way to navigate through profiles. Different ways of framing problems will result in different products, some likely more creative than others.

Psychologists use problem finding as an umbrella term that refers to two groups of thinking processes. The first is *problem identification*. Problem identification entails discovering or noticing problems, even when others in the same situation do not notice them or choose to disregard them. Often, identifying one problem leads to another, one project growing into another. When we identify a problem, we tend to feel inspired by the experience of noticing it and then inspired to act on the problem. Dr. Kati Kariko identified the study of mRNA as her problem. Having noticed that these molecules could be used to instruct cells to make any protein, she was on fire with inspiration for pursuing new applications, eventually leading her to foundational research making mRNA COVID-19 vaccines possible (and earning her the Nobel Prize in medicine in 2023).

The second thinking process is *problem construction*, or exploration and experimentation to determine how to frame the problem. It goes from deciding (or being asked) to paint a still life to exploring what objects will be part of the painting and how they will be put together into a unique whole. Even if we don't need to identify a new problem because it has been given to us, we have to construct the problem specifics.

IDENTIFY PROBLEMS: FIND YOUR INSPIRATION

Sylvia Baer is a college English professor. She noticed that students in her women's literature class did not appreciate the work of Emily Dickinson. Sure, they could analyze it formally, but they did not get it viscerally in a way we do when we are touched by poetry. Sylvia identified a problem that she did not want to let go: helping students connect with the poet. Dickinson's work examines, as Sylvia put it, "what it is like to be inside of your own brain," and she was convinced that with the right approach, students who are young adults developing their own sense of personal identity could come to relate to Dickinson's poems.

Identifying a problem worth pursuing is inspiring, and often suggests potential solutions all on its own. The problem Sylvia identified was that her students could not personally relate to the poet's work. She reasoned that we become able to relate to others when we get to know them as individuals. And a spark of an idea was born. "I just decided one day to walk in as Emily Dickinson," she told me. "I found a cheap wig. I put on an all-white, long gown. I was delighted to have visitors."

The students loved it, and Sylvia started exploring and refining her role. She had a friend create a replica of the dress Dickinson frequently wore, and she invested in a real wig. In the classroom, Sylvia remained completely in character as Emily Dickinson. She read poems, talked with students about them, and spoke about her brother and his mistress and the latest events in nineteenth-century Amherst, Massachusetts. For the first time, Sylvia's students saw a real person rather than a disembodied writer from a distant time. Emily Dickinson's poems came to life for them in a new way—as did the poet herself. "My students felt like they actually met Emily Dickinson," Sylvia said. "Words matter when they're connected to a person."

In Sylvia's case, the problem was there—it existed in the world—and she identified it as worth solving. Chances are that her students were not unique in being unable to intuitively relate to Emily Dickinson's poetry. What was unique was Sylvia's decision that this problem was worth approaching creatively. Doing so was not required for her to do her job of teaching students about the poet's work. She wanted to go deeper. And this problem needed a creative solution.

Where to Find Inspiration?

Problem identification means recognizing that something has to be done or could be done (*Ah, here is a challenge to take on*). The first rule of identifying problems is showing an interest. Luckily, this is not hard because when it comes to creativity, identifying a problem feels inspiring. Sylvia noticed her students' difficulty in relating to Emily Dickinson. She was bothered by it but also curious and determined. And she was inspired to do something about it. Similarly, artists identify their problems by engaging with the art of others, by traveling, and by learning about the world. In-depth studies of the creative process show that artists spend much of their time in a receptive state that enables them to notice problems that others simply don't see.

In *A Treatise on Painting*, Leonardo da Vinci described finding inspiration all around him. "I will not omit to introduce among these precepts a new kind of speculative invention, which though apparently trifling, and almost laughable, is nevertheless of great utility in assisting the genius to find variety in composition," he wrote. "By looking attentively at old and smeared walls, or stones and veined marble of various colors, you may fancy that you see in them several compositions, landscapes, battles, figures in quick motion, strange countenances, and dresses, with an infinity of other objects. By these confused lines the inventive genius is excited to new exertions."

Problems do not come from all around us only for artists. Scientists build on their own observations, identifying problems worth pursuing in the inconsistencies or gaps in research that came before them, in what they read in articles or books, and in discussions with colleagues. They present their work to other scientists, informally in lab meetings and formally at conferences, and the questions that emerge from the ensuing discussions lead to identifying other problems.

Entrepreneurs identify problems by noting the frustrations or unmet needs of life—each one presents an opportunity to create products and services that will make life easier or more convenient. Apoorva Mehta disliked everything about the grocery shopping experience—from the fluorescent lights to the organization of the stores to the checkout lines. All of it was a problem to him. And he realized he wasn't the only one who thought so. He identified a problem that could and should be solved and was inspired to create the grocery delivery service Instacart.

Doctoral student Kaile Smith and professor of psychology Jennifer Drake at the City University of New York studied more than 300 people, half of whom were immersed in creative work, either professionally or as hobbyists (let's call them creative doers), and half of whom were not routinely creative. For two weeks, the researchers sent the participants daily surveys asking how much inspiration they experienced, what inspired them, and what they did with their feelings of inspiration.

They found that those who were immersed in creative work got inspired more strongly and more often than those who were not creative doers. They were open to noticing what others might not. And once they noticed something inspirational, creative doers responded by doing and making. In other words, they did not just *feel* inspired, they *acted* on the feeling. They also intentionally sought out inspiration by proactively engaging with the world with curiosity—reading, observing, discussing—and then put effort into developing those sparks into something concrete.

One reason creative individuals experience more inspiration is that identifying one problem and working on it leads them to identify new problems. News of Sylvia's innovative teaching method got around, and when a local newspaper published an article about it, Sylvia realized her act had struck a chord. She then identified another problem—making Dickinson's poetry accessible more widely, beyond the confines of a college classroom. Her solution was to develop and act in a play based on Dickinson's life, just her onstage with a basket of props and poems. Some months of work later, she performed at colleges, in theaters, and even at a military base, in front of hundreds of officers and their spouses.

Sylvia's life exemplifies what Columbia University psychologist Howard Gruber called *networks of enterprise*. Identifying one problem spurs a task, a task grows into a project, one project inspires another, and then everything together grows into a lifelong network of enterprises. She identified the problem of helping her students relate to the work of Emily Dickinson. The task of bringing the poet to life in her own classroom grew into bringing Dickinson's poetry to others outside the college where she teaches. The problem of bringing poetry into people's lives found other outlets too—Sylvia shares her own poems with children at Halloween (along with candy), she translates poetry, and she has curated a Yale University exhibit of the haiku poet and photographer Roberto Fernandez. Her life work is organized around nurturing others' creative endeavors in diverse ways, spanning multiple enterprises, from teaching, to being the founding editor of an interdisciplinary journal in the humanities and social sciences, to founding and curating a New Jersey gallery that hosts multimedia artists.

The realization that identified problems can become projects and that projects can grow into enterprises can be liberating. It means that you do not have to plan out what you are going to do five or ten years from now. Indeed, if your goal is creativity, you are unlikely to be able to plan in such a way. Instead, you need to pose more questions.

Create Your Luck

Problem identification might seem unimpressive, even obvious. Sylvia did not have to do much to identify the problem of students not appreciating the poetry of Emily Dickinson. The problem was right there in front of her. But often we do not see problems and opportunities that are staring us in the face.

British psychologist Richard Wiseman devised a clever experiment for a BBC show featuring two people, one who described himself as lucky (a "good things happen to me" type) and one who described himself as unlucky (a "good things happen to others" type). Each person was asked to go into a coffee shop and order a drink. Unbeknownst to them, Wiseman had prepared two pieces of good fortune: the first was a £5 bill he placed on the pavement just outside the coffee shop, and the second was having a successful businessman seated at the counter.

The self-described "unlucky" person was focused on the task. He entered the coffee shop, placed the order, enjoyed his drink, and left. He did not notice the £5 bill, and though he sat right next to the businessman, he did not start a conversation with him, or anyone else for that matter. When asked about his experience later, he said going to the coffee shop was uneventful.

The "lucky" person, however, looked around, noticed the money, and picked it up. Feeling cheered, he started a conversation with the businessman and ended up leaving the coffee shop with his card. When asked about his experience, he spoke of good luck and a possible job opportunity.

Luck, as it happens, is like problem identification: both require that we first *notice* the bit of good fortune and then follow through and take advantage of the opportunity.

Some enterprises get started through serendipity—seemingly lucky chances. But, of course, luck is not enough. As French chemist and microbiologist Louis Pasteur said, "In the fields of observation, chance favors only the prepared mind." In terms of contemporary psychology, the prepared mind is one that is receptive and open to new experiences.

A different version of this idea says that chance favors the bold. And both versions are true. To notice an unexpected opportunity, the mind needs to be open and receptive, and to turn it into something creative, we need courage to accept the risk inherent in taking on something new. Through openness to new experiences and possibilities, coupled with bold action, we can create our own luck.

To be more like the self-described lucky person in the BBC documentary, you need to be aware of your surroundings—the less we operate on autopilot, the more we will notice problems. Professor Matthijs Baas and his colleagues at the University of Amsterdam found that the ability to observe and notice features of our thoughts and feelings and the world around us is related to more flexible and original thinking, more creative action, and greater creative achievement. Because people vary in their observational ability, researchers wondered if training through daily meditations that help people observe the present moment and become aware of their thoughts, feelings, and bodily sensations would also lead to greater creativity. And indeed it did.

Although a meditation practice can help, it is not the only way to make yourself receptive to noticing what is around you. Consider the groundbreaking art of Salvador Dalí. He collected art, was fascinated by philosophy, the (then) emerging science of psychology, and the practice of psychotherapy. Learning about these intellectual disciplines provided problems for his art: How could he make the confusion of dreams vividly visible? How could he evoke the terror of death and decay? He would come back again and again to these problems and find his solutions in the repeated use of images of melting clocks, sex, and insects.

After World War II, Dalí found artistic problems in new theories in physics and molecular biology, as well as in his Catholicism. He was deeply shaken by the atomic bomb dropped on Hiroshima and later remarked, "Thenceforth, the atom was my favorite food for thought." It became his main problem to explore in art. Dalí subscribed to scientific journals and had a library of books covering scientific disciplines from evolution to quantum mechanics, many of which feature his notes and observations in the margins. Nuclear physics provided a new problem: how to show matter as made up of empty space interspersed with subatomic particles. His solutions were paintings composed of spheres or dematerializing objects.

You will notice more when you do what not just Dalí but other artists, scientists, and writers do: read, watch movies, listen to and wonder about stories, talk to colleagues, attend professional events, and engage more broadly than focusing on your immediate task, work, or interest.

Stockpile Inspiration

The realities of work ask for creativity on demand, which means a readily available source of problems. Although problems can come from anywhere and at any time, there is no guarantee that they will come exactly when we need them. Scientists might come across a call for research proposals on specific topics on which they are not currently working, designers can get approached by clients with a particular need, and theater producers look for particular kinds of plays.

To deal with the trouble of identifying problems on demand, creators tend to stockpile problems or sparks of inspiration that come at different times (at the discretion of the muses). They write them down in notebooks and computer files, or they collect physical samples, such as scraps of fabric or colored tiles, that could be used directly in their future work. Problems or inspiration that emerge during one project can end up being used in another one. Leonardo da Vinci's notebooks are full of drawings that he later used in paintings, observations, and diagrams related to his inventions and devices.

Of course, you do not have to carry around notebooks. The early twenty-first century brought pocket-sized computers into our lives. Author and podcaster John Green in his book *The Anthropocene Reviewed* describes how he uses the *Notes* app on his iPhone. He writes whatever strikes him as interesting or important in a moment. Looking back at the notes, he is not always clear about what he was thinking at the time or what relevance he imagined his impromptu notes would have at a later time. For instance, in 2011 he wrote, "They're painting the ceiling of the Rijksmuseum?" but later could not recall why he jotted that down or what he intended to do with it. Perhaps he'd originally intended it to be a line or a plot point in a story, but it never became one. Other lines were inspirational. In 2016, he wrote, "No bright line between imagination and memory." That line not only became part of his best-selling 2017 book *Turtles All the Way Down* but inspired its plot about, in Green's words, "a kid who is constantly remembering what she imagined and imagining what she remembers."

When you write or otherwise record questions or bits of inspiration, some of them are likely to find a home in your work. This can happen shortly after the feeling of inspiration strikes, as with Green's line in *Turtles All the Way Down*, or it can happen much later. In one study on stockpiling inspiration, an architect described coming across a pink terrazzo tile she found striking. But it did not fit any of her current projects. Only years later, as she worked on a new hostel, did she think of it again. It took repurposing, but the tile found its home. Don't worry if the problems you identify do not find immediate use. Inspiration does not have an expiration date.

CONSTRUCTING PROBLEMS: PLAYING WITH INSPIRATION

Whether we identify a problem that inspires us or are given a problem, how creative our work on it will be depends on how we think about it. What aspects of the problem can we focus on? How can we frame it? When we do this, we are constructing the problem we will focus on from the multiverse of all possible ways an overarching issue can be viewed. Unlike constructing a bridge from a precise blueprint, constructing problems takes trial and error and much change.

I heard a popular YouTuber say that Pixar's movies start as horrible ideas and gradually transform into masterpieces. The undertone was "It is hard to believe that Pixar, a company that produces one gem after another, could start with poor ideas."

The truth is that Pixar's story is not unique. There is a kernel of something in the beginning, a problem identified, a spark of inspiration—something that is worth trying out. But that does not mean that any of it will make it into the end product. And that is the story not only of Pixar but also of creativity.

Pixar's story is remarkable in one regard. In his biography of the company, *Creativity, Inc.*, former Pixar president Ed Catmull dared to describe the company's creative process in its messiness. He had the courage to admit that creativity is about taking problems and developing potential solutions—which includes undoing some work when needed, abandoning some when necessary, and either redoing bits and pieces or only keeping bits and pieces.

The original problem from which my favorite Pixar movie, *Up*, came to be, for example, had to do with escaping life when it becomes overwhelming, inspired by director Pete Docter's experiences growing up and having difficulties navigating social situations. The story was to center on two brothers from a floating city on an alien planet fighting about who was going to inherit their father's kingdom.

You don't remember it like that? That's because the movie ended up being about a grumpy elderly widower on a quest to fulfill a promise to his late wife. He ties balloons to his house to fly to South America and by accident takes along a boy. They meet a talking dog and a giant, colorful flightless bird that is being hunted by the old man's childhood hero, a famed but eventually disgraced explorer. The only idea that survived through the changes in the storyline was the bird around whom much of the adventuring revolves.

How do two brothers become an old man and a boy? By the creators engaging in exploration. They tried out many different images that evoke the contrasts between the frustrations of everyday life and the fantasy of escape. The main character emerged after many, many sketches, until finally Docter drew an old man with smiling balloons, and something just clicked. The grumpy old man had come about after being given space for change and growth, and the end result was a character that children could relate to, like they connect with their grandparents.

The Power of Exploration

Problem construction can take the form of arranging and rearranging thoughts or ideas (sometimes literally), or it can be formal testing of different possibilities. In a classic study, psychologists Mihalyi Csikszentmihalyi and Jacob Getzels set up an art studio in their laboratory at the University of Chicago and invited art students to create still life drawings. Researchers provided more than thirty objects for artists to choose from and observed as they selected objects, arranged them, and worked on the drawings.

Some artists spent more time than others picking up the objects, feeling their weights and textures, and trying to work any mechanical parts. They would arrange them, step back, and rearrange them. They would try sketching, look at the sketches and their physical object counterparts, and then come back to the arrangement and change the composition, the problem for their work, moving the placement of some objects, removing others altogether, and adding ones not previously included. They spent time playing with the elements of the still life before committing to a specific composition.

Other artists spent less time playing with objects and quickly got to work on their drawings. They decided what to do and spent the majority of their time doing it.

After the researchers examined the completed drawings, they found that the artists who engaged in more exploration in their process of creation were judged by well-known artists and art critics as having produced more original and appealing drawings. These artists investigated what their still lives could be and delayed making the final decision about what to draw until they had thoroughly explored different objects and their arrangements. The fundamental problem—creating a still life—was already given, but it hid many possible specific problems. They were constructing their individual problems—what could the still life be—by exploring different combinations of objects and various ways they could be put together. Each of the arrangements they tried was a problem constructed, in this case quite literally built.

It turns out that the amount of time spent on exploration to produce a new business venture is similarly fruitful. Researchers at the Wharton School at the University of Pennsylvania examined the trajectories of start-ups for which extensive information was available in a database of more than 1.2 million companies across the United States. They were interested in what could predict the effectiveness of company scaling.

Scientists defined the start of company scaling as the point when the resources within the team of founders were no longer sufficient to continue developing and implementing ideas. To continue operating, companies would need to recruit managers and sales staff. Examining the timing of job postings for manager and sales positions provides a convenient way to measure when scaling starts to happen. Researchers were thus able to analyze 38,217 companies and 6.3 million jobs.

The results showed that early scaling was related to company failure: compared to those that scaled after two years from founding, companies that started scaling in the first six or twelve months were 20 to 40 percent more likely to fail. And this effect remains significant even after accounting for differences in timing across industries, the year of founding, and the place of founding.

Researchers hypothesized that experimentation was key to success. To test this hypothesis, they recorded whether companies employed A/B testing tools, which enable comparing different attributes of the business idea at scale. Employing these tools means experimenting with various product features, learning whether idea A or idea B results in better performance, and thus informing next steps. As they suspected, such experimentation was related to a lower chance of failure.

The implications of this research are very practical. For best results, do not settle prematurely on solutions, no matter how reasonable they might seem. Rather, explore how to approach your problem. How exactly this will look will depend on the nature of your work. Sometimes experimenting can take the form of arranging objects, as with the artists in the still life study. At other times it can look like testing that compares the effects of different product features, as in the study of start-ups. Or it can have a different form specific to what you do.

Redefining the Problem

Problem construction also happens through redefinition.

Amelia Winger-Bearskin is a thought leader in the digital technology space and an innovator in how to apply digital technologies in the arts and business alike. She grew up around creativity. Her father was a researcher in innovation at Kodak and her mother a storyteller for their Haudenosaunee (Iroquois) tribe, focused on decentralized community practices. "I really wanted to build things that were in people's hands, like the way that George Eastman did," Amelia told me. "His true innovation was not inventing the camera. It was inventing the camera for everyone. Once he put that object into the hands of millions of people all over the world, photography changed, and our world changed as a result—the way we thought of reality, the way we thought of measurement in the world, the concept of documentation. Everything was changed by this camera."

Amelia saw George Eastman and the democratization of photography as an example of how the intersection of art and technology could influence the world. And her career has always been at an intersection of fields. One of Amelia's major projects was the Interactive Digital Environments Alliance (IDEA), focused on virtual reality (VR) applications. IDEA was approached by the City of New Rochelle to develop technology-enabled means for urban planning.

In contrast to symbolic interactions, such as when urban areas and structures are represented by blocks or small-scale models, VR does not have to rely on our ability to imagine the world but engages us to be fully in it, both mentally and physically. Through VR technology, people could walk around different features in their city, experience them in a realistic way, and provide informed feedback.

IDEA first defined its problem as helping New Rochelle's city planners in their jobs by using VR tools. That was a productive direction, as city planners successfully used the tools, but Amelia and her colleagues soon realized that city planners were already able to imagine their designs in city spaces. Although VR was helpful, it was not a game changer.

Amelia and her IDEA team realized that unlike professional city planners, citizens don't spend their days thinking about and picturing different structures and how they could be incorporated into the city landscape. For them, immersive technology *could* be a game changer. It would be much easier, for example, to answer whether they would stop at a downtown park when walking by it in a virtual environment than thinking about this scenario in the abstract. Being able to experience city features in a simulated environment made them feel real, and citizens could now provide valuable feedback. The IDEA team redefined the problem they worked on to include citizens in the process of city planning.

Another way they reframed their problem was in the choice of the technology used. Virtual reality had proved helpful to both city planners and citizens. However, creating VR environments takes substantial time and resources. Another form of immersive media, augmented reality (AR), requires less time and equipment to develop.

AR is a form of immersive experience that combines real-world and computer-generated virtual content. Perhaps the most well-known example is the Pokémon Go game in which players look into the world around them through their phone camera and can also see 3-D, computer-created imaginary creatures (Pokémon) as if they were a part of their environment. When AR is applied to city planning, people can look through the phone camera into the city as it exists and also see computer-generated features that are in the process of being designed and planned. For example, they can see a park or a library as if it were already built in front of them. Now, even those who otherwise would have a hard time imagining a new building or park could contribute an informed opinion about how those features fit into the city. And this could be done without the need for expensive VR environments.

Amelia's story of how problems are defined and redefined and change is typical of the creative process. Organizational psychologists have even been able to put a number on how much time problem-solving teams spend on such problem construction. Although they expected that teams would spend the most time generating ideas, they found that teams spent 53 percent of their work time on problem construction. Successful teams spent most of their time framing and summarizing the problem through discussion—talking through disagreements about the nature of the problem and sharing past experiences relevant to the problem that could illuminate a particular aspect of it—and less time creating the actual solution.

Problem Construction Leads to Solutions

Scientists in the Netherlands dove into how solutions emerge from the ways in which problems are constructed. They asked experienced industrial designers to say aloud whatever went on in their minds as they worked to redesign the trash disposal system on passenger trains. This is the closest we can get to peeking into what goes on in people's minds as they are going through the creative process.

When they analyzed the designers' process, researchers found that it was a back-and-forth game between defining and redefining the problem on the one hand and, on the other, taking steps toward possible solutions. Evaluating the steps toward solutions often leads right back to considering whether the problem could and should be opened up and redefined. One designer, for instance, early on asked whether trash bins were necessary at all. What if there was just a hole in the train floor? Thinking of opening a hole in the floor was his way of dramatically departing from how trash disposal was done at the time. As he asked more questions, he learned—to his horror—that the train toilets indeed simply opened onto the tracks. His outrage inspired a new way of looking at the problem. He now viewed waste disposal as broader than litter, to include bathroom waste as well. This redefinition meant he was looking not only at where litter could be placed but also at what to do with it so it did not accumulate on the train *and* so both litter and bathroom waste would not simply be released into the environment, causing pollution and contamination. Solution? A system that sucks and compresses waste of all types.

Reframing the focus of the problem is a defining feature of the design process. And it is increasingly important the more open-ended the problem. Experienced designers undertake diverse projects in their work, in roles ranging from technician to collaborator. In cases where designers are asked to be technicians, they enter the work at the end of planning, have little involvement in either formulating the problem or generating solutions, and have little space for iteration. They are simply asked to execute the client's ideas or solutions, and the work is routine and conventional. By contrast, as collaborators, they join the process in the early stages of development, are active in formulating (and reformulating) the problem, and explore solutions through much iteration. These are the truly innovative projects.

If this is the case, why don't all clients engage designers as collaborators? It comes back to the willingness to take risks. Designers know that when a client is represented by middle managers, it is more difficult to establish true collaboration because the managers are trying to imagine what their bosses want rather than being fully present in the project formulation. They want to prevent criticism and end up being averse to taking reputational risks. Middle managers' actions often suggest that they are contrasting productivity and originality, which biases them against truly novel ideas and significant innovation.

Experienced designers try to purposefully broaden how the problem is defined as they work with clients. Indeed, what sets experienced designers apart from novices is their understanding of the importance of problem construction and how they guide clients through this process. They focus on changing the conversation from the specific to the more abstract. To help, they use mood boards—curated collections of images, materials, notes, or patterns—that evoke the design's style. The exact pieces in this collage do not have to explicitly be part of the final design solution. They can simply be a set of unrelated objects or symbols that capture or suggest the overall character of the problem. If you focus on broad ideas and concepts, rather than any concrete feature, you will open up the conversation to exploring multiple possible problems.

Integrate Contradictory Problems

Professor Roni Reiter-Palmon is an organizational psychologist at the University of Nebraska at Omaha who systematically examined how problem construction influences the creativity of solutions. She and her research team presented study participants with a fictionalized scenario called "Becky's Problem." Becky was arrested for shoplifting a few years before and is now glad to have a job at a pizza restaurant. She is grateful to the owner for the opportunity, is doing well in her job, and has even been offered a promotion to manager. The trouble is that she has noticed that her coworker Jim—who is also her roommate—has been making lots of mistakes and treating customers rudely and recently has begun stealing from their employer. Becky's problem is that she feels the need to do something about

Jim's behavior, but he is a good friend, and she also needs him to keep his job to be able to afford their monthly rent. She cannot think of a good solution.

Before developing solutions, people were asked to reframe the problem in as many ways as they could. Their task was to transform one broad problem (*What should Becky do?*) into many others that could focus their search for ideas.

Researchers found that the creativity of solutions was not related to how many different ways people thought of to reframe the problem. Rather, it mattered *how* they reframed the problem. People who devised the most creative solutions drew on contradictory problems. For example, they could have addressed in their solution both the question "How can Becky keep her roommate?" and a contradictory problem, "How does Becky make sure she doesn't get fired?" Thinking in this way, one participant offered a creative solution: "When initially reading this, I wondered why there was no mention of Becky confronting the roommate. He needs to know how much the boss has helped her out, and that he gave her a chance because he saw she needed one. Becky must also be assertive, though, and demand that the roommate does his job and improves within a short amount of time because letting the boss down is not an option. And, if he doesn't make the appropriate changes within the next pay period (or whatever she feels necessary), she'll be looking for a new roommate." Instead of forcing a choice between loyalty to her roommate or her boss, as many other participants did, this solution considers a wider range of possibilities and reaches a more original and effective resolution.

This research suggests a specific strategy you can put into practice. If you incorporate seemingly opposing problems in your solution, you are likely to strike creative gold. This is what product engineers did when they looked at washing machine design from a new angle. Washing machines use spin cycles to better clean the clothes and to remove water at the end of the wash process. To keep the machines safely in place during the intense spin cycle, heavy concrete blocks are fitted inside the casing. But this makes the machines heavy to transport (increasing polluting emissions) and heavy to move when installing in a home. For a long time, it was assumed that machines just had to be heavy—the weight solves the spin-cycle stability problem. However, recently engineers constructed the problem in a new way and came up with a new solution. They asked how the machine could stay in place when running but also be lighter. And they asked what if the machine were heavy when it needed to be and light when it needed to be. After all, it does not have to be heavy and light at the same time. When the problem was posed in a new way, aiming for apparently contradictory goals (make it heavy *and* make it light), a new solution emerged too: replacing the concrete block with a container filled with water. In transport, the container would be empty (and the machine lighter); after installation, it would be filled (making it heavier when necessary).

BE PATIENT

Experienced creators are aware of the importance of problem finding, and there is strong evidence that problem finding makes the difference between failure and success. So, why does it fail to happen so often? The answer lies in a bit of a misconception about the nature of creativity—and a large measure of discomfort about not making progress quickly enough.

The misconception about creativity goes back to what we discussed earlier: the mistaken assumption that creativity is about solving problems. Implicit in equating creativity and problem-solving is the belief that problems are out there as fully formed entities in their own right. We only have to discover them, take them on, and run with them. From there, it is reasonable to think that to do something creative, we have to get our act together, stick with it, and avoid playing around.

A lack of awareness about the importance of prolonged problem finding is a common barrier to finding creative solutions. The same is the case when designers describe some of their clients as wanting no deviation from their narrow way of presenting a problem or when organizational leaders impose project deadlines so tight that they preclude experimentation.

The second reason extended problem finding is often skipped relates to how it makes us feel. It is uncomfortable. If we don't close in on one way of looking at a problem, we feel like we are wasting time. We feel like we're flailing, oftentimes while the clock is ticking and the deadline is looming. We are unsettled because we are not settling on an idea, feature, or prototype, and we are not building the product. When we are exploring and experimenting with problems, we are in a pool of uncertainty. The pressures we feel are real.

Yet, in the absence of space for exploration and problem finding, creativity is unlikely. It takes courage to accept this discomfort and skill to manage it. To resolve this creativity conundrum, the next chapters address how to manage the emotional ups and downs of creative work.

6

Harnessing the Power of Emotions

If you ask him, Jan Kinčl says he is a music producer. But he is really a musician and an entrepreneur—a composer, performer, house and techno DJ, engineer, and music label owner. Sometimes his work is highly technical, sometimes he's focusing on the business side of music, and other times his work is very artistic. It's easy to wonder how he manages it all.

So, how does he do it? As I learned when we spoke, a big part of it is harnessing the power of emotions to fuel his creativity.

Jan knows that creativity requires long periods of exploration and time to focus on the work. But he also knows that life has a way of imposing demands. Clients want to discuss the latest project; collaborators reach out to connect; colleagues want to "just check one thing." Each of these little demands activates us—often in a good way, by spurring us to find effective ways of solving problems. But constant mental and emotional activation can be troublesome. As the time needed for trying out new ideas, testing, and developing them gets interrupted and shrinks, productive activation can turn into irritation, tension, and stress.

Understanding this, Jan is not reachable on Wednesdays. "[That's] the day when I don't open my computer inbox in the studio," he told me. "I don't check my phone." No point in emailing, calling, direct messaging, or sending smoke signals—he will not respond. His colleagues, collaborators, and clients know it, and this time is not negotiable. Wednesdays are studio days, and he reserves the time for engineering work, playing with new ideas, or trying out a new instrument. "I call it research and development," he said. "Often in this play, something very interesting happens—something very workable and useful. And if I am constantly scheduled and finishing something, this play will not happen."

By blocking out his Wednesdays, Jan removes small sources of stress that psychologists call *daily hassles*. Any individual email or call is not a big event. But such small daily hassles can accumulate, collectively cause stress, and also preclude the long spans of uninterrupted time required for the flow of creative work.

Another way Jan creates the psychological and emotional conditions for his creative work is to reserve the evenings as a time for trying out new musical ideas. By then he is starting to feel a bit tired and unfocused, but Jan has found that in this state he can be open to seemingly random associations, letting one thought lead to another, and he can be playful, even silly, without self-consciousness. "I dim the lights, and I start to play without any thinking," he said. "I am usually too tired to think. I make something, and at some point this something can become very interesting.... If it becomes cool, I stick with it. And then I build."

This is a time for playfully throwing all he has against the wall. In this stream of consciousness state, ideas rarely (if ever) emerge fully developed, but he follows them where they lead and jots them all down or records them on his phone, knowing he can return to them later and refine them if he chooses to. He describes this approach as "piling words" or "splattering colors." After an hour of such work, his day is done.

Assembling the piles of ideas into a coherent whole that leads to something recognizable as a song only happens the next day. In the mornings, Jan feels focused and serious. He listens to what he recorded the night before. He discards some ideas ("Maybe I throw out a bit because it is too wild") and recognizes others as promising ("Then I figure out how I can channel what I made into something that makes sense"). He can now start developing the ones he deems worth keeping. Details start taking shape, and he weaves different idea strands together. Quiet and serious mornings are a time for analytical thinking and patient combining of pieces of the musical puzzle.

LEVERAGE YOUR EMOTIONS

Jan intuitively understands the power of emotions to fuel creativity. He recognizes how different situations trigger various feelings and realizes that some of these feelings help one kind of thinking, whereas others are helpful for another kind of thinking or task. And he knows that he can create moods conducive to his creative work. Psychologists call what Jan is doing the ability to use emotions to facilitate thinking and problem-solving. To use emotions effectively, we need to start by understanding what they are telling us and how they influence our thinking and then apply this knowledge in practice.

Recognize Emotions Are Information

When I speak to parents and CEOs alike, their first reaction to the biggest lesson of emotion science—that feelings can be helpful for thinking, problem-solving, decision-making, and directing our action—is resistance. Problem-solving and decision-making demand rational thought, after all! How could listening to our emotions help?

It is easy to think of times that our emotions led us astray—when we lose our patience and say something we regret to a coworker, run dangerously close to a deadline after getting carried away by curiosity, fail to perform at our best when we get very anxious, or don't share ideas in a meeting and lose the project we want because we succumb to self-consciousness. Chances are, most of us can add a plethora of personal examples to this list. The idea that emotions can direct and assist our thinking and decision-making goes against everything we think we know about emotions and what they do.

Emotions move us. They make us cringe, recoil, jump with joy, approach with interest and curiosity, seethe with anger—all this we know. But science tells us they also contain messages we can learn to read. Jan intuitively realized the basic principles of what scientists call *feelings-as-information theory*. He came to understand that each emotional state provides different information—and can be useful for different parts of the creative process. When he felt tired after a long day at work and was in an almost dreamy, unfocused mood, he learned it was a good time to record ideas without any self-censoring. When he felt somber and critical, he learned to immerse himself in technical and detail-oriented studio work.

Feelings-as-information theory describes emotions as signals that tell us what is going on around us and within our minds. For instance, dissatisfaction says we are not there yet; we have not reached the goal in the way we aspire to. Happiness is a sign of mission accomplished; all is well with our world. Frustration tells us something is not working well. We might have hit a wall or there might be an obstacle in our way. Disappointment means that our expectations have not been fulfilled. Anxiety means that we are facing uncertainty. And the list goes on.

By reading these signals, we can decode the information contained in our emotions and use it as we would any other kind of information to guide our thinking, decision-making, and behavior. Once the idea that emotions are information sinks in, it becomes clear that emotions should not be disregarded, discounted, or resisted. We all know that thinking and decision-making are helped by having more information. And as creative work is rife with uncertainties, additional information can only assist in that endeavor.

Identify Your Emotions

To use the information inherent in your feelings for creative purposes, the first challenge is to accurately and precisely identify what you are experiencing. Many of us see our feelings as little more than nuisances in our everyday life, especially when it comes to unpleasant feelings like confusion, anxiety, or anger. Like *Star Trek*'s Mr. Spock, we might wish to rid ourselves of "illogical" emotions and be guided purely by reason. The truth, though, is that when we push emotions down and suppress them, they tend to come back. They become visible in fleeting, unconscious expressions and drive our actions without our awareness. When we push away feelings or do not allow ourselves to experience them, their causes and consequences stay with us and can hurt our well-being and goals alike.

It turns out that knowing what we are feeling is a surprisingly difficult task. Much of the time, we tend to think about and talk about feelings in very general terms. Consider what you answered last time you were asked how you were doing. Chances are you said something like "good" or "fine," or perhaps "stressed," or maybe "tired." The problem with these words is that they do not give us much information. Does "good" mean that we are content? Or happy? At ease? And by "stressed," do we mean challenged? Or overwhelmed? Perhaps tense?

How we reply to the *How are you?* question, of course, depends on who is asking, the nature of our relationship to that person, and the context in which the question is asked. We are more likely to share details of our feelings with close friends and family than with coworkers or bosses. Sometimes we understand what we are going through emotionally but decide not to share it. But sometimes we get caught in overly general thinking about emotions even if we are only trying to answer the question for ourselves. It can be difficult to pinpoint and describe what we are feeling. We are rarely taught about shades of emotional meanings or given feedback about finer distinctions among similar feelings.

Yet, the feelings that might be hiding behind the generalized "fine" or "stressed" are specific and are trying to send different signals. To get information that can be helpful for more effective creative thinking and decision-making, we have to identify our feelings as specifically as possible. Scientists call making such nuanced distinctions among similar feelings *emotional granularity*.

Start by considering two questions. First, how pleasant or unpleasant do you feel, from strongly unpleasant, to relatively neutral, to very pleasant? And second, how activated are you in your body, from very subdued, to somewhat jittery, to highly worked up? Emotions vary in how pleasant and how activated they make us feel, constituting four major categories:

Pleasant and activated. We might be amused, interested, playful, or hopeful. Feeling more intensely pleasant and activated, perhaps we are enthusiastic and joyful, inspired or elated.

Pleasant and not activated. These feelings range from being calm and at ease, to comfortable and content, to peaceful and serene.

Unpleasant and activated. Two big groups of emotions in this category relate to fear and anger. The fear family ranges from feeling nervous and anxious to being afraid or panicked. In the anger family, emotions can range from being peeved, annoyed, or irritated to frustrated, angry, and even livid or furious.

Unpleasant and not activated. These feelings are sad or pessimistic, discouraged or lonely, hopeless or depressed.

Sometimes, just identifying an emotion clarifies what we need to do. If we are confused, we need to learn more about something. When we know that frustration alerts us that we've hit a wall, we apply this knowledge by making the decision to try something else: scale the wall, walk around it, build a ladder, discontinue what we're doing. Boredom signals that our surroundings are not stimulating or meaningful. We can do something else or try to look at what we are doing in a fresh way (*perhaps there is a purpose to what we are doing after all*). Anger warns us about an injustice and nudges us to address it.

Different Emotions, Different Thinking

Emotions not only convey information about what is going on with us and around us but also affect how we see and process the world.

Imagine walking down the street in New York City. Let's examine three hypothetical scenarios.

Scenario 1. You are happy. You are looking around, delighting in seeing the sights. You look up and spot architectural details you never noticed before. Normally, you would take the subway uptown but decide to walk through Central Park. An excited child is feeding a squirrel. This gives you an idea for a logo you are designing. You saw a gray squirrel, but the logo will be orange-red to evoke energy. And the squirrel tail can make a monogram *C* you wanted in the logo.

When happy, we view the world through rose-tinted glasses. We are more likely to remember pleasant and positive news and to see opportunities around us. Our thinking is broader and more expansive. In bright, happy moods, we can make connections among ideas that are not obviously related. We can be playful in our thinking and readily come up with new and unexpected ideas. Hey, we can even try out something silly. All is good with our world, so why not?

Scenario 2. You're feeling grumpy, and you are focused on slaloming through the crowd of busy-looking passersby and confused tourists. You notice piles of trash and in your mind tell people to get out of the way. There is no time for detours or pauses. Mentally, you are struggling with a work problem. You do not think the proposal you are preparing works yet, and issues with it continue to jump out at you.

When somewhat irritated or sullen, we are better able to see problems. In these moods, it is easier to find mistakes we have made and see potential obstacles. We see discrepancies and gaps between what is and what could or should be, and we want to fix them.

Scenario 3. Perhaps you are on your way across town and feeling down. The city looks gray. How long is this going to take? Really, you just want to jump in a cab. But you know that will take longer. You will just get stuck in endless traffic. OK, what can you do? You get into a problem-solving mode. Focus. Sure, you don't feel like getting onto a subway or a bus, but, well, it makes more sense.

Gloomy moods narrow our focus and make us think critically. In these moods, we zoom in on the details and review them as a set of propositions to reason through in an "If this, then that" fashion.

When we identify specific feelings, read their messages, and know the kinds of thinking that are dominant in different emotional states, we can put these pieces of the puzzle together. Interest and curiosity will propel us toward meaningful pursuits. Feeling grumpy, frustrated, down, or sad is not pleasant, but these moods can make us better at finding problems, seeing mistakes, or identifying those little somethings that prevent our work from coming into its own. Creativity has many tasks and demands, and there's an emotional state that can help us with each of them. In other words, creativity is not helped by one kind of feeling or mood, but different challenges we face in creative work can benefit from different emotional states.

Different categories of emotions are not mutually exclusive, and we can experience more than one feeling at a time, such as being anxious and curious or frustrated yet determined. Complex emotions contain seemingly incompatible sides, such as when we feel bittersweetness or have a love-hate relationship with something. Complex emotions help creativity by pointing to multiple perspectives. For example, the climate optimism movement was born out of a feeling of urgency to act on the climate change crisis and also a sense of hope that a set of solutions could be devised.

CHANNEL YOUR EMOTIONS

The simplest way to use your emotions for creativity is to allow them to influence your thinking and action. Pablo Picasso meant this when he said, "The artist is a receptacle for emotions that come from all over the place: from the sky, from the earth, from a scrap of paper, from a passing shape, from a spider's web." When we look at Picasso's *The Old Guitarist*, the sadness is palpable. His *Femme Écrivant (Marie-Thérèse)* is intimate and dreamy, full of longing. Picasso channeled pain and despair after the Nazi bombing of the Basque town of Guernica into possibly his most famous painting. Standing in front of it, we are overtaken by anguish. And Picasso was hardly the only one to draw upon and express emotion in art. Pierre-Auguste Renoir's *Luncheon of the Boating Party* exudes exuberance. Edvard Munch's *The Scream* reverberates with terror. Gustav Klimt's *The Kiss* radiates passion. Francisco de Zurbarán's *St. Francis* imparts reverence.

In my lab, we conducted a study of creative individuals working in different mediums and disciplines—painters, sculptors, composers, writers, designers—and asked them what emotions they used in their work. They talked about love and joy, happiness and excitement, wonder and awe, but also sadness and fear, nostalgia and longing, pain and anger, among many others. A composer described one occasion in which he channeled his emotions to create a new piece when he had just arrived at his girlfriend's home. "I was glad to be there, was feeling relaxed because our weekend was just beginning, and felt loving toward her and loved by her," he said. "I stood at her piano and just allowed all those feelings to flow through me into the relationship between my fingers and the piano, which I recorded on my iPhone."

We can easily imagine artists channeling their emotions into paintings, sculptures, or performances. And people in creative industries like advertising or design can do this too. But this way of using emotions in the service of creativity happens in other domains of work as well. Many successful innovations, for example, started with an experience of empathy. The OXO Good Grips kitchen products were born when Sam Farber wanted to help his wife, Betsey, who suffered from arthritis and was struggling with traditional kitchen utensils. He recounts being on vacation in France and Betsey complaining that the peeler she was using when making an apple pie hurt her hands. He channeled the empathy he felt for his wife's plight into designing—together with her—a vegetable peeler with a better handle. The list of innovations that have grown when a seed of empathy drew someone's attention to a problem is very long—from employees of GE HealthCare noticing the distress of children going through MRI scans and redesigning the experience into a pirate adventure to Airbnb building its business by imagining the kinds of information travelers need to make them feel comfortable renting a room or a house.

Channeling emotions can also be a key signal in communicating about creative work. Researchers at the University of Tennessee studied this in entrepreneurs. In one experiment, they showed investors recorded pitches from founders and asked them to rate various indicators of emotional expression, such as the extent to which presenters showed animated facial expressions, talked with varied tone and pitch, exhibited energetic body movements, or had rich body language as they described their ideas. Investors also indicated how passionate and enthusiastic the founders appeared and rated their interest in the new venture.

The results showed that investors were more likely to show interest in the ventures presented by entrepreneurs who channeled emotions into their pitches. The investors said that these entrepreneurs showed commitment to and energy for the endeavor being considered, that they had "an infectious quality that brings in talent and money," and that their demeanor suggested they would keep going in the face of obstacles and early failures.

Both excited (positive, high activation) and fiery (negative, high activation) presentations were seen as passionate, while entrepreneurs who exhibited a positive, calm (low activation) voice or a negative, energetic (high activation) voice came across as better prepared. If the amount of funding pledged depends on passion *and* preparation (it does!), what should you do? The researchers uncovered a very practical piece of advice from their work: for optimal results, when communicating or advocating for your creative ideas, you would be wise to use a voice that evokes fiery determination. This way, you will be perceived as both passionate *and* prepared—which tends to translate into the capital to fund your projects.

FOLLOW THE DISCOMFORT

To best utilize your emotions, you first have to allow yourself to experience them and linger on them a bit to find the sparks or cues for action. Normally, our emotions are somewhere in the background of our awareness, occasionally breaking through when they're strong enough to grab our attention—as when feeling angry, afraid, or amused, for example.

Let's imagine a different scenario—one in which we deliberately pause and consider our feelings, reminding ourselves that emotions convey vital information. Yes, frustration is unpleasant. But it tells us there is a problem, that something needs our attention and skill. So, what if we allow ourselves to actually linger in that sense of frustration—if we do not distract ourselves or do something enjoyable to feel better in the moment? We just may find that this unpleasant emotion could reveal an opportunity or insight we would not have otherwise.

Nineteenth-century socialite Josephine Cochrane was frustrated that her servants kept breaking her favorite china when washing it. Because she often entertained guests in her home, broken dishes posed an ongoing problem. She could have hired new staff who would be more careful or complained about the housekeepers to friends over tea. Instead, she took the creative route. She started working on developing a dishwashing machine—a new and original means to wash dishes without damaging them. This socialite had become a Pro-c-level creator.

Noticing and then reflecting on the frustration of chipped and broken china sparked a process that led Josephine to patent her design for a mechanical dishwasher in 1866. In 1893, after many improvements and enhancements along the way, she exhibited her machine at the Chicago World's Fair and won an award for "best mechanical construction, durability and adaptation to its line of work." Orders from hotels and restaurants followed. The company she founded was purchased after her death by KitchenAid, which, 100 years later, is still going strong. The basic design she developed continues to be used in modern dishwashers.

Josephine was not educated in the sciences or engineering, but she was a daughter and granddaughter of engineers and inventors who worked with the latest technologies of the day. Her father was a civil engineer who supervised multiple woolen mills, sawmills, and gristmills, and her grandfather held the first patent for a steamboat in the United States. Thus, she was not a stranger to technology and was primed to think of technological solutions to problems. Still, the process was not easy, and it took decades to identify the problem, decide on a potential solution to pursue (mechanical washer using a water jet system), create a prototype, and finally reach the turning point she experienced at the World's Fair (commercial sales of the new machine). It all started with frustration she did not ignore or suppress, but channeled into action.

When entrepreneurs listen to their emotions and linger on those feelings, they ignite the problem-finding process. Melissa Butler was frustrated by the state of the beauty industry. As a Black woman, she did not see options for colors that worked for her skin tone. This frustration was a problem to solve for herself and others. She launched The Lip Bar in 2010 with a goal of providing affordable vegan and cruelty-free options for diverse skin tones; by the end of 2020 the brand appeared in more than 500 stores and counting, even in the middle of a global pandemic. Steve Kaufer was inspired to start Trip-Advisor, one of the world's largest travel advice networks, after a rather unpleasant experience trying to research a vacation. The list of inventions born from frustration or dissatisfaction reimagined as a challenge or a problem to be solved is virtually infinite.

Stories of entrepreneurs' creativity are so familiar that they can now seem obvious and are easily taken for granted. But does what works for entrepreneurs also work for the rest of us? One of the most inspiring creative stories that I encountered in my work came from a surprising place: the food services department at the Ottawa Hospital in Canada. Michael Knight, supervisor in the department, noticed the irritation and dissatisfaction of workers assembling patients' food trays. They had to bend to reach food items, and the lists of what should be on patients' plates were inconveniently placed. Workers were getting tired, they complained of physical pain, and the demands of their jobs made them emotionally stressed. They felt burnt out.

Their frustration indicated there was a problem. And Michael paid attention to it. Rather than suggesting that the workers needed to get better at handling frustration or become more resilient to stress, he worked with them to figure out how to design a food assembly line that would remove the points of annoyance and strain. Result? A new work process that did not require workers to bend, stretch, or strain to reach things. The redesigned work area and flow made workers happier and improved their accuracy in assembling the food trays. It delivered two successes: the workers' frustrations were alleviated, and patient safety was enhanced. Noticing frustration and dissatisfaction led to innovation with far-reaching positive consequences.

Creativity was not necessarily in Michael's job description. But he (1) noticed and attended to the feelings of his staff, (2) understood and accepted that their feelings indicated a problem, (3) made the decision to explore the problem, and (4) invested time and effort in creating a new workflow. These steps for harnessing the power of emotions for creativity by lingering on them and acting on what they tell us are not unique to Michael. This very book was born from a sense that something was missing from the existing books on creativity. I realized that this persistent feeling signaled a problem as well as an opportunity. Once I decided to explore what was missing and how I could fill this gap, the book started taking shape. After a year of writing and editing—with plenty of stress, occasional times of doubt, but also great enthusiasm and joy—I finished the book.

The feelings that will nag you might be different and the problems they point to certainly will be, but the steps that will take you from feeling to outcome (notice the feeling, identify the problem, explore the problem, develop the solution) will remain largely the same.

MATCH YOUR EMOTIONS TO YOUR TASKS

As music producer extraordinaire Jan Kinčl demonstrates with his work patterns, we can also harness the power of emotions by playing a matching game. Different feelings can make particular ways of thinking easier and more effective. We can therefore match the knowledge of what emotions are good for with tasks that benefit from those particular moods.

We do not always have the choice of what we do when, of course, but for times when we do, this matching game can boost our creativity. As a scientist and writer, I regularly match my moods to tasks on my to-do list. I am not a morning person. In the mornings I tend to be irritated (why, oh why, is the world arranged to the benefit of larks?) and sullen. Everyone in my house knows I am not fun first thing in the morning. But being grumpy improves one's ability to make a contrarian argument, and there are certainly times when we need to be contrarian. My morning mood makes it easier to take the perspective of peer reviewers or readers, for example, and notice problems in my writing like inconsistencies or incomplete stories and figure out how they can be improved. Then, in the mid- to late afternoon, my energy level increases, and my mood shifts from downcast to more optimistic. This is the time to come up with new ideas and write.

My morning low is a symptom of what scientists call our *chronotype*—our preferred times of activity and sleep. People can be strong morning types (most alert in the morning, going to sleep early), strong evening types (most alert later in the day, going to sleep late), or anywhere in between. Although the rhythm of our lives is often dictated by external demands and obligations—such as school schedules, commutes, and work hours—we generally have a sense of when we'd prefer to go to sleep and wake up, if we were entirely free to plan our days.

During our preferred times of activity, when our energy is highest and our mood most elevated, we are better able to generate creative ideas. At other times, we might be better able to perform tasks that require critical thinking, talk with colleagues or collaborators, or search for information we need.

Of course, time of day is not the only factor influencing our moods. They can be triggered by the circumstances around us, our interactions and relationships with others, and events in the larger world. The COVID-19 pandemic, for example, affected people across the globe, triggering anxious and depressed moods in millions of people. These difficult feelings, however, spurred people to engage in more creative activities both in their personal and professional lives. We found novel ways to connect and communicate with friends and family, collaborate with colleagues, complete work remotely, and make use of our leisure time (remember the collective obsession with sourdough starters and baking bread?). Other events that create collective moods can be national tragedies or political events. In the United States, the murder of George Floyd by the police in 2020 angered people across the country, and this collective anger inspired creative action to call for racial justice and police reform.

Most sources of our daily emotions are more personal. Feeling overwhelmed when there is more on our to-do list than can fit in a day, for example. The anxiety of anticipating a performance review. Curiosity and interest in a new project. Dissatisfaction with what we are doing, something just not seeming right. Many of these feelings—yes, even the unpleasant ones we normally want to avoid—can be matched to different tasks and used to help our creative work. When I feel anxious, I make my work plans. Not only will I be better able to foresee risks or obstacles and figure out how to deal with them, but having a plan relieves some of the anxiety. When curious or interested, I go on a reading spree to learn about the latest research in my field. And when dissatisfied with a new study idea, I come back to consider it, seek advice from colleagues, and look for another approach.

Once you attend to your feelings and identify them, you can start playing the matching game and choose those tasks from your to-do list that can benefit most from a particular mood. With the feelings you experience routinely (your typical morning versus afternoon mood, for example), you'll be able to plan for them in advance. Other moods will depend on the daily flow of events and experiences, and you can match them on the fly with tasks on your to-do list. Being flexible in what you do at which times, aided by your emotions, will pay off in the form of greater ease in the execution of those tasks and a greater likelihood of success.

STEP BACK TO EVALUATE YOUR WORK

Jan only considers a project truly done months after its initial completion. Such an approach gives him time to create distance from his work, see it afresh, and mull over how it can be improved. Why? He understands that the initial elation he feels after finishing a song or album can be deceiving. The delight at a finished product can make us see the big picture—*This is something truly original!*—but it can blind us to the specifics that need tending to. Feeling happy feels good, but the downside is that it can prevent us from paying attention to details and minimize any signs of trouble. Inserting a buffer of time between finishing a project and deciding it's truly done (and releasing it to the world) allows Jan to preserve the ability to see a new way of improving a project and experience the pride of knowing he has done his best work.

If emotions can be helpful in evaluating our creative work—is it truly done, or does it need further attention?—the logical question might seem to be *which* emotions. When in high spirits, we can see the potential of our work. On the other hand, when we're feeling down, we're better able to see its problems. If we rely only on the view through our rose-colored glasses, we will not notice potential issues. But if we rely only on the gray-colored glasses, we will not see the strengths and possibilities. So, are we back to the conclusion that emotions cannot and should not be relied on when making decisions? Not at all. It turns out that the question of which emotions are helpful and which will lead us astray is not the right question—nor is either optimism- or pessimism-fueled decision-making the only option.

When evaluating our ideas and making decisions about them, we need to remember that *all* emotions tell us something worthy of attention and that all emotions can be used to help us evaluate our work. The trick is to step back and consider what you can learn from the multiple perspectives provided by different feelings, both pleasant and unpleasant. For the same project, there will be times when we feel optimistic and times when we feel more cautious or even pessimistic, usually because we focus on different aspects of it. Each emotional perspective tells a part of the story but not the whole one.

Unlike when playing the emotion-task matching game (one mood is best for a particular kind of thinking and problem-solving), when we use emotions to help evaluate our work, no single kind of feeling is to be trusted alone. Those points of nagging dissatisfaction? They are a sign we can still improve our work. Those points of happiness we experience when we alight upon a clever solution? They show the potential. Considering both ensures that we optimize the decision of when we are done.

We often do this intuitively. Imagine applying to school, either to pursue a degree yourself or to support a child in doing so. A competitive process can be quite challenging. Chances are, you will not apply only to a single school, no matter how desirable it might be or how optimistic you are. Rather, you will consider uncertainties and your own doubts and create a list that includes safety schools that should be well within reach. You will also consider your strengths and hopes and be inspired to create a list of aspirational schools. Finally, schools that are in between these two poles will also find their place on your final list. There is no guarantee of getting accepted to any individual one, and there is no ideal formula for creating the perfect list, but you will do best if you decide to sample from different groups, taking into account different feelings as they relate to this process.

Using emotions in evaluating your work is similarly a balancing act. Perfectionism, with its exceptionally high standards and obsessing over even small dissatisfactions with our work, is an enemy of getting that work done. On the other hand, if you focus too much on the excitement of the moment, you can fall for the trap of settling prematurely, not giving enough time to exploration and testing of different ideas. These poles might seem incompatible and nearly impossible to reconcile, and there is certainly no foolproof way to achieve an ideal balance. As with so much of creative work, this is a case of learning to tolerate ambiguity. But take heart: an abundance of information is hidden within the range of your own emotional perspectives.

WHEN THE FEELINGS YOU HAVE ARE NOT THE ONES YOU NEED

We can use emotions that we spontaneously experience by allowing them to influence our thinking, by matching them to the tasks in front of us, and by using the different perspectives they provide us to make balanced decisions about our work. But there are times when our naturally occurring moods are not exactly ... convenient.

Imagine being tired and down as you enter a brainstorming session. Brainstorming calls for broad thinking and pulling together ideas from unexpected corners of your knowledge and expertise, as if from thin air—but feeling blue narrows our attention, which makes brainstorming less successful. Or let's say you get great news, but you have to critically dive into and polish a big presentation before an important meeting. In this joyful state, you see all the strengths of your work and can imagine multiple directions it can take. But it is hard to focus on or care about the minutiae of the presentation. In both cases, your feelings are not a good match to your tasks in the moment. They're inconvenient. Nevertheless, the work must be done; the show must go on.

Although we tend to experience feelings as something that happens *to* us or is imposed upon us, the surprising feature of emotions is that we have agency and can influence them and even create different moods. And we can purposefully create feelings that are a better match to our needs.

This is what scientists do when they employ techniques of mood induction and create specific moods in the laboratory. For example, in a series of studies, professor of psychology Constantine Sedikides and his colleagues at the University of Southampton asked people to recall memories that made them feel nostalgic or to think of an ordinary day. Nostalgia is a complex emotion that includes feelings of pleasure or attachment to something or someone in the past and also wistfulness or sadness about events, places, or people who are gone or far away. After remembering something nostalgic, participants wrote stories. In one experiment, the story had to include a princess, a cat, and a race car, and in another experiment, it had to start with a sentence setting up a mystery: "One cold winter evening, a man and a woman were alarmed by a sound coming from a nearby house."

After bringing to mind nostalgic memories, people indeed felt nostalgic. And they wrote stories judged more creative than those who had thought of an ordinary day. Nostalgia includes multitudes—bittersweet fondness, melancholy, longing. Researchers found that nostalgia enabled people to see multiple perspectives and include them in the stories, which made them more creative.

We can take a cue from the psychology lab and purposely choose to invoke different moods for our own creative purposes. Professors Joel Cohen and Eduardo Andrade demonstrated that people sometimes deliberately choose to create moods that will be the best match for the tasks in front of them. In a series of studies, they first created different moods in their participants by showing them movie scenes that were happy (a clip from *American Pie 2*), tense (a plane accident scene from *Top Gun*), or neutral (a travel documentary). This mood induction enabled researchers to know exactly what the mood starting point was for each participant.

Then, they told people they would work either on "a challenging cognitive task that required carefulness, precision, and analytical and logical thinking" or "a challenging cognitive task that required intuition, creativity, outside-of-the-box thinking, and imagination." The analytical thinking task was chosen because it benefits from negative moods, whereas the brainstorming task is helped by happy moods.

Before taking on the tasks, participants were offered a choice to listen to happy or sad music. Listening to music can influence our moods, and in this way participants could decide to make their mood either more positive or negative. As the researchers hypothesized, people were purposeful in their choices. Those who faced an outside-the-box thinking task were more likely to choose upbeat music to put themselves in a more positive, energized mood that broadens thinking, especially if they started out in a negative mood after watching a tense movie scene. By contrast, those who expected to work on an analytic task were more likely to choose sad music (and put themselves in a more negative mood that focuses thinking).

Just like in the lab, we can decide to induce moods in ourselves too, even on the spot. Remembering emotional events makes us mentally relive them. At different times in our lives we have felt nostalgic, sympathetic to someone's misfortune, angry about an injustice, or optimistic about our ability to do something difficult. Remembering such events will not feel exactly the same as the actual experiences did. But we will be able to recapture enough of the feelings to assist us in the present. A short story writer in one of my studies described it this way: "The act of writing often feels lonely anyway, but while I was writing, I would try to draw on that feeling to capture the loneliness that each of the characters felt; I would try to stay in that frame of mind while working on the piece. Also, I would try to conjure up memories from my own family's losses to get details right for the story—maybe go to a cemetery to see what details/memories would come back. Actively conjuring emotions and memories from those times." This is the same process employed by actors when they use personal emotional memories to create vivid and believable portrayals of their characters.

When you harness the power of emotions, it is key to remember that you are searching not for a specific feeling that is uniquely helpful for *all* of creativity but for specific emotions that could be helpful for discrete tasks on the path from having ideas to making them happen. At different times, creative work requires broad thinking (when seeking new ideas) and analytical thinking (when reviewing your work and searching for ways it could be improved and developed). The challenge is to find your own way of getting into the right mood for a particular task in front of you. When I need to get into a more activated mood, I tend to schedule meetings with colleagues, because I know that I will become more excited and enthusiastic as we discuss our work. And when I need a little smile and boost of feeling good, I write a postcard to a friend (which is why I always have a stack ready). Some techniques can work for many people—like recalling memories or music—but others might be more specific to you. My postcard writing is rather unusual; it might not be your cup of tea, but it is very effective for me.

Acknowledging the creativity-enhancing power of emotions does not, of course, deny that emotions can also get in our way. Who hasn't been overwhelmed to the point of paralysis? Or stressed trying to get through a bottleneck. Or desperately stuck. Or discouraged into wanting to give up. At those times, we need to get out of the emotional glut that pushes us into a creative rut. The next chapter examines how we can do something about our emotions when they threaten to impede our progress.

When Emotions Get in the Way

Katja Forbes is a human-centered designer, business owner, and organizational leader. She founded her own design company, building it from a single client to a host of marquee clients, from the airline industry to financial services to government. After eight years, she sold it to one of the leading global technology service and consulting organizations. Katja ran the acquired company for three years through the COVID-19 pandemic and did not lose a single employee in that time.

She caught the attention of a large multinational bank and was recruited as the head of client experiences for corporate, commercial, and institutional banking. Attracted by the opportunity to have impact through an organization dedicated to financial inclusion for frontier markets and unbanked people, she accepted the offer and moved from Australia to Singapore. She now works with complex capital and financial market products, trade products, and trade finance products in fifty markets around the world. Katja is in charge of creating content that helps managers sell products and allows a way for clients to directly interact with the products and services to move money around.

A former ice hockey player, Katja is very competitive (she says no one can ever criticize her as hard as she can criticize herself) and always looking for ways to improve her game—on and off the ice. In her new role, she's found challenges pertaining to the design of complex systems and also social and emotional challenges related to being part of a large organization. Her husband compares her career change to going from being the lead guitarist and singer of her own rock-and-roll band to becoming a member of an orchestra, where everybody follows sheet music together.

In her role as a designer in a large financial corporation, there can be times when not everyone understands or is aware of Katja's value. There are hierarchies to navigate, and she needs to convince an audience that isn't necessarily attuned to design of the importance of her contributions. Doing that demands energy. She likens these interactions to papercuts. Individual papercuts aren't so bad, but suffer enough of them, and one can bleed—or experience the work equivalent, burnout. This is why Katja is careful to be proactive in managing the emotional toll of the occasional "papercuts" before they can accumulate and grow into something that significantly interferes with her job. Because she believes deeply in her organization's values, she has developed strategies that help her take action and persist in her work.

To deal with her critics, inner and outer, Katja leans into her strengths. At work, Katja said, "I'm going to really amplify the things that I'm great at, [such as] communicating, speaking, being strategic and having futuristic thoughts, and being able to think outside the box for the organization." Reminding herself to cut herself some slack helps too. "You actually have to be really intentional and be able to sit with yourself, sit with yourself uncomfortably, feeling like you haven't done enough or you've done wrong," she said. Katja is describing a skill well known to emotion scientists: the ability to proactively manage emotions to both boost well-being and pave the way for successful creative work.

Another proactive way she manages her feelings is seeking feedback and considering it a tool for growth. Early on in her career, Katja worked at a company with strong organizational values around employee growth. At the end of every meeting, people would be asked about what went well in their work and what was a delta. Katja took the term "delta" to heart. It's commonly used in mathematics and science to denote change in a variable. Similarly, her company used delta to denote areas in need of improvement. Katja loved the neutrality of the term: it does not reference problems or negatives, which opens people up to learning from the feedback. "We're quick to take things that we think are bad or that we think are critical and then ingest them into ourselves and go, *Therefore, I am bad*," she said. But with a shift in language, we prevent feelings of shame or defensiveness and put ourselves in a receptive state where we can take in feedback and improve. Suddenly what we hear is thought provoking rather than threatening, generative rather than deflating. And thought provoking we can manage and even welcome.

The emotional demands of Katja's work are many. They range from adjusting to being part of a large organization after years of heading her own company, to the demands of designing and building ways for customers to interact with complex financial products, to managing a team of designers. While the exact challenges and triggers we experience are unique to each of our situations, the course of creative work is an emotional roller coaster for all of us. Just as they do for Katja, some of the challenges we encounter come from within (our inner critic who's always ready with an opinion), some come from others around us, and still others stem from the very nature of creative work, which, by definition, means we are doing something new and difficult. The success of creative work to a large extent depends on how we manage the emotional challenges that are part and parcel of every creative effort.

CREATIVE WORK TAKES MANAGING EMOTIONS

Katja Forbes understands that to be successfully creative, she needs to manage her energy, support the creative staff she leads, navigate the challenges of product design, and effectively communicate her team's work to stakeholders in her organization and outside it. Just as we can induce certain feelings to help with a particular task at hand, we can manage our difficult emotions, those that might be in the way of our continued commitment to creativity.

Of note, there are emotional experiences that are so powerful that they overwhelm us in the moment. Traumatic events, times when we experienced a profound shock or an immediate threat to our survival, can trigger strong emotions even years later. Extreme emotions are normal reactions to abnormal situations. In such cases there are limits to our ability to manage our feelings. But in most everyday situations, we have agency to influence and regulate the course of our emotions.

When I asked a diverse group of creators what emotions they experienced in their daily creative work of transforming ideas into products, they described a mix of frustration, excitement, and joy. Other research shows that creators describe the daily doing, undoing, and reworking toward the final creative goal as painful or even full of anguish. In other words, creative work is stressful.

Everyday experience makes clear that stress is unpleasant. Research in health psychology has amply documented how stress, especially when chronic, predicts both physical and mental health problems. But research also shows that unusual or unexpected experiences—which are inherently stressful—often inspire and motivate creative work and creative achievement. Effective emotion regulation is the ingredient that can help mitigate the negative effects of stress and precipitate recovery from stress, which unlocks the doors to creativity.

Let's unpack. Stress is a psychological consequence of dealing with significant demands. We could be facing a difficult project at work, experiencing a conflict with a coworker, or living through a broader social crisis, such as a pandemic or political turmoil. Importantly, there isn't a one-to-one correspondence between these events and people's experiences of them. The same event can be experienced differently depending on how we interpret it and what we anticipate its effects to be. If we interpret the event as a threat—something that we expect to be dangerous or harmful—our experience of stress escalates, and the emotional and psychological effects will be negative. And if stress becomes chronic, we will be at risk of emotional exhaustion and burnout and less effective in responding to the demands in front of us. But if we interpret the event as a challenge—something that may be difficult but that we believe we can overcome with effort, time, or help—the negative consequences are usually averted.

WHAT IS EMOTION REGULATION?

Regulating emotions means being able to manage our feelings to get desired results. We intuitively think of regulating emotions as aimed at feeling better than we currently feel or simply being happy. However, that is only one possible goal. Sometimes regulating emotions has a goal of achieving something we consider important. When our goal is creativity, most fundamentally we have to tolerate the risks associated with creative work. This means that our task is not to make ourselves feel better but rather to accept a certain level of uncomfortable uncertainty. At other times, the goal is to improve our work. In this case, we will need to manage our emotions so as to be able to sit with a sense of frustration for a while. Though that emotion is unpleasant and we naturally want to move away from it, it is our window into realizing what is not working and how to improve it. Choosing to stay in that uncomfortable state is an act of emotion regulation—we are prolonging a state to learn from it.

We need the full range of emotions when it comes to creative work—but we also should not become overwhelmed by emotion.

That's where emotion regulation comes in. You may regulate emotions by strategically finding ways to get into a specific mood (e.g., enthusiasm and eager anticipation), decreasing the intensity of what you are feeling (e.g., anger or anxiety), changing the nature of what you are feeling (e.g., moving from frustration to curiosity), intensifying your feelings (e.g., moving from pleasure to excitement), or maintaining feelings that otherwise might dissipate (e.g., sustaining interest on a project). To understand how we regulate emotions, it helps to deconstruct the course of emotions.

Emotions unfold through a series of steps, starting with a triggering event. This event can be something in our environment, such as a task or a project we are assigned or an interaction with someone. But it can also be something internal to our mind—doubt about our ability to be creative or a persistent expectation of something negative happening.

The next step is attention. If we do not notice an event, we will not experience any feelings about it. Perhaps the most straightforward example of this is in our social interactions. Although sitting in the same meeting, one person can notice the undertone of disapproval in a colleague's comments and be affected emotionally by it, while another person might not notice it and have no reaction at all (which can be a source of misunderstandings that create a whole chain of other emotions!).

If we do notice something triggering, we next have to interpret it. What does the event mean for us? Even if it might be challenging, can we respond to it successfully? Do we think we can solve a problem or rise to the occasion? Or is the situation so difficult that it poses a threat to our reputation or even our safety?

Finally, our emotional reactions emerge as an outcome of the situation-attention-interpretation chain and include physiological responses (e.g., sweating of palms, heart palpitations, muscle tension when we get activated), psychological reactions (anxiety or fear, curiosity or wonder, sadness or disappointment), and behavioral reactions (jumping with excitement or yelling in anger, among a virtually infinite list of actions).

HOW TO REGULATE EMOTIONS

We have more control over our emotional experiences than we think we do. More specifically, we can influence each step in the process described above. You can do something about the triggering event, such as try to prevent it or change it. You can decide what you attend to and focus on. You can change how you look at the situation or shift your perspective on it, which will influence how you interpret its meaning. Finally, when you are already in the midst of an emotional experience, you can alter that feeling by choosing to influence your physiological responses (e.g., relaxing muscles eases tension inherent in stress) or by being mindful about how you react (e.g., perhaps refraining from speaking your mind in a heated situation). Let's look at each step in more detail.

Select the Right Situation

It might seem counterintuitive, but one of the most effective ways to manage our feelings is to start dealing with them before they ever happen. Which is to say, we can choose to put ourselves in some situations and say no to others, thereby selecting for certain feelings and preventing others. Emotion scientists call this strategy *situation selection*. When Katja leans into her strengths and invests more time in the aspects of her job in which she can express her passions and feel most accomplished, she is using this strategy. Similarly, scientists choose which questions to research, usually because they find them interesting or stimulating or because they find the inconsistencies and gaps in existing knowledge frustrating and want to address them. By picking their research topics, they create work that will be energizing. In our workplaces, we might volunteer for a project that aligns with our personal goals, making it more motivating for us.

Every time you make the creativity choice—whether in the beginning of a project or at another point when you recommit to it—you are selecting situations. Sometimes these selections are energizing in the long run, such as projects where your eyes are on a distant prize (e.g., a published book or a five-year growth strategy). But making creativity choices can also be challenging or stressful in the short run (a pitch to a potential client or a project that requires a quick turnaround). When you select those situations, you are temporarily entering less pleasant states but at the same time investing in creativity down the road.

Modify the Situation

When we find ourselves in an inevitably stressful situation—let's say we have to deal with the demands of multiple tasks or projects, each of high priority—we can regulate our emotions by modifying the situation. One such way is to choose to change your physical environment. In writing this book, I had to juggle working full-time as a research scientist managing several grant-funded projects with meeting publication deadlines. To me, it was difficult to transition mentally from my "day job" of data analysis and technical writing to writing for nontechnical audiences, which created unhelpful stress. So, I modified the situation. Instead of writing at my desk, I started writing at my local Barnes & Noble bookstore. The new environment signaled that it was time for a different task with different objectives, which eased the stress, and my progress in writing became much more consistent.

At work, we can modify our job situation through the process that management scholars call *job crafting*. Professors Amy Wrzesniewski and Jane Dutton coined this term to describe ways in which people change the attributes of their jobs to better fit their goals. This includes negotiating greater autonomy, seeking support, volunteering for projects that stretch our skills, and asking for development opportunities. When we are proactive in looking for better ways to approach work and when we choose to work for organizations that provide training, reward effort, and allow us a level of autonomy and authority to fulfill our responsibilities, job crafting will make us feel empowered and result in greater creativity.

We can also modify situations by preparing, even rehearsing, for the occasion. Katja described doing this when she had to lay off a staff member. Knowing she'd be heartbroken over the loss of this person (and dreading saying "those awful words, *I'm sorry you don't have a job here anymore*"), she prepared by planning out and practicing exactly what she was going to say. Her goal was to be as kind as possible in managing an employee's exit from the company so, as she put it, "it doesn't feel like they're being cast out or thrown in the bin." Laying off someone is never easy, but Katja managed her emotions by meticulously planning her words. Later, she felt at least somewhat better after receiving a note from the former employee acknowledging that Katja had handled the difficult conversation with grace and even saying that she would gladly work with Katja again.

When you modify your situation, you actively create conditions that enable creative thinking and doing. You can modify the stressful situation of conflict at work by directly addressing it with a coworker (interpersonal conflict is a sure creativity killer). You can modify the crisis situation, such as dealing with unexpected feedback, by working to solve the problem sooner rather than later. Or you can change the situation of facing a problem alone by bringing colleagues or collaborators to the table.

Redirect Attention

Another set of strategies for regulating emotions involves directing or redirecting our attention. We probably all know from personal experience that distracting ourselves from physical pain helps to ease it. Distracting ourselves works with emotional pain in much the same way. If we become overwhelmed by frustration while discussing the direction of a project, for example, taking a break and doing something different will not only lessen the aggravation but might even provide the distance necessary to see the value of a different perspective.

In one study, researchers demonstrated the benefits of switching attention when people have multiple tasks to accomplish. Participants in the experiment were given two creative thinking tasks, one asking them to come up with ideas for an extraordinary business trip and one in which they had to think of ideas for a new refrigerator. Between these creative thinking tasks, they were asked to examine sets of four words and decide which word did not belong in the group. This was not difficult but required focus. Furthermore, some people were not given specific performance goals, whereas others were given challenging goals (i.e., generating at least fourteen ideas on the creative thinking tasks and solving at least 100 out of 160 word sets for the analytical task). Finally, researchers were interested in learning whether it made a difference if people could switch between the creative and analytical tasks at their discretion or not.

The results showed that people were most creative in their thinking when they had difficult goals and when they were able to switch between tasks. Having performance goals helped focus their attention and motivate their effort, and having the ability to switch between tasks enabled them to refocus attention from one task to another.

Importantly, not everyone who was given an option to switch tasks chose to do so. Those who did not switch came up with similarly creative ideas to those who did switch. However, they were more exhausted afterward. Switching tasks provides a respite from challenging work, reducing the tension we experience. When we get back to the task we switched from, we feel a bit fresher. Though not switching (and thus not regulating the tension) did not undermine creative thinking in this laboratory test, in everyday life, when the demands we face are much higher than those experienced in a thirty-minute research session, accumulating exhaustion starts becoming detrimental to creativity.

This research might seem paradoxical. It's true that switching requires some time to mentally tune into the new task, which can temporarily reduce productivity. This is why we need chunks of uninterrupted time to do focused and deep work. However, this rule is not absolute. It applies to situations and tasks we are well capable of and that we simply need to buckle up and do. However, creative thinking often comes in waves, with ideas flowing and real progress occurring for a while, then slowing or even ceasing for a time. At that point, switching to a different task will be a way to reduce the tension and worry that the ideas have dried up. If you continue to work in the name of sticking with the plan, you will only increase stress. When you take a break, you will interrupt that stress cycle, cut tension, and get your ideas flowing again.

Reappraise

A powerful way to regulate emotions is by altering how we interpret situations. When Thomas Edison famously said that he had not failed but simply found 10,000 ways that something did not work, he was using a strategy called *reappraisal*, or the process by which we reframe what is going on and what the situation means for us. When we think we have failed, a host of strong emotions ensues, from disappointment to discouragement and from frustration to despair. And these emotions can block us from regrouping and trying again. But when an experiment or a prototype does not achieve its originally intended goal and we interpret the outcome not as a failure but as the discovery of a route we need not try in the future, we end up with emotions that energize future effort rather than getting in the way of it.

In one study examining the effects of reappraisal, researchers recruited relief workers and their leaders after the Wenchuan earthquake in China, commonly known as the 2008 Sichuan earthquake. This work was especially suited to benefit from reappraisal—relief workers had to interact with people on the ground who were stressed and scared and might have reacted in less than constructive ways. If someone was yelling, for instance, instead of interpreting their behavior as rude or inconsiderate and feeling aggravated or angry, workers could look at these reactions as influenced by exceptionally difficult circumstances.

The researchers found that workers who tended to reexamine how they thought about the crisis were better able to consider different perspectives in their jobs. They tried to imagine how other people felt before criticizing them and tried to consider multiple sides in a disagreement before making their decisions. In turn, this perspective-taking increased workers' creativity in solving problems on the ground, as judged by their supervisors.

Or consider public presentations. Oftentimes, publicly presenting ideas or products is part of the creative process. Alas, studies repeatedly find that public speaking is among the most commonly feared situations. And creators are not immune to this anxiety. Being overly anxious will interfere with a successful presentation. So, what to do?

Lily Zhu at the University of California, Irvine, devoted her doctoral research to examining what helps entrepreneurs ease their nerves before pitching ideas. She surveyed semifinalists in annual new venture competitions at two major business schools in Southern California, each with $100,000 in cash prizes. Just half an hour before they were about to deliver their pitches, entrepreneurs described what strategies they were using to manage their anxiety.

When entrepreneurs framed their anxiety as a signal that they very much cared about their ideas (rather than viewing it as a lack of confidence in their performance), the judges saw them as more passionate about their ventures. In turn, their perceived passion was associated with higher funding potential. This was the case even when controlling for how much presenters prepared (which can ease anxiety and increase confidence) and other emotion regulation strategies. How entrepreneurs interpreted their anxiety made a concrete difference in their ability to raise funds, which is a necessary step on the way to transforming creative ideas into products and services.

When reappraising the situation, you are choosing to take a step back and being curious about what is going on, looking for alternative explanations. Why are people you are interacting with reacting in a particular way? If you interpret their actions as reflecting disinterest or lack of care, for instance, chances are you will get irritated. But if you ask, "What if they do not have the relevant information?" you will not. You can also reappraise triggers of your own feelings. We can feel activated and jittery because we are anxious but also because we are deeply invested and care about something. Anxiety often begets more anxiety and can spiral, but care signals we are in the state of full alertness that boosts performance. Finally, when reappraising, you can ask whether you can learn something. How will you look at the critical feedback you received? As irritating? Or as a way to help strengthen the work? Reappraisal can help you focus on hidden meanings or opportunities in a situation. You might realize that the closing of one door could also mean the opening of another, such as when failure of one intended application of a product gives way to an exciting unanticipated application.

Change Your Reaction

Alas, there are times when we cannot put ourselves in the ideal situation, change a less-than-perfect situation, distract ourselves with a different task, or reinterpret the event. Sometimes we have no choice in the matter—we must be in a particular place at a particular time and face a particular difficulty. At these times we cannot prevent unwanted emotions or create helpful ones. The only option then is to attempt to change our *reactions*—whether physiological or behavioral—in response to the emotions we are feeling. If we receive unexpected highly critical feedback when we present our product in a work meeting, for instance, choosing to take a few deep breaths will lower our physiological activation and enable us to get into a more favorable state of mind for a measured reaction.

When we have to change what we are already feeling because it is not helpful or appropriate for the situation, such as when we interact with clients or customers, we are engaging in what scientists call *emotional labor.* Perhaps we are tired but have to appear enthusiastic and pleasant. Or we might be aggravated but need to show patience, be accommodating, and creatively solve a problem at hand. We have two options: pretend we are experiencing the feelings demanded by the situation (called *surface acting*) or put effort into trying to change our feelings to truly experience the emotions and attitudes the situation demands (called *deep acting*), using any of the options above. Katja engaged in deep acting when she meticulously planned out what she would say in her difficult conversation with an employee. Doing so allowed her to evince and actually experience the equanimity and compassion she knew were important.

Whereas surface acting is related to stress and emotional exhaustion and, in turn, less creative action, deep acting is related to the experience of motivating challenge and commitment to work, which helps boost creativity. Strategies from situation selection to situation modification, distraction, and reappraisal can lead you to deep acting. It is often an effortful process but one that pays off in more creative and effective thinking and action.

REGULATING EMOTIONS HELPS PERSISTENCE

Creative work takes persistence. Entrepreneurs build their ideas into products and services and take them to consumers over the course of months to years. A scientific project can take a year or longer, from coming up with research ideas, to designing studies to test them, to collecting and analyzing data, to reporting on the findings. After research reports are submitted for publication, the peer-review process of responding to comments and completing necessary revisions can take several more months (or even longer!). Stories of persistence can go from impressive to dramatic. Mathematician Yitang (Tom) Zhang worked on a problem in number theory for three years without making much progress (and also worked as a bookkeeper at a Subway restaurant to help make ends meet) before having a big breakthrough that took him from lecturer to full professor and recipient of a MacArthur Fellowship (popularly nicknamed "the genius grant").

To make it successfully through the long process, creativity requires emotion regulation strategies for the (relative) short term as well as for the long term. In the short run, regulating emotions helps expand our thinking. Researchers tested how changes in mood influenced creative thinking that lasted less than ten minutes and creative thinking during the course of a workday. In one study, scientists recruited master's students to take part in an experiment in which one group was first induced to feel a negative mood and another group was induced to be in a neutral mood. To do that, participants in the negative mood group were asked to recall in vivid detail and write about an event that had made them feel either afraid, distressed, or nervous; the neutral group participants were asked to describe everything they had done the previous day. After that, all participants were asked to describe something that made them feel happy, inspired, and enthusiastic. Finally, participants thought of creative ideas about how to improve the quality of teaching in their university department. Their ideas were evaluated by two judges for their originality and flexibility (the number of different kinds of improvements mentioned, such as involving ideas about teaching materials, facilities, teachers, or other categories of potential changes).

The study showed that the students who were made to feel unpleasant emotions followed by positive emotions were more original and flexible in their thinking than students who were first made to feel neutral and then positive.

To test whether this beneficial effect of a shift in feelings created by scientists in a lab also happens for people at work, researchers studied a group of professionals working full-time in a variety of jobs that require creativity. Participants completed short surveys at the beginning and again at the end of their workdays for one week. First, they were asked to what extent they experienced each of six positive feelings (excited, interested, strong, active, inspired, and alert) and eight negative feelings (scared, guilty, distressed, afraid, nervous, hostile, upset, and angry). Then, participants indicated how creative they were that day, whether they came up with work ideas that were both novel and useful, and whether they were a good role model of creativity.

Researchers learned that the most creative days were those when people experienced a mix of positive and negative feelings in the morning, which then changed during the day so that positive feelings intensified and negative feelings weakened.

Most creative people benefited from an opportunity to use information conveyed both by negative and positive moods. Negative moods inform people of potential problems in their work. For example, feeling guilty signals they've done something wrong, and feeling nervous or scared tells people that what they have done might not work and needs more attention. On the other hand, positive moods broaden thinking and open people to unconventional ideas. Researchers concluded that creative thinking is boosted by two distinct ways of managing our daily feelings: we have to be able to both *tolerate* negative feelings (to learn the lessons they provide) and *regulate* these feelings so that they do not take over.

Let's consider creativity on the long-term scale, beyond a single task or day of work when the major challenge we are facing is to sustain interest and persist in spite of difficulties along the way. Imagine you are working in a large food and beverage company. You and your colleagues tend to like your jobs, and you appreciate being part of creating products that people enjoy. You identify gaps in the product lines that leave some customers dissatisfied—most canned or bottled drinks, from sodas to iced teas to coffee-based drinks, are highly sweetened. One morning during a pitch session, several original ideas are suggested to extend well-known brands in different directions, such as implementing reusable bottles with customizable flavor packets and seltzers containing real fruit juice. Everyone agrees that the ideas are creative and have potential to be successful.

But, of course, not all ideas will get developed and see the light of day. Getting from idea to actual product will require maintaining interest in and motivation for the idea, despite any frustration, bumps in the road, or criticism you may encounter along the way. You have to get approval to use material and human resources to start working on the idea and maintain support through product development and testing.

This is where the ability to effectively regulate emotions is key for long-term success. If you're not skilled in the strategies to tolerate stress or even boredom (which may indeed occur over the long course of transforming a creative idea), you're more likely to lose interest after the initial excitement. Doubt that is common in any creative work, when not managed, can diminish our motivation and creative self-efficacy. If you're not skilled in the strategies to take off the emotional edge of frustration, criticism, or rejection, a high-potential idea may fall by the wayside because you are not able to scale over or dig under that wall. But if you are more adept in applying regulation strategies, our research shows that this skill in dealing with emotions becomes the resource that can push you over bumps to make creative ideas happen. You will be able to sustain your interest and persist.

WATCH FOR EMOTIONAL CONTAGION

The need for emotion regulation is even more obvious when creativity involves working around and with others. Have you ever become sad when a friend shares a story of misfortune? Been in a bad mood until you have a conversation with your perpetually upbeat, optimistic colleague? Whether we realize it or not, our emotions affect the emotions of those around us, and the emotions of those around us influence how we feel. To put it another way, emotions are contagious. This emotional contagion happens even in short encounters. And it certainly happens all day long at work. Think about how much creative work happens in teams, such as groups of scientists who collaborate on research projects, teams of designers and engineers in technology companies, or writers, animators, and technical specialists in creating animated feature films. We have all been in team meetings and know that the mood of the group is not only palpable but can spread quickly.

Now think of emotional contagion in the context of leadership. Because leaders set the tone for their teams, they significantly influence how others feel. They signal what is acceptable and what is not, what is valued and what is not, what will be rewarded and what will be discouraged. Based upon the leader's verbal and nonverbal cues, most employees will be able to quickly ascertain whether their work environment is "creativity friendly," which is to say, a place where they are given free rein to share novel ideas and even critical thoughts without being ignored or castigated. Leaders ease or bring tension to the emotional atmosphere through how they frame tasks and feedback.

When I spoke with Katja, she shared a very simple strategy she uses with her team members. She starts each meeting by asking how people are doing. She is not interested in stock answers of "fine" or "busy." Katja is a leader who genuinely wants to know how people are. It takes effort to break from the temptation to jump to the business of to-do lists, but it pays off by making everyone feel seen and valued. One employee shared that in their previous organization, meetings started with the question about *what* people were doing. Just that one word—"how" instead of "what"—made a world of difference.

Katja is also deliberate in considering what motivates her team and bringing those elements into the workplace. "People are motivated by autonomy, being able to make decisions about what they do and how they do it; mastery, some sense that they're actually achieving something, that they are becoming a master of the thing that they're interested in, or the thing that is their work; and a sense of purpose," she said. "I put a lot of time and energy into ensuring that I'm connected with the people and that the people feel valued. Not only valued in that I say *I value you*, but valued by showing that *the organization values you and wants to invest in you*." If growth makes motivated and creative workers, sometimes it can come down to asking directly what training people would like and in what directions they aspire to develop.

These strategies are not unique to Katja. In a large study my lab conducted, we examined how supervisors' behavior influences their employees' creativity at work. We asked three groups of questions. First, we asked people to describe how their supervisors act around and about emotions. For example, how often do supervisors notice (and acknowledge!) if someone is feeling upset about a work decision or worried about changes at work? How often do they generate enthusiasm to motivate others? Do supervisors understand how their (or the organization's) decisions affect people? Are they able to manage their own emotions and help others cope better with work challenges? Collectively, answers to these questions enabled us to assess to what extent supervisors acted in emotionally intelligent ways—ways that showed their ability to accurately identify emotions, understand and use them to help thinking and problem-solving, and effectively regulate emotions.

Another group of questions were about people's own emotional experiences of work. We asked our participants to describe how they typically feel about work in their own words and also how often they experienced a long list of specific emotions, from feeling content, respected, and proud to feeling frustrated, angry, or discouraged (and more!). Finally, we asked to what extent they had opportunities to grow in their jobs and how often they were creative at work (e.g., contributed new ideas or original ways to achieve work goals).

We found that supervisors' emotional intelligence is a resource for their employees. Employees described dramatically different experiences of work if they had supervisors who acted in emotionally intelligent ways or not. Two-thirds of the top feelings mentioned by those whose supervisors acted in emotionally intelligent ways were positive, whereas 70 percent of the top feelings mentioned by those whose supervisors were not emotionally intelligent were negative.

The details are even more revealing. Those whose supervisors acted in emotionally intelligent ways say they are happy about their work three times more often than they say they are stressed. They describe feelings related to the creative drive, from being challenged and fulfilled, to feeling motivated and enjoying work, to feeling appreciated. By contrast, those whose supervisors do not act in emotionally intelligent ways describe their work experience as marked by anger—they say they are irritated, aggravated, annoyed, and mad. And they often feel underappreciated or unappreciated.

A more positive work experience for employees is valuable in and of itself, but the benefits of supervisors' ability to manage their emotions and influence the emotions of others does not end there. Workers also see that they have greater opportunities to grow and report coming up with creative solutions to work problems, suggesting new ways of achieving objectives, and developing ways to implement these ideas.

Finally, studies have found that leaders' ability to regulate emotions not only helps facilitate and support the creativity of those with whom they work but also translates to greater profitability and higher growth. Leaders who more successfully manage their own emotions create a climate that is open, oriented toward growth, and not plagued by tension. Thus, if you are a leader, it pays off, quite literally, to invest in building emotion regulation skills. When working with others, these skills will leverage the power of emotional contagion to build the emotional climate that not only makes creativity possible but encourages it to thrive.

BE FLEXIBLE. THERE IS NO BULLETPROOF STRATEGY

Earlier in this chapter, I described a host of strategies to regulate emotions. We can lean into energizing situations, try to change our circumstances, strategically distract ourselves, or think about challenges in a different way. It seems reasonable to ask what is the most productive way to manage those feelings that might impede our ability to persist on the long way from having ideas to actualizing them. The truth is that no one strategy will work at all times. Key to managing our feelings is flexibility. What works in one situation might not work in another. Having multiple strategies on which to draw is essential.

Reappraisal is an affective emotion regulation strategy in many circumstances. However, using a lot of reappraisal to deal with difficult feelings can be unhelpful in some situations. In one study, researchers recruited entrepreneurs from a pool of applicants to a seed-funding program run by the Flemish government. All ventures were contacted a year after their application, making them comparable in their development stage. Researchers administered a survey to the company founders asking about how they managed their emotions and about their prior entrepreneurial experience, as well as about their companies (industry sector, founding team size) and their success (company survival a year after seed money application, entrepreneurs' ratings of company performance). Results showed that reappraisal was related to less likelihood of venture survival, especially for companies that did not perform well.

Why can the same strategy be effective in some instances and harmful in others? Specific strategies are not beneficial or detrimental in the abstract. Rather, how helpful they are depends on the demands of the situation. Reappraisal helps entrepreneurs facing challenging feelings in the early stages of a new venture by reminding them that challenges are to be expected in the creative process, and the tendency to see silver linings can enable people to persist through the strain of creative work.

By contrast, reappraisal might not be helpful when companies are already established and facing make-or-break difficulties. Reappraisal now could mean that entrepreneurs are interpreting poor company performance as less serious than it actually is. Instead of reappraisal, focused attention on the stressful work of what might be going wrong is essential for venture survival.

Furthermore, some strategies work only for certain people. Generally, brainstorming benefits from positive energized emotions and from regulating emotions to feel more energized (such as by listening to your favorite upbeat song). But there are exceptions to every rule, including this one. People who tend to be nervous and apprehensive tend to come up with more creative ideas if they think of something worrisome before they start brainstorming. Feelings that match our personality can give us a boost in thinking because they are familiar.

As you make choices about the best emotion regulation strategies in the course of your creative work, ask yourself a series of questions:

Can I be proactive? It is much easier to manage emotions before they take shape than to deal with full-blown frustration, disappointment, or anger, for example. When we build awareness of what situations relate to particular feelings, we can start anticipating (some) emotions before they happen. With greater attention to situation-feeling connections, you can discover that you feel unhelpfully anxious before meeting with a certain colleague or that you tend to be energized and inspired when different teams present their project progress. When you can prevent situations that will trigger unhelpful feelings or lean into those that enable you to shine, your creative work will be less bumpy.

Can I change the situation? When there is no way to prevent difficult situations, it might be possible to do something to make them a bit more manageable. Consider ways to modify situations, from job crafting, to preparation, to solving the problem that triggered your stress (such as dealing with conflict or an unexpected crisis sooner rather than later). We can have agency in relation to our emotions even when it does not feel we do. And trusted others—friends, family, coworkers, coaches—can help us both assess the situation and its importance and devise regulation strategies.

What can I do about my own reactions? Even if all else fails and you do not have much control over the situation itself, you can still have control over how you interpret and react to it. Perhaps you can reappraise and find lessons for the future (like Edison's unsuccessful attempts at the lightbulb) or think of some positive aspects of what is happening. Reaching out to others can both help us reappraise and be a check of our reappraisals in a second-opinion kind of way. Finding a different perspective on a situation can sometimes inspire new ideas and avenues for creativity.

Now for a word of caution: It is easy to think of regulating emotions as a means to make us happy and less stressed. Alas, the reality is more complex. Successfully choosing emotion regulation strategies that match situations in which we find ourselves helps us feel happier and less stressed, but it does not mean that we achieve a state of permanent, tension-free satisfaction that enables steady and (relatively) smooth progress. When your goal is creativity, you will experience a mix of positive, energized feelings (such as happiness, excitement, and pride) along with negative ones, particularly stress and frustration. Striving for creativity means at times deciding to enter situations and pursue work that is difficult and challenging. Doing so means not that you desire these stresses and difficulties or become comfortable with them but rather that you accept them as necessary for creativity to happen.

Overcoming Creative Blocks

Andrea Portera is a contemporary music composer. He has written more than 160 pieces of music, which have been performed across countries and continents by prestigious orchestras such as the Tokyo Philharmonic Orchestra, the RAI National Symphony Orchestra, the BBC Philharmonic, the national orchestras of Greece and Estonia, and many others. Andrea's works have been commissioned by major international foundations and festivals, and his music has won awards in competitions from Italy, Spain, Finland, Poland, Russia, and Japan.

When I spoke to him about his creative process, Andrea surprised me by saying he starts not with sound but with visual imagery. He begins by sketching abstract designs in a notebook. His experience is synesthetic—a perception of one sense linked with another—and for Andrea, colors are associated with the sounds of different musical instruments. He sees yellow and hears a flute, for example, or sees purple and hears a violin. When he is writing music in this way, he is fully immersed, does not feel fatigue, and can even forget to eat or sleep as one musical image flows into another. He told me that in the middle of composing, the experience is pure joy.

At the beginning, however, there is frustration. He has a sketch in mind, but it is not yet a full or truly good idea. At this point, he is in search of the main theme of the piece and looking to develop it. Andrea describes this part of the process using a simile. His work, he says, is like a circle. He starts on the outside of that circle and has to get to the center. The circle can be entered from any point—there isn't a single correct method or approach. Once he manages to find his way inside, he can see the music and write it down. The issue is how to enter. In his experience, the quality of the initial writing does not matter. The important thing is beginning the creative process.

Lucija Ivšić has been writing music, performing at major music festivals, and touring the world with her postpunk indie rock band, Punčke, for more than ten years. Punčke released five critically acclaimed albums and were nominated for an MTV European Music Award. But in the back of Lucija's mind were other passions too. She pursued her love of science and got a degree in geoinformatics. Eventually she found a way to bring together her various interests through sound design, performance, and research at the intersection of art, science, and technology. Her mixed-media and virtual reality work explores the nature of identity by examining memory, our sense of place, and its physical expressions.

Lucija described her creative process on a recently completed performance piece as a wild roller-coaster ride. It started smoothly, she said, with an exciting idea built through intense, focused work, and climbed steadily up to a series of successful performances. The problem she tackled emerged after several months of postpandemic touring, feeling alone as a solo performer and contemplating the meaning of community and personal identity. She decided to build what she referred to as an "artificial technological ensemble" of sixteen custom-made humanoid singers that sensed movement and would participate in a call-and-response music piece with her. To complete it, Lucija had to learn how to write computer code to program the singers, taking the risk of doing something she had not done before, and find engineering support for their physical fabrication. And she did it all, making steady progress on an ambitious project. When she performed the first version of the piece, the singers were arranged in a circle six meters across, with the audience positioned inside it. These performances were by any measure very successful—audiences were emotionally moved and inspired to reflect on how the presence of others influences us.

Yet, Lucija knew this was not the final version.

This is where the problems started. The roller coaster that climbed up now came precipitously down. A period of deep dissatisfaction with the piece took hold, and Lucija became preoccupied with using AI. She could not shake the thought that AI was the way to be current and relevant. Lucija made some attempts but knew that they were not what she was after.

As she found herself in the middle of the project and in a rut, she started an artist residency in a small town just outside Florence, Italy, determined to figure out what was troubling her work and to make progress on it. Lucija continued to work but was still unhappy with the piece and felt she'd arrived at an impasse.

During her residency, Lucija followed a routine. Every morning, she wrote in a stream of consciousness journal, went for a run, got tomatoes, burrata, and a focaccia in town for breakfast, and then settled in for a day of work. Then, one day she had a realization.

It struck her how her simple breakfast of tomatoes, cheese, and bread made for a perfect meal, and suddenly Lucija had a moment of clarity: she needed to simplify her work. It needed to be simpler to be more effective.

She drew the entire storyboard and proceeded to work on the reconceived piece as soon as she was back in Australia. The doubt was still there, but she was re-energized and making progress again.

When the head of the lab where she works finally saw the finished piece, he was so touched that he cried—the highest praise to an artist and performer.

Both Andrea Portera and Lucija Ivšić intimately know and vividly demonstrate that creation is not a smooth process. Daily creative work will always be challenging, but when we hit a creative block, it can feel downright impossible. A creative block is the experience of being stuck. Formally, scientists define it as a failure to make progress on a creative project that is not due to a lack of ability, desire, or commitment. It is so common that it can be considered an unavoidable, and perhaps even integral, part of the creative process. In interview studies, scientists have recounted periods marked by an inability to solve or even understand a problem. Artists have described starting their work from an urgent desire to make art and a need to "incarnate" their ideas but also feeling a sense of being plagued by an inability to clearly conceptualize their ideas or to make them tangible, which usually results in a period of wandering, as if through a void. Composers and writers have described the anxiety of facing the blank page. Regardless of what we do, we should not be surprised if at some point we get stuck.

NOT SEEING THE FOREST FOR THE TREES

The problem when being stuck is that we become so close to the work and the details of it that we lose track of the big picture and the possibilities in what we are doing. Imagine starting a new project. Perhaps you are sitting in a conference room and a team leader is presenting the project goals. The leader describes the desired end results, as well as the major constraints and obstacles that can be anticipated, and concludes with a set of dos and don'ts before inviting questions and discussion. Everyone seems to be on the same page. Still, as people start sharing their ideas, some of them are clearly not heeding the list of dos and don'ts.

In a classic set of experiments, researchers wanted to see how common this experience is. They gave different design tasks to engineering students—to create a versatile and easy-to-mount bicycle car rack, a measuring cup for the blind, or a spill-proof coffee cup. In each case, one group of students reviewed an example design that included several features that would prevent the final product from meeting its goals, whereas another group of students saw no sample designs before starting their work. For example, when designing a coffee cup, students had to create a disposable spill-proof cup that was durable, could be used with one hand, and did not have a straw or a mouthpiece. An example design showed a cup that used a straw and a mouthpiece and would leak when on its side. Researchers wanted to see if students would unconsciously be influenced by the example they saw and fixate on the design features presented in the examples.

Regardless of the particular design problem or whether or not they saw example designs before starting their work, participants came up with the same number of ideas. However, many of those who reviewed sample designs beforehand *did* become fixated on their specific features. This was the case even though the sample designs clearly did not follow the goal specifications. For instance, although the instructions explicitly said the coffee cup should not include a mouthpiece or straw, 39 percent of designs by those who saw the sample included a mouthpiece and 17 percent included a straw.

These results were replicated multiple times in various studies, but researchers wanted to conduct another, more stringent test. They wondered whether the same effect would happen among professional engineers in a structural design department of a major corporation. These engineers had more expertise and more experience than the students. It stood to reason that they would be better at designing according to a set of given specifications. The results showed otherwise: they were just as susceptible to fixation as the engineering students.

We can get unconsciously fixated on examples, turning something that is intended to help the creative process into something that gets us stuck. Alternatively, we can be unwilling to consider new ideas, fixated on our existing knowledge and experience. Whatever the exact cause, we need to step back from the individual trees and see the forest. We need to find ways to broaden our thinking.

If you have noticed that people on your team do not always follow the list of given dos and don'ts, your predicament is not unique. They may be blocked or stalled in generating solutions that are original and useful or effective. But the experience can be a temporary one. The team can regroup and go back to the drawing board. However, jump-starting the blocked creative process will require you to draw on all that you know about creativity. Think of it as an exercise in applying everything you have learned up to this point in the book.

HOW TO GET UNBLOCKED

Understanding the nature of creative work, including its difficulties, blocks, and failures, is step one. For some, this understanding can be implicit, meaning that we have an unspoken recognition that bottlenecks are a normal part of the process and not indicative of our (permanent) lack of ability. For others, the understanding is explicit, a realization born out of experience and practice that we can put into words and share with others. One artist I interviewed for a study described it aptly: "Failure is the most common experience in creation. When you create enough, you realize that doubt, feeling paralyzed, is a part of the process. I've done enough pieces to know that failure and feelings of uncertainty can be overcome in ways that are not always immediately visible. When you have enough breakthroughs, you trust the process more and are less daunted by creative block."

This understanding of the creative process helps people do what needs to be done. It helps them persevere rather than give up when they get blocked. I surveyed more than 400 people, some of whom were recruited without regard to their creativity, whereas others were recruited because they were professionally creative within a broad range of fields, including the arts, the sciences, education, technology, and business. We asked all participants about their understanding of the nature of creative work. Participants also rated how much they used different strategies and approaches when working on creative projects. And finally, we assessed their motivation, well-being, and creative achievement.

The results showed that creative professionals had a better understanding of the creative process as involving ups and downs than those who were not creative in their jobs. Going into a creative project, they knew that things would not always go as planned, and they expected to feel frustrated at times. They understood that some days would just not be productive, and they accepted this as a part of creative work.

Moreover, understanding the nature of the creative process was related to how effectively people approached their work. Those who were aware of the challenges of creative work, including running into obstacles and impasses, were likely to flexibly adjust their approach as necessary, such as trying new strategies when encountering bumps in the road, engaging in a trial and error process when navigating blocks, and, when stuck, trying to work on a different project for a while. In other words, they knew to resort to problem construction and reconstruction. Also, those who recognized that the creative process is nonlinear were willing to take informed risks and continued to be driven by an interest in their work and a sense of challenge they found in it. They did not necessarily experience less stress or anxiety, but they had qualities of resilience—the ability to manage these difficulties and bounce back.

Once you realize you are in a state of creative block, the question becomes, now what? A rut might seem so deep that we cannot see over it into clear territory where we can move freely and take one step after another. Although no one bulletproof set of steps will get us out of the rut, three major groups of strategies can help nudge us out. Just like when a car gets stuck in mud or packed snow, you might need to do a bit of going backward and then a bit of going forward until you gain sufficient momentum to break free. You might get lucky and the first wiggle gets you out, but, more often than not, a few tries will be necessary to get you back on the road. The first set of strategies focuses on the difficult emotions associated with being stuck. The second set of actions is about ways to broaden your thinking again. And the third is about getting busy and buckling up.

PRACTICE SELF-COMPASSION

Creative block is an emotionally overwhelming experience. When I asked creative professionals to describe it in their own words, "frustration" dwarfed all the other feelings. For some, this frustration is tinged with anger, for some with disappointment, and for some with anxiety and doubt, which can range from uncertainty to a sense of personal inadequacy and guilt. People can feel like they're drowning in a sea of frustration—and those feelings can easily grow into more pernicious self-doubt, helplessness, and even depression.

The key to coping with any difficult emotion is to remind ourselves that these feelings are not permanent, even (and perhaps especially) when this does not seem to be the case in the moment. When we are overwhelmed by the frustration of being stuck, our goal is not to transform the jumble of confusion, anxiety, and dissatisfaction into peace or happiness. Rather, the goal is to move far enough out of the emotional havoc to be able to get a different perspective or reach out for one. Emotion regulation strategies, from redirecting your attention to changing your reactions, as we examined in the last chapter, will help. But even before we reach for specific emotion regulation tools, we need to give ourselves a little break and act with self-compassion rather than criticism.

People who are highly self-critical are judgmental toward their flaws and even their passing inadequacies. When times are difficult, they tend to be tough on themselves and are often intolerant and impatient toward themselves when something does not go as they want. To make things worse, they tend to obsess and fixate on what is going wrong, which makes coping more challenging. Also unhelpfully, they tend to isolate themselves from others who could potentially be a source of ideas and support. This attitude of self-criticism can get generalized beyond a single situation of being at an impasse and diminish a sense of creative self-efficacy. In turn, less confidence in your ability to be creative can become a self-fulfilling prophecy—what we fear becomes reality as anxiety gets us deeper into the hole.

The opposite of self-criticism is self-compassion. This is an attitude of kindness toward ourselves. When we practice self-compassion, we keep our challenges or failures in perspective and remind ourselves that the pain or frustration we are experiencing is not unique to us. In the case of creative work, hitting bottlenecks is simply a part of the process.

Psychologists Darya Zabelina and Michael Robinson ran an experiment in which they showed how self-criticism and self-compassion affect a crucial aspect of creative thinking: coming up with original ideas. They hypothesized that boosting an attitude of self-compassion would enhance creative thinking and do so more strongly for those who were highly self-critical and might otherwise self-censor novel or unusual ideas.

To test this, researchers first assessed people's tendency to be self-critical. Then, they asked them to write about a personal experience in which they felt bad about themselves—"something that involved failure, humiliation, or rejection." Participants recalled this event in vivid detail, describing what led up to it, what happened, who was involved, how they felt, and what they did at the time of the experience. People in one group were not given any additional instruction. But in another group, participants were also asked to write about the experience in a way they would talk to a friend going through a similar situation. Because we tend to sympathize and show kindness to those who are close to us, this was designed to evoke the attitude of compassion toward oneself. After writing about the experience of failure or rejection, all participants took a standard test of creative thinking asking them to imagine consequences for hypothetical scenarios (e.g., if people could walk on air) and completed a set of sketches.

Researchers found that the least original ideas were generated by those who were highly self-critical and had been asked to focus on the experience of failure. This is exactly what happens in times of creative block. We get caught up in a loop of self-doubt and criticism. However, when self-critical people focused on viewing their experience from the perspective of self-compassion, they came up with ideas as original as those who were not critical of themselves.

People differ in their tendency to be self-critical and self-compassionate in their everyday lives and in relation to different life experiences. Some of us more easily assume the attitude of self-compassion. For others, doing so might take a conscious choice and effort to see setbacks from a more balanced perspective, while constantly reminding themselves of our common humanity and the challenging nature of creative work.

Self-compassion in practice means cutting ourselves some slack. One writer in our research spoke about coping with the creative block as being "like self-therapy." This is an apt comparison. The crucial ingredient in successful psychotherapy is the quality of the therapeutic alliance—the relationship between a therapist and a client based on respect and empathy. By analogy, successful self-therapy has to start with respect and empathy for oneself. Building on this basis, the rest of the work of getting unstuck can unfold. As this writer described, "These blocks pass, just like all emotions! I use trust, grounding in the process, and habit to get me out of the block.

It's a mix of patience and self-starting. It's a blend of waiting and seizing the day. When a block occurs, I still show up to do the work, but I might need to accept that some days the work is not as good, or not as productive. When things are bad, it's like a dance between inspiration and practice."

Showing compassion to ourselves can be a tall order, especially when we realize we have made mistakes (and think we should have known better) or are at an impasse while the deadline clock is ticking. Thinking of what you could have done differently can throw you into self-recrimination. There will be time to reflect on the creative process and what you could or should learn from any particular project and your experiences of it. But being critical at the time of a creative block will not make it better. This is the time to imagine what a good friend would tell you.

BROADEN YOUR THINKING

It is clear that broadening our thinking helps to overcome a creative block or impasse. You are fixated on something unhelpful and need to step away from it. However, this is easier said than done, considering that creative blocks breed frustration, and when we are frustrated, our thinking narrows.

Creators often develop personal strategies that broaden their thinking and their range of perspectives when they are facing difficulties. When I spoke with Andrea Portera, he detailed working on a composition commissioned by the Kymi Sinfonietta, a Finnish orchestra. He had a vision of a spider as a personification of the unconscious but not a specific image that he could translate into music. So, he engaged with a broad range of topics in an effort to expand his thinking. He went to see an exhibition about spiders at a local museum. He read books about the Jewish Kabbalah and the tree of life. Andrea followed an image that emerged from these threads and then chose fixed segments of notes—twelve notes in the same order—as a constraint. He described this self-imposed structure as a prison. But without those guardrails, he said, it would be like being lost in a labyrinth. His eventual composition, titled "Arachnomancy," was born of following a wide range of influences and exploring where they might lead.

Researchers tested a number of strategies aimed at broadening our thinking to get out of the states of fixation and creative block and identified a set of tried-and-true approaches. As is the case with emotion regulation, however, there isn't a single, never-failing strategy. To find what works for you in a particular situation, you will need to engage in some trial and, chances are, some error.

From Function to Form

At times, people experience the creative block at the start of the creative process, before they have working ideas, just like Andrea recounted. Psychologists study this kind of creative block in the laboratory by presenting their participants with problems such as the so-called candle task. In this problem, people are taken to a room with a table set against a wall. On the table are a candle, a book of matches, and a box of thumbtacks. They have to affix a lit candle to the wall in such a way that it does not drip onto the table.

This task is hard. As a rule, people try out ideas that turn out not to work, such as attempting to use tacks to fasten the candle to the wall or trying to apply wax as glue to stick the candle to the wall. Instead, the effective solution is to use the box as a candle holder and attach it to the wall with thumbtacks.

The problem is difficult because people tend to automatically perceive the box as a receptacle for tacks. They do not see it as an object with properties independent of its original, obvious function. People become fixated on the obvious function, a cognitive bias known (not so creatively) as functional fixation, which prevents them from seeing novel potential applications. To successfully complete the task, people have to restructure what they see and know as given.

When researchers asked study participants to say out loud without self-censoring everything that came to their mind as they worked on the candle problem, they found that getting blocked was a common experience. People reported that they were out of ideas or their mind had gone blank, said they were confused about the problem, and showed clear frustration.

They would no doubt be happy to learn that in laboratory experiments, functional fixation can be reduced (and the creative block removed) relatively easily—indeed, with the smallest of changes.

The candle task's standard instructions describe the materials available as "a candle, a book of matches, and a box of thumbtacks." But then in one study, researchers changed this description to "a candle, a book of matches, a box, and thumbtacks." Now, instead of "a box *of* thumbtacks," we have "a box *and* thumbtacks." This change is very slight, but it makes a big difference. It breaks the mental image of a box of thumbtacks as a single unit that highlights its function (holding tacks) into two independent concepts—a box and tacks. With the original instructions, only 20 percent of people solve the problem successfully in the time allotted, and those who solve it take an average of nine minutes. The modified instructions result in an 80 percent success rate, and participants complete the task in an average of 4.5 minutes.

We are not consciously aware that we are fixated on an obvious function, making it hard to tell what is going on in your specific creative block. But if you are working on a problem that has familiar elements, consider whether you can deconstruct features that have common functions into their objective descriptions.

Reconstruct the Problem

When we are in a state of creative block, our problem-solving process has failed. We have to go back to the drawing board to sketch the problem anew. This, you will recall, is a process of problem construction.

To help explore and construct problems, designers interact with objects and materials, manipulate them, and test different features as they develop new products. And they create spaces in which this exploration process can happen more easily. Similarly, Pablo Picasso's studio spaces were full of cavasses in various stages of completion, as well as many objects that he found stimulating or inspiring, ranging from ceramic vases and metal plates to African masks, Iberian sculptures, and works by other artists such as Henri Matisse, Auguste Renoir, Amedeo Modigliani, and Alberto Giacometti. These seemingly chaotic environments in which we can interact with objects or physical representations of our ideas help get the creative process going or get it restarted.

Research supports what many creators have discovered intuitively. When designers work in a space where they can manipulate materials, they broaden their thinking and break the hold of specific details on which they might be fixated. Observations of designers at work show that they spend most of their time interacting with the items at their disposal. Working with design materials enables the discovery of their different features and new potential applications, which broadens thinking.

I had the sense of this book in my mind for a while, but just as the sense of knowing your material is not always a reliable indicator of how well you can demonstrate what you know on a test, a mental sense is not enough to actually get the content of a book onto the page. It was very challenging, for example, to find the right organization and structure for certain chapters. Paradoxically, this was especially the case for those chapters that were closest to the research in my own lab. I simply had too much I wanted, and thought I needed, to say. In those cases, I would seek refuge in our spacious and airy back room, print out the sections I had already written, take scissors and physically cut them, spread them all out in front of me, and arrange them in different ways. I quite literally deconstructed and reconstructed the chapters.

When creative block brings you back to the proverbial drawing board, bring props. Clean environments can reduce distractions when you are working on straightforward tasks and increase your productivity. But when you are looking for a way to broaden your thinking, some mess actually helps get ideas flowing. Just as I cut out pieces of my chapters and kept moving them around until the puzzle came together, try to find ways to make your work physical and tangible. When you move the pieces around, you will see them in a broader context, and at some point they will snap into a new picture.

Reach Out

Working with other people can serve a similar function as exploring and reconstructing ideas. With effective communication, the group of coworkers or collaborators can become a vehicle for opening up your thinking. Other people are able to contribute different perspectives on the problem, and potential solutions can emerge from the combination of shared ideas, whether your impasse happens early on in idea development or at the very end, when you cannot decide whether the work is really done.

When Lucija traveled from Australia to Italy, this different physical place opened a way to move forward. Her insight about how to restart the project and build momentum arrived in a manner that was almost straight out of a made-for-television movie. The delight of a simple daily meal in the Tuscan countryside sparked in her mind an analogy that moved her to simplify her project.

But even as she continued to make progress after the initial insight, Lucija was still unsure. Finally, she reached out to the head of the lab for help. After an intense period of work, strategies that at other times can help us take a different perspective and a fresh look might not work anymore. We are too close to the work to truly step back and see it with detachment. At these times, you need other people to hold the torch. In Lucija's case, the lab director was the voice that made clear the piece was just right. He could approach it with fresh eyes, and from his reaction of awe, Lucija knew that she had finally achieved her goal.

Take Breaks

When you have tried and tried again and still not managed to get over a bump in the road, the best thing you can do is take a break and do something different. Researchers hypothesized that this works because a break serves an incubation function—it allows for unconscious processing of the problems and ideas we have previously worked on, which may lead to new insights.

After reviewing and analyzing results from 117 independent studies, psychologists Ut Na Sio and Thomas Ormerod at Lancaster University found that people's creative thinking improves after a period of incubation if they first spend longer (versus shorter) amounts of time struggling with the task. The practical takeaway is not to break from your work at the first sign of trouble or frustration. Sit with it, stare at it, and struggle with it for a good while first.

Furthermore, not all breaks are created equal. Simply resting or doing something completely passive and undemanding does not do the trick. For best results, you should break to a task that requires some effort but is not very demanding. In everyday life, this is easy to do. Knowledge workers, for example, can take a break from problem-solving by catching up with email, working on a report, or doing other paperwork that's been lingering on their to-do lists. Artists can order supplies or mix up some paints; writers can jot down ideas for a new story. These are all work-related ways of taking a break, which give us the benefit of still being productive, yet allow us the mental space we need to get unstuck.

Let Your Mind Wander

There is a saying that great ideas occur in the shower. In fact, one study found that 30 percent of insights people have happen in the shower. We come up with new ideas specifically because our mind is off the task on which we are stuck. Psychologists at the University of California, Santa Barbara, studied professional writers and theoretical physicists to examine this effect. Both groups have to be creative in their work, but the nature of their work is quite different. Whereas physicists' work is restrained by having to obey the laws of physics, writers can take their ideas in virtually infinite directions.

For two weeks, at the end of each day, study participants described their most creative idea and answered a set of questions about how they came up with it. First, they answered whether at the time the idea occurred to them they were absorbed in the problem or thinking about something unrelated. Then, they indicated whether they were actively working on the project for which they had a creative idea, were working on another project, or were doing something unrelated to their work. And finally, they specified whether the idea was about a new problem, something on which they were making steady progress, or something for which they were at an impasse.

Two-thirds of the time people were making steady progress on their creative work. But the experience of impasse was familiar to both physicists and writers; 14 percent of their workdays were best described as being stuck in some way.

Most ideas occurred as people were absorbed in the work, but a substantial number—about one in five—arrived when their mind was wandering and not focused on the problem. What's more, creative ideas conceived after experience of an impasse were significantly more likely to be a result of mind wandering than were ideas for projects on which people were making steady progress. When we are stuck, insights can come from unexpected places, and we are more likely to be open to both seeking and noticing connections from unexpected sources because none of the usual ones have worked.

The clear advice is to let your mind wander at times. Yet, our society is obsessed with productivity and how to increase it. We seek time-saving tips, mind hacks, and tools to be ever more focused and productive. However, mind wandering means time not spent focused on tasks, and therefore, it is not actively productive in the moment. The paradox of creative productivity is that, in order to achieve more in the long run, you must sacrifice time spent on tasks. Professor Jonathan Schooler, who pioneered research on mind wandering, proposed to replace this term with "mind-wondering." If you let your mind wander, it will also wonder—playfully ask questions and explore what-if scenarios. Without effort, your thinking will broaden.

BUCKLE UP

The truth is that sometimes we can try all the strategies to open our mind and broaden our thinking and still remain stuck. When we find ourselves in this predicament, the only remaining option is to work anyway.

Neil Gaiman is a writer who has won every existing science fiction, fantasy, and young adult fiction award for his novels, graphic novels, short stories, and screenplays. In a reading celebrating the tenth anniversary of his masterpiece *American Gods*, he was asked about writer's block. He started answering by questioning the very notion of it. "First of all," he said, "I really don't believe in it. Radio broadcasters do not have radio broadcaster's block. You're not allowed to come in and say, 'Today I cannot talk, I'm sorry, the words are not there.' Shoe salesmen, no shoe salesmen block, gardeners do not have gardener's block, cellists do not have cellist's block, but writers, because we're clever, have writer's block. Because it's so much fancier than saying, 'I'm stuck. Story's not really going anywhere. I don't know what to do ... Leave me alone. I shall drink tea and contemplate the infinite.' It'd be lovely."

Of course, Gaiman was (half) joking. He does get stuck at times. He was commenting on a romanticized notion that getting stuck is unique to writing or similar artistic endeavors and that this experience of being blocked is a special form of artistic suffering that gives writers permission not to do their work.

Instead of being a generalized experience, which is implied by the term "writer's block"—the inability to write at all—writer's block, Gaiman said, is specific to a particular piece. "If somebody had real writer's block, they wouldn't send you emails grumbling about having writer's block," he said. "There would be no words. But the words are there."

From understanding the nature of being stuck come some solutions. Gaiman continued,

What I tend to do is one of two things when I have writer's block. Thing one is I always like to have more than one thing on the go. Whether it's an introduction that I ought to be writing, whether it's a short story, whether it's a script. If I have something else, then when I get stuck, I can just go and work on the thing that I'm not stuck on. And thing number two that I'll do, which is really no fun and a very dispiriting thing to do, but it does kind of work, is you write anyway. Writing on days when you're stuck and it's bad is horrible. It's like writing through a headache. Every word seems stupid. If in a normal day you manage to do a thousand words, let's say, this day you do 200 words and you think they're all stupid. Except that the next day you come in and you look at what you did, and you move a comma around, and delete a line and change something, and you have a perfectly usable 200 words. What really gets strange is that a year later, you finish the book, you can remember that there were days when you wrote and it was magical and you wrote as if diamonds were dripping from your fingers and you were inspired and the gods were talking through you. And you remember there were days when you pushed through horrible writer's block and it was all awful. But you can't actually find them on the page. It all reads like it was written by the same person.

What Neil Gaiman shares from personal experience and practice is not just his individual preference or unique hack. The first option he described is the strategy we discussed above—taking a break (while still being productive on another task). Doing something different can create enough distance to provide a broader perspective. Gaiman would occasionally hit a wall and not know what Shadow, the main character in *American Gods*, would do next. At these times, he would write short stories about how old-world Gods came to America that were inserted as special boxes in the novel. By the time he finished these stories and came back to the main plot line, he had figured out how to continue.

But he acknowledged that at other times you simply have to buckle up, continue working, and steadfastly plug away, systematically trying out possibilities. Even if you don't make much progress, *some* might still happen, ultimately contributing to the creativity of the overall work. This is the path of continuing to sweat and getting perhaps 200 of the usual 1,000 words in a day. That is only 20 percent, but it is more than nothing. You might be working as if "through a headache," but you might move rather than standing in place.

Creative work that feels more like hard labor than joyful flow of ideas is common. Even after Lucija's insight that broke the hold of her creative block, she continued to be displeased with her progress. But she would get up every day, go to the lab, sit at her space, and work. She was not happy, but she was determined, and she continued the work, even if the process was unfolding more slowly than she was hoping.

Although there is much we can do to dig ourselves out of the hole when progress is slow or not satisfactory, often we need a little help from our friends and family (mentors, colleagues, leaders). Creativity is social even when it does not seem to be. We will turn to this sometimes hidden aspect of creative work next.

PART THREE

Creativity in Context

With a Little Help from Your Friends

When Steven Spielberg won his first Oscar for Best Director for *Schindler's List*, he expressed gratitude to many who had directly or indirectly contributed to the film.

> Let me just start by saying that this never could have happened, this never could have gotten started without a survivor named Poldek Pfefferberg who Oskar Schindler saved from Auschwitz, from Belsen. He's the man who talked Thomas Keneally into writing the book. I owe him such a debt—all of us owe him such a debt. He has carried the story of Oskar Schindler to all of us. A man of complete obscurity who makes us wish and hope for Oskar Schindlers in all of our lives. . . . I want to thank Sid Sheinberg for giving me the book. Thank you, Sid. I want to thank Steve Zaillian for a screenplay of inordinate restraint. I have great actors in this movie. Liam, thank you. Ralph, thank you. Ben Kingsley, thank you. I want to thank my wife, who's here with me tonight, for rescuing me ninety-two days in a row in Krakow,

Poland, last winter when things got just too unbearable. And my mom who's here, who is my lucky charm, whom I love very, very much. And to the six million who can't be watching this among the one billion watching this telecast tonight. Thank you.

Spielberg's acceptance speech highlighted the often overlooked social side of creativity. We tend to romanticize the notion of the lone genius creator but the truth is, all creativity is social. Spielberg could not have made his award-winning film (*Schindler's List* garnered a total of seven Academy Awards that night) without a Holocaust survivor who told the story, the author who wrote a book about it, or the executive who brought the book to his attention. He could not have made a movie as powerful as *Schindler's List* without the screenwriter and actors who brought their own creativity to the production. And in thanking his mother and his wife, Spielberg was acknowledging another kind of contribution from those around him: emotional support.

Creativity is not social only in the case of those who work directly with large groups of people, such as a film crew, or those who are part of an organization. All creative endeavors, even those completed alone, emerge from a larger social milieu. Writing, for example, may be a solitary activity. But this book hardly came to be in a social vacuum. I developed my research examining the creative process over the last twenty-five years through innumerable interactions with other scientists. Some of those interactions were direct—talking with colleagues at conferences and developing collaborations—while many more were indirect, through research articles and books that I have read. Then, during the writing process, when I got stuck on a chapter about, of all things, getting stuck, I reached out to several colleagues who helped me untie the unnecessarily complicated knot I'd got myself into. And although my husband could not help with the generation of the book's ideas (he's an oceanographer), for months he made it possible for me to go out and write in late afternoons by taking on more than his share of homework help and cooking, not to mention providing emotional support when I wondered what I was doing.

Much of creative work happens between these two social extremes—large collaborative projects, such as thousands of people contributing to a major motion picture, and (seemingly) solitary endeavors such as writing, composing music, or painting. When I spoke to Matt Kursh and Andrea Hoban, cofounders of Oji Life Lab, a digital skills training platform for individuals and organizations, it was evident that their creativity is not just *helped* by interactions with others but actually *comes to be* through those interactions.

Matt is a serial entrepreneur. The first company he started in college was acquired by Apple. His next company was an early e-commerce platform that he sold to Microsoft. He's also run a nonprofit foundation and served on numerous boards of public, private, and nonprofit organizations.

His original goal for his current company was to create programs and resources to teach life skills to teenagers. Matt wondered, "What if we had hundreds of locations where high school students could learn those skills?" It turned out that adolescents were not the right audience. As much as they could have benefited from building life skills, teens were simply not interested. Right there, on the heels of realizing that his original idea wasn't going to work, the first social spark for the next version of the idea happened. Although high schoolers were not aware they needed these skills, another audience was keenly aware of their importance: professionals running businesses. Matt saw an opportunity but did not have the right expertise.

He turned to his network for advice and help. A mutual friend introduced Matt to Andrea. She worked at an international staffing company running their job training division globally and was getting certified as a coach. Matt had been looking for advice about corporate learning and development, and in Andrea he ended up finding just the right cofounder.

The challenge before them was how to bring the skills trainings to those who needed it. Andrea happened to have a conversation with someone in her network that highlighted the need for a flexible technology solution. In large organizations it was difficult to bring people to the same place at the same time for training in person. At around that same time, Matt had a conversation with another learning specialist who mentioned a meditation and mindfulness app as a model for a learning program that did not require any special arrangements to start—one could simply sign up and go. Andrea and Matt at first had misgivings about the idea, because many of the e-learning programs available at the time were not high quality, promising more than they delivered. But they took on the challenge and set off to design a digital training experience that would be useful and engaging, in which people would be guided rather than lectured to, and, very importantly, that would incorporate meeting people live (because that is essential for truly learning human skills).

The Oji Life Lab was born. The problem they identified was serving what Andrea describes as "the big middle." Typically, training programs are designed for leaders or new hires, but Andrea and Matt wanted to design effective learning solutions for those who tend to be left out by traditional programs. The question before them was how to make this happen.

Andrea used her knowledge from the field of corporate learning. "Our ethos around learning is that I will be much more likely to change my behavior if I do something for a short period of time daily, but do that daily behavior for a longer period of time," she explained. "I will definitely have a greater chance of working a new muscle and using it. So, spaced repetition, spiral learning, revisiting topics over time with greater depth—that's the way we approach a learning sequence." As their first program on emotional intelligence skills was successfully applied in organizations as diverse as a medium-sized manufacturing firm, a large healthcare system, and a global technology company, Oji Life Lab developed additional programs to teach decision-making skills and a multitopic bundle of skills for new managers.

Andrea is in charge of content, and Matt is in charge of software. But that dichotomy oversimplifies their partnership. Matt describes it with an analogy. "I think like in screenplay writing, some people think it's the plot that matters and the characters sit on top of it, and some people think it's the other way," he said. "But really, they're intertwined. There's no way to separate the plots and the characters. They both impact each other."

"We're really generally aligned," Andrea went on, "but it's not always that we agree on everything. What I think has been the mark of our very fortuitous partnership is an unequivocal knowledge that we always have each other's best interests at heart. To let that creativity loose is to be in an environment where you feel safe and trusted."

Creative work is enabled by seemingly paradoxical social forces. On the one hand, creative work benefits from strong relationships characterized by support and respect. On the other hand, close relationships make us want to please others to maintain harmony, which makes being original in thinking and unconventional in action more difficult.

How do we reconcile this apparent contradiction? By availing ourselves of both strong, close relationships and what scientists refer to as weak ties—the contacts, acquaintances, and colleagues with whom we do not interact frequently and with whom we might not have deep emotional attachments.

Research points to strong relationships and weak ones serving different functions for creativity. Strong social relationships form a support network that encourages creative work and lifts us up and pushes us to persevere when the going gets tough. Weak ties, on the other hand, help inspire new approaches and inject fresh thinking, especially when we reach a creative impasse. For creativity to happen, the task is to balance strong and weak relationships and draw on them in the most beneficial ways to boost creative work.

DRAW ON CASUAL RELATIONSHIPS

After the first key insight of pivoting the network of learning centers for adolescents to professionals, the question for Matt became what form the building of human skills in organizations might take. That spark came during another casual conversation with a professional acquaintance in their network. That person pointed to the need for technology-enabled solutions.

The benefit of weak ties is that they connect people to different social circles. These contacts can have backgrounds and experiences that are quite distinct from ours, thus providing a source of information and ideas that otherwise would not occur to us. Having access to weak ties can expose us to a greater variety of information or perspectives and broaden the reach of our thinking. We cannot know whether any single weak tie will ignite that crucial spark, but collectively such ties can create enough leads to light the way to novel and fruitful ideas.

Access to information and different perspectives is important to jump-start creativity, but alas, the simple accumulation of new knowledge and fresh perspectives is not enough. Rather, it matters what we *do* with that knowledge once we have it. When Matt learned that businesses would like a training app and that a popular meditation app provided a good example of what could work for them, he could have easily dismissed it. Oji Life Lab was not looking to create a wellness program, after all. But Matt and Andrea went beyond the surface irrelevance. They stripped the example of the specifics and focused on the "download and go" aspect of the app for their programs. They took from it the focus on starting the learning process with no special arrangements; users could proceed at their individual pace.

Jill Perry-Smith, professor of organizational behavior at Emory University, studied social networks of scientists at an applied research institute focusing on new technologies, from aerospace engineering to information technology. Creativity was central to these scientists' job descriptions; they were solving hard problems, and their customers were looking for original and effective solutions. As part of a study, Perry-Smith and her team asked scientists to list people with whom they communicated on work-related topics. Because people tend to omit those with whom they have only occasional contact, they were prompted to include anyone they discussed work with, even if their interactions were infrequent, informal, or limited. After making their lists, scientists were asked about how close they were with each person, for how long they'd known them, and how often they communicated.

Colleagues the scientists had known for less than five years, whom they described as acquaintances, distant contacts, or just friendly colleagues, and with whom they communicated a few times a month or less, were considered weak ties. By contrast, the people whom scientists had known for more than five years and with whom they interacted several times a week were considered strong ties. In addition to counting the number of weak and strong ties each scientist had, the study measured the diversity of backgrounds in each one's network based on their roles and tenure at the institute.

Results showed that scientists who were judged to be more creative by their supervisors had more weak ties than those who were less creative in their jobs. Why? A greater number of weak ties made it more likely that scientists interacted with others with diverse backgrounds, which was a boost to their creativity.

So, does this mean we should strive for ever more weak ties with whom to discuss work-related topics? Professor Jing Zhou and her colleagues wondered whether there might be a point of diminishing returns or even a downside to too many weak ties. It takes time to meaningfully engage another person in a discussion, and too many discussions can take time away from other work. Also, after many conversations and many different perspectives, it might start to be difficult to integrate all the new information and ideas and bring them meaningfully together. Too many perspectives can become a "too many cooks in the kitchen" situation, creating more confusion rather than sparking inspiration.

Zhou and her collaborators conducted a study in a high-tech firm in China to test their ideas. Employees were provided with a roster of names of everyone at the company and asked how important each person was for them as a source of professional advice when they had a work-related problem.

The results of this study reaffirmed the relationship between weak ties and employee creativity: weak ties did boost creativity. However, this happened only when employees' networks were "right sized." Having either too few or too many weak ties was related to less creativity. The sweet spot was somewhere between these two poles.

Zhou and her team also found that not everyone benefited equally from their social ties. Those who were not very concerned with fitting in with others were best able to take advantage of weak ties. But for those who valued conforming to the expectations of people around them and who wanted to show restraint in their actions to uphold these expectations, it was more difficult to accept new ideas or perspectives.

This research has very practical implications. If your goal is creativity, remind yourself that trying to fit in is not actually helpful. Concerns about performance reviews and promotions can tempt you to "color within the lines" in the context of work or to try to anticipate what decision makers and evaluators are looking for and then to perform according to those standards. Such concerns are valid, but they run counter to what makes creativity possible. Excelling means being proactive and creating value. Your creativity will depend on a decision to seek new angles on problems and engage with novel ideas.

Your weak ties at work will not only give you access to diverse information but will also enable you to consider myriad perspectives, many of which will depart from the usual ways of doing the job. Your strong ties, meanwhile, will provide support in an entirely different way.

RELY ON STRONG RELATIONSHIPS

Strong relationships are for creativity as health is to people—their importance becomes most apparent when something is not quite right. Just like health, supportive relationships are important at all times, but we don't necessarily notice them unless there is a problem.

When something is not right at work, dissatisfaction sets in. Many of us are familiar with that nagging sense of being unhappy at work, which can range from not wanting to be there to positively dreading it. When this state sets in, we can react in different ways. One option is to quit and look for another job. In the United States, after the COVID-19 pandemic, a record number of people did exactly that. In what came to be called the Great Resignation, 47.8 million workers quit their jobs in 2021, and 50.5 million quit in 2022. This can be a productive and energizing option, inspiring greater enthusiasm in new positions and endeavors. But quitting, of course, is not always possible. Sometimes staying in a job is a matter of necessity.

It turns out that even when we're stuck in a job we find unsatisfying, we can still find ways to be creative, and one of the primary resources for doing so comes from our close colleagues. Research shows that the power of strong relationships for creativity is such that dissatisfied workers who must stay in their jobs because quitting is not an option are able to be just as creative as those who are happy at work and have other choices than to stay in their current positions.

Strong relationships with coworkers help us be creative in two major ways. The first is through their actions, and the second is through how they make us feel. What our coworkers do can directly support our work—they can jump in and lend a hand when we fall behind, willingly share their expertise, and act as peacemakers if disagreements or conflicts arise. Our coworkers can help us have a voice. They also provide valuable information and feedback that help us improve our job performance. With this support, we can creatively solve problems.

Strong work relationships also make us feel a certain way. Most of us would readily agree with the poet Maya Angelou, who said, "I've learned that people will forget what you said, people will forget what you did, but people will never forget how you made them feel." We viscerally and instinctually recognize that emotion is at the core of what is important in how we describe relationships.

Research shows us that at work, the most important and influential emotional descriptor of relationships is *respect*. Relationships marked by respect are those in which people communicate that they value one another. We feel respected when we experience being seen and heard, when we feel included and taken into account, when we feel acknowledged and recognized. In relationships of respect, people are available to listen to each other, they express genuine interest in each other's thoughts and opinions, they appreciate and emphasize one another's positive qualities and contributions, they value each other's time, and they make requests of others rather than demands. By contrast, we do not feel respected when we experience being spoken over, disregarded, excluded, or devalued.

Respectful relationships create a virtuous cycle. They give us a greater sense of vitality at work—we feel alive and full of energy, we feel eager to act, and we are confident in our ability to act. Respectful relationships give us a little extra strength to do what needs to be done. These subjective feelings not only motivate us but also help us be more successful in our creative work.

Another important effect of respectful relationships is that they boost people's ability to bounce back after setbacks. Because creative work by its very definition includes obstacles and frustrations, impasses and points of failure, if we want to see the journey from an idea to its realization, resilience is necessary to persist rather than giving up or falling back on noncreative solutions.

When colleagues and team members engage with respect, we all become able to reach out to each other to reflect on and discuss work productively. Respectful engagement demonstrates to others that we are present in our interactions, and it communicates that we value one another. In such an environment, we feel able and willing to share what we know and what we are working on with others. Respectful relationships take the edge off the reputational risk concerns and those *What would others say?* questions that pop into our minds as we weigh the decision whether to share original ideas or not. Respectful relationships also enable us to try out new ideas, ask what-if questions, or raise concerns about something on which we are working. These discussions can serve the function of extended problem finding: we explore ideas, hash them out, question them, and seek and share feedback. In this process, we can identify previously overlooked issues and notice opportunities we otherwise would not have.

Research studies conducted with a broad range of people at work, from knowledge workers developing high-tech products to CEOs and their immediate teams, show that the result of respectful engagement with team members is greater pursuit of creative goals, greater ability to solve problems creatively, and the ability to make creative ideas happen.

When we spoke, Matt kept coming back to the topic of respect and trust when describing his relationship with Andrea and their ability to build Oji Life Lab. He talked about how influential the book *Cognition in the Wild* by Edwin Hutchins was for his thinking. The thesis of the book is that cognition is not just an individual and internal mental process. Rather, the true unit of cognition is "us together." He takes this very much to heart. In their creative work, Matt and Andrea have an unspoken trust in one another. They are not focused on who came up with an idea or who made what specific contribution. Matt does not even think attribution is meaningful because of how mutual the creative process is.

Discussing their ongoing work as a key to creativity is very clear in Matt and Andrea's process. When they launched the first Oji Life Lab program, Andrea would run live sessions with users and afterward come back to the office and reflect on them. She shared her excitement about inspiring ways the program they built affected users' lives. After Andrea shared a number of these examples, she and Matt realized that a new opportunity was hidden in them. These conversations sparked an idea for a new feature they called *stories*. They built this feature to allow users to capture something that is meaningful to them as text, audio, or video on their phone and tag it to indicate what kinds of benefits they got from the program. Some people end up describing ways they were able to lower stress; others tell about better decisions they were able to make; still others describe how they achieved something difficult. When organizations adopt Oji programs, users can decide to make their stories visible to employers or others at the organization, making them into little sharable wins.

As important as relationships with our coworkers and team members are, relationships with supervisors can be even more powerful in coloring our creative drive and in influencing what we do and how. When scientists jointly analyzed results from dozens of studies, they found that the quality of relationships between leaders and employees reliably predicts employee creativity and innovation at work. High-quality relationships are those in which employees know where they stand with leaders. They trust that leaders understand their job problems and needs, will use their power to help solve problems at work, and will stand up for them, even "bail them out" if necessary.

When researchers analyzed what specific features of the employee-leader relationship contribute to employee creativity, the answer again came down to respect: employees who had professional respect for their supervisors, admired their knowledge and skills, and were impressed with their supervisors' overall job competence were more creative. Often, we think of inspirational leaders as those who are likeable or charismatic. But our instincts can be misleading. Charisma is only skin deep and not sufficient for lasting impact. If you are a leader, the key thing you can do to inspire creativity in employees is to be a role model of work excellence and to cultivate relationships marked by respect.

WHOM TO REACH OUT TO AND WHEN

If the creative process can be helped by weak ties, as well as by strong relationships, how do we find the right supports around us and the right balance of weak and strong ties? What can we do to boost our creativity through our relationships, all the way from coming up with ideas and deciding to act on them to developing and building them into something tangible?

The good news is that we can be proactive about reaching out to different individuals and groups. The trick is to know what creative work calls for across different phases of the journey.

Sample Different Perspectives

To get the creative process started, we need *cognitive flexibility*—thinking of different perspectives and sampling different classes of ideas. Imagine a simple problem such as the ones researchers often pose to subjects in their laboratories—for instance, thinking of different uses for a common object, such as a brick. Being cognitively flexible means coming up with ideas in multiple categories, such as using the brick as a building material, using it for decoration, using it as a weight to hold something down, and using it to break or smash something. These are all different categories, with many possible ideas within each one (e.g., within a breaking-something category, you could smash a nutshell to get to the meat, smash a car window when you have locked yourself out in a remote location where you cannot call roadside assistance, or break a glass door to save an animal trapped in a cabin on fire).

Now imagine a much more complex problem in a professional setting. An organizational leader might be thinking about how to alleviate employee burnout. An educator could be looking for ideas on how to improve student engagement and outcomes. A brand manager might be figuring out how to extend existing products to new users. Exploring different kinds of possibilities broadly helps with finding the best ideas.

Oji Life Lab founders needed to come up with categories for topics to cover in their skill-building programs. The idea for the first program arrived serendipitously, sparked by a conference Matt attended that convinced him of the importance of emotional intelligence. Then, Matt and Andrea heard from multiple leaders in different industries that they needed training programs in decision-making and managing people. The idea sparks for their programming came from weak ties in their networks. Matt and Andrea reached out, listened and heard the needs of those they aimed to serve, and were able to build innovative products unlike anything else in corporate training and development.

We can certainly consider different categories when thinking on our own. But conversations with acquaintances and colleagues from diverse backgrounds will extend our mental network of knowledge and information, which can provide the seedbed for cognitive flexibility. This is where networks with a large number of weak ties will be a great resource and where reaching out across the network will expand our thinking into areas we could not have conceived of alone.

Importantly, when we think of social ties that affect work creativity, we tend to think of professional networks. However, relationships that affect our creativity go beyond professional networks and also include our personal and family ties. Nora Madjar, professor of management at the University of Connecticut, found evidence that employees are more creative in their work when others in their unit and outside work share their knowledge, expertise, perspectives, and ideas with them. Employees are also more creative when they receive support for creativity from others at work (both in their primary unit and elsewhere in the organization). For those who are less predisposed to think in original ways, encouragement by friends and family to introduce creative ideas or solutions at work is especially helpful.

What exactly the most creativity-boosting social network will look like depends on the nature of our work. My husband, Jamie, the oceanographer, conducts research on how currents influence the ranges of various marine species and on what drives those currents. An ideal social network for him will be smaller than the ideal social network for my research on creativity across different industries. Jamie can broaden his perspectives by having conversations with ocean physicists and biologists. The knowledge and expertise of his psychologist wife, his historian parents, and his management consultant and artist friends would not be relevant. On the other hand, I have learned much from and been inspired by many of these very people, as well as other family and friends. In addition to creativity scientists in psychology and organizational behavior, I have learned from a creative director turned scientist, social and tech entrepreneurs, exhibition designers, educational leaders, and many writers and artists.

You might wonder how many contacts to establish as you build your social network. Alas, there is no specific formula to identify the "correct" number for optimal creativity—your network needs to be extensive enough that it provides you with enough people with whom you can discuss problems and ideas, and it needs to extend beyond your immediate colleagues or teammates so you will have access to diverse information. Of course, you are not going to build personal relationships with one eye on how they can help your work, but personal and family relationships you already have can be a surprising and enthusiastic source of support, in providing both new perspectives and encouragement. When you reach out beyond the closed circle of close colleagues, collaborators, and friends, those contacts will have their own networks, stretching your potential pool of information even further.

To see whether you are on the right track, consider how you can broaden the perspectives of your creative work. What do you need to know? What might you want to know? Whom could you reach out to? Inspiration can come from unexpected sources, and we cannot precisely and reliably plan for it. But we can decide to sample broadly. Chat about work with people on different teams in your organization. Have conversations at conferences not just with those who work on problems similar to yours but also with those who are pursuing different areas of interest and specialization. Interesting ideas often emerge when you can make an association or draw an analogy between different issues.

Develop Ideas: Leverage Support

Once we have a collection of diverse ideas, the challenge is to judge how good they are. Which bits and pieces among them are promising, and which are not? We have to see the ideas in their entirety, such as when we first organize pieces of a 1,000-piece puzzle for one of those blizzard-weekend projects. Of course, our task of judging ideas is much harder than building a puzzle, as we don't have the benefit of a box top to reveal the full picture of the finished product. In our creative work, we might have (some) pieces of the puzzle, but the picture we are building is of our own making. To complete the picture, we can leverage our weak *and* strong relationships to help us refine and develop our ideas and evaluate whether we are on the right track once we start shaping them.

When working to elaborate and develop initial ideas, we need emotional support and encouragement. Because the ideas we start with tend to be vague, it is common to experience doubt. For some, this manifests as questioning the ideas themselves, while for others, it can cross into questioning their creative abilities. Support from strong relationships with friends or close colleagues boosts our sense of creative self-efficacy and helps us maintain our creative drive even in the face of uncertainty.

But support does not mean being told that everything is awesome. Rather, emotionally supportive relationships enable us to share ideas that are not fully developed and still need work and guiding feedback. These relationships allow us to share without censoring ourselves or trying to frame our thinking in ways that aim to make us look competent or in control. We can trust that we will not be harshly criticized.

As we develop ideas, they will expand and evolve. Creators will be able to test these developments to some extent. But more critical eyes will usually mean more opportunities for improvement. To be helpful, feedback needs to enable growth and include specific suggestions that build on existing ideas.

Matt described his partnership and work with Andrea as just the right mix of support and constructive feedback to improve on the products they are building. "[One day] we were talking about conspiring with one another, and we were talking about sparring with one another," he said. "And somebody misspoke and said *conspar*—we need to conspar. And now it's a thing we all use. It's like, okay, we're going to collaboratively disagree." Diving into such collaborative "consparring" becomes invigorating and can end in pure creative magic. "To me," Matt went on, "one of the most wonderful things that happens in any creative project is when somebody shares an idea that I think I can't make any sense out of, or that I think is bad, and then I ask them to clarify it. And then, that feeling like a revelation is occurring. That's where the juice is."

To develop and build your ideas, you will need a personal version of "consparring" with trusted others. As you do that, it is important to remember that having supportive relationships is helpful, but it will not eliminate challenges or unpleasant feelings. At times, interactions with those we are close with can even heighten temporary frustrations and anxieties. But in these cases, our feelings are a by-product of moving along the creative process and actively solving difficult problems. Not only are they to be expected, but their arrival is a sign that we are actively engaged in the creative process and on the right track.

The Key Is Switching Between Weak Ties and Strong Ones

Because creative work requires both weak and strong relationships at different times, moving from our initial vague ideas all the way to successful products and performances calls for the skillful use of our social capital.

When organizational behavior scholars set up studies to pinpoint how social relationships help creativity in the stages of coming up with ideas and developing them, they found that maximizing the success of the full creative process requires strategically switching between weak and strong relationships. In one experiment, researchers first identified strong relationships in a group of business school students. They asked students to list the names of those with whom they informally discussed a range of issues and then followed up by asking how emotionally close they were with each of those people. For the second part of the study, researchers paired participants with either strong or weak ties. Some participants were joined by two people from their list with whom they had strong ties. Other participants were paired with two weak ties—randomly chosen people who volunteered for the study and were not on participants' lists of contacts.

Each group was then asked to design an object that could be sold in the university's gift shop. Together, they generated multiple ideas, selected one they considered most creative, and then proceeded to develop this idea. Some participants interacted with people with whom they were paired while working to come up with ideas, and some interacted with others while elaborating and developing one idea they had selected. The creativity of the new item was evaluated by judges who knew the university shop well and could tell what was relatively commonplace and what was original.

The results showed that interactions with different kinds of social ties benefited creativity—but that weak and strong ties did so differently. Working with weak ties helped with idea *generation*. By contrast, working with close contacts helped with idea *elaboration*.

When we are close with someone and they know our goal is to develop a particular idea, they do two specific helpful things. First, they provide support by acknowledging the value of the idea. This can be quite subtle, such as starting with "Oh, that's great!" or "Nice!" Then, they offer suggestions aimed at elaborating on or improving the idea. This could mean clarifying the nature of the proposed product, recommending new features, or offering a twist that makes it fresh or surprising. The results of the study pointed out that not only were strong relationships beneficial during the elaboration phase, but weak ties were detrimental at this time because those people kept sharing their own new ideas instead of engaging with the creator's ideas. They were not truly present and invested.

To maximize creativity, we need to purposefully choose whom we reach out to depending on the phase of our work. As you are first generating ideas, you should reach out to your weak ties—those with whom you are not very close and with whom you do not interact very often. Once you select the ideas to pursue and develop, you need to turn to close colleagues. Failing to switch can have negative consequences for the end product. Relying only on close relationships increases the chance that you will come up with and become attached to a not very creative idea. The opposite can happen if you put your faith exclusively on weak ties: highly creative ideas can emerge, but they are less likely to be developed to their full potential because it is hard to discern what could be useful and what is not.

According to the science of creativity, the ideal social network to support creative endeavors would include a large and diverse group of weak ties, who can help inspire creative ideas, and also a set of strong relationships with close colleagues, who can provide support and feedback when we're building out those ideas and making them into products and performances. One of the more painful aspects of work, however, is the reality that building such a network is not equally possible for everyone. Research from my own lab, for example, shows that it is more difficult for women to get support for creativity and have the experience of being valued and respected at work than it is for men. And there are the perennial challenges stemming from socioeconomic inequalities—those with greater access to capital, education, and powerful social connections have easier access to most resources, and that includes the ability to build the ideal network necessary to create the best conditions for creativity.

The fact remains that if we want to achieve greater creativity for everyone, organizations and societies need to address the problems of unequal access to social capital. Leaders can work toward this end by creating environments that encourage others to speak up and share their ideas and by providing individualized and empowering consideration to those they lead. In the next chapter, we will examine how these social forces can enable sustained creativity and innovation.

Building Creativity at Work

Start-ups burst with energy that is the engine of innovation. Their desire and willingness to play with ideas, test them, develop them, or abandon them as necessary provides ideal conditions for creating groundbreaking products and solutions, and they can get there relatively quickly. If large organizations are ocean liners, start-ups are speedboats. Large organizations can reach creative destinations too, of course, but they move more slowly and with an eye to balancing what is new with what is already in the pipeline.

This is why large organizations often carve out smaller innovation studios and labs that run on start-up spirit. I spoke with Meredith Arthur, chief of staff at TwoTwenty, the Pinterest product incubation lab. Her job is to define and position the lab's work within the larger company and ensure TwoTwenty is successfully communicating what they do, while also making sure the lab is operating smoothly and her team is creatively engaged.

When I asked Meredith what it was like to work at TwoTwenty, she lit up. Her first response was to describe the team as extremely engaged and curious. But then she paused to reflect. "Relieved," she said. "I'm just so glad I'm on TwoTwenty."

This seems like an unusual word to describe one's experience of a work environment. But Meredith has enough years of experience working with both start-ups and large companies to know that not every team is full of enthusiasm and energized by their work. She is grateful to be with a team that plays with ideas together and builds together and where every person feels ownership of what they are doing. And she is grateful that as a senior person, she still gets to build products that are meaningful to her.

Meredith was recruited specifically to nurture a culture of innovation. You see, TwoTwenty is fully remote. Having team members in San Francisco and Warsaw, Munich and Barcelona calls for a deliberate building of an entrepreneurial and empowering culture. As trite as it might sound, Meredith kept coming back to communication being the key. Sometimes, the most important tasks seem the most obvious. Yet, when it comes to creating the conditions for creativity and leading teams toward innovation, what might sound obvious or trite requires great skill. As chief of staff, Meredith meets individually with each of more than two dozen team members twice a year. Her goal is to understand—*really* understand, she stressed—what drives everyone. "What's exciting you, what's inspiring you?" she said. "A lot of our culture at TwoTwenty is around tuning into that."

The practical requirement for tuning into individual employees' sources of creative drive and inspiration is a communication infrastructure. Meredith developed ways to keep everyone in the loop. She compared her leadership to being a crossing guard: she works to enable people to get from one place to another. "It's not about me fixing problems," she said. "It's about me making sure the right people are talking to each other about the problems."

Meredith has created two operational pillars of culture at Two-Twenty. The first is monthly remote funnel reviews, which are central to the product development process. Their goal is to make sure that everyone on the team gets an overview of what is happening across all projects and phases of projects. This is a time for review and reflection rather than decision-making. Reviews ensure that everyone on the team understands the range of projects in the funnel and that team members know each other's strengths sufficiently well to know how to pull people into particular projects at the right time. This is the time to jump onto a project or to ask for input, expertise, and collaboration from others.

At the top of the funnel are projects in the *Investigate* phase. These are projects in the idea spark stage, and there might be just one or two people working on any of them. As ideas prove to have worth and potential, they move into the next part of the funnel, the *Prototype* phase, and finally the *Market Launch* phase. Launching a product can take the form of releasing a stand-alone app, such as TwoTwenty's *Shuffles* or *How We Feel* apps, or a product that could land at Pinterest.

The funnel review process is intentionally quite open. "We work culturally to teach people how to raise their hands and be their own leaders around the projects," Meredith said. "You have to communicate what your needs are. And if you have the bandwidth, you are saying, *Hey, I think my skill set would be helpful for this project.*" Meredith works to ensure everyone on the team has a chance to voice their thoughts and ideas, while empowering them to have autonomy and take initiative.

The second pillar of culture at TwoTwenty is onsite events. These are intensive in-person affairs, usually a week long, modeled after hackathons—accelerated collaborative engineering events. Two-Twenty's on-sites are a bit like sleepaway camps for engineers and developers, who are excited to create something they care about. As Meredith said, "Of course, you have meals where you're spending time together, but we also try to have an activity together. We're builders and you can actually bond the most by building together."

The team developed an intuitive strategy for how to assess, prioritize, and make decisions on projects based upon people's enthusiasm. Their internal code names for this process are "pretty pony" and "dead horse." "Pretty pony" means that team members are excited about what they're working on, believe in it, and are eager to get to it every day and make progress on it. Unsurprisingly, "dead horse" means that team members do not feel the project is going anywhere. That said, one person's feeling that a project is a dead horse at any given time does not necessarily mean it gets abandoned. It is possible to simply have "a dead horse day," Meredith explained. A day of doubts. The team puts such feedback into perspective: it's an important piece of information, but they do not act on it immediately. If the feeling persists and a critical mass of people consider an idea or project to be a dead horse, a decision to abandon it becomes more likely.

On the other hand, if the whole team considers something a pretty pony, it's taken as a good sign that a project is on the right track. "Tuning into where that energy and excitement is, is something that we talk about, which is unusual for a team," Meredith said. "We'll say to each other, *Are you dead horse on this? Are you pretty pony?*" There was consensus that the *Shuffles* collaging app, for example, was a pretty pony. And their feelings were spot-on. When the app launched in late July 2022, it quickly started climbing Apple's App Store rankings. It went viral on TikTok and in a single week shot to the top five in the United States among lifestyle apps and reached the top twenty in all non-gaming apps. Users loved the slick cutout feature, the ability to combine images into collages, and the ability to add music and animation. TwoTwenty's pretty pony level of enthusiasm for the *Shuffles* app is an excellent example of how relying on their emotional energy strategy for assessing a project's merit bore fruit. Emotions offer crucial information in creative work, and skilled leaders know how to harness it.

CREATIVITY IS BUILT ON PSYCHOLOGICAL SAFETY

At the core of how the team at TwoTwenty operates is active participation: speaking up to pitch new ideas, building and improving on others' ideas, and jumping into projects for which any individual has skills, interest, and time. This approach might seem rather simple. Just do it. Just raise your hand. Join in! Share your opinion, whatever it may be.

However, the simplest-seeming things are rarely easy to achieve. Chances are that you've been in meetings, just as I have, where you're not sure whether you could or should share your thoughts and ideas. Would your ideas, especially critical ones, be met with annoyance or anger? Are you willing to put yourself in a position where you may be seen as stepping on toes, being out of line, or having a bad attitude? Could there be other, more tangible negative repercussions?

These and similar questions that we ask ourselves concern what organizational behavior scholars call *psychological safety*. Amy Edmondson, professor of leadership and management at Harvard University, conducted pioneering research on psychological safety and defined it as a sense that our interactions with others—whether leaders or team members—will be respectful, that we can speak freely and without self-censorship, and that we can experiment or take risks in suggesting new and original ideas. When we feel psychologically safe, we are willing to voice opinions, even if they are unpopular or different from the majority consensus; we are able to share information and ideas with team members, raise critically important concerns, and disagree with others on the team about what is being done and how. This is exactly what we saw happening at TwoTwenty, thanks to Meredith's efforts to create a culture of open communication.

It is crucial to also note what psychological safety is not. Psychological safety is not an atmosphere of permissiveness in which anything goes. It does not give team members license to speak and act with no regard for others. Rather, it is an assurance based on shared trust among team members that everyone will be treated with respect and that any sparring will focus on tasks and ideas, not people (i.e., disagreements aren't personal). Psychological safety is also not about being "nice." If we were to teleport into a work meeting of a team in which people feel safe, we might be surprised by how argumentative it can seem at times. This is precisely because people trust that they can bring up problems and issues, voice conflicting viewpoints, and argue for their positions.

Psychological safety enables us to make decisions that involve risks to our reputation or standing within a team, share information that may be helpful but might not be well received, propose ideas that diverge from the group's popular views, and highlight issues that need improvement or further development. In many ways, this list mirrors the key requirements for creativity. There is no creativity without the sharing of information and ideas, without critical assessment of what works and what might not be ready quite yet, or without debate about how to develop ideas and build on them.

Organizational behavior professors Ronit Kark and Abraham Carmeli wanted to test how psychological safety colors people's emotional stance about their work. They studied a group of part-time graduate students who worked in different fields, from banking and insurance to the communication, electronics, food and beverage, pharmaceutical, and medical equipment industries. They asked how much positive energy people have at work, how much physical and mental strength, and how well they feel in their jobs overall. They called these feelings of vitality. Two weeks later, people completed another survey, which asked them whether they had taken risks with ideas they shared, developed new uses for existing work methods or equipment, managed to solve problems that caused issues for others, and come up with original and workable ideas.

Kark and Carmeli found that employees who had a greater sense of psychological safety at work also felt more energetic and alive in their jobs. In turn, these feelings of vitality were motivating and sustained workers to pursue opportunities for creativity.

Another question is how psychological safety affects what people are able to do at work. Professor Lu Chen and colleagues asked employees in technology research and development departments about psychological safety on their teams. If one makes a mistake, is it held against them? To what extent are team members able to bring up problems or discuss difficult issues? Is it safe to take risks? How difficult is it to ask others on the team for help? How much are individuals' unique skills and talents valued and utilized? Then, these same employees took a survey about their daily effort in creative work. Do they spend considerable time trying to understand the nature of the problem on which they are working? Do they think about the problem from multiple perspectives? Are they searching for relevant information and ideas from a variety of sources? To what extent do they try to devise ideas or solutions that move away from conventional ways of doing things? Finally, researchers asked supervisors about employees' creative ideas, actions, and achievements.

The results showed that the employees' sense of psychological safety on their teams predicted how much they engaged with creative work. Psychological safety enabled them to seek more information, explore problems longer and more deeply, and generate both a greater number of ideas and more diverse ideas. In turn, this engagement became obvious to supervisors, who knew nothing about how employees felt about their teams. Greater psychological safety boosted the kind of work that is necessary for creativity to become visible.

Psychological safety not only supports individual creativity but also boosts team creativity. Studies that ask employees to indicate their level of psychological safety at work and solicit leaders to evaluate the creative contributions of their teams consistently show the benefits of psychological safety for team performance. Moreover, these findings are reliable regardless of who is being studied, from business student teams, to research and development teams, to manufacturing project teams and healthcare teams.

In one study, Professor Yuwen Liu and colleagues studied research and development teams. Each team member answered questions about psychological safety in their jobs, as well as about the initiative climate—whether people on the team do more than they are strictly required to do, whether they take chances to get involved when opportunities present themselves, and whether they actively attack problems if something goes wrong. They also surveyed team leaders about how much each member shares their expertise and know-how with others and to assess the creative performance of their teams.

As they expected, researchers found that a greater sense of psychological safety opened people up to willingly share their knowledge, which in turn boosted team creativity. Team members were most likely to share information when teams were built on mutual expectations of individual initiative. Just like Meredith described for the TwoTwenty team, when people have a sense of psychological safety, they have a collective sense of ownership. Sharing expertise and ideas not only helps others but also contributes to joint success.

Collectively, organizational behavior research shows three major ways psychological safety establishes conditions for creativity. First, when people feel safe to take risks and trust that no one will deliberately undermine them, they are willing to voice concerns and discuss mistakes. A sense of safety diminishes worry about being labeled a naysayer or attracting blame for admitting to errors. The importance of this function of psychological safety becomes particularly obvious in instances when it is lacking, resulting in the development of products that are deficient. This could range from relatively minor annoyances, like poor user interfaces, to fatal flaws, such as with the Boeing 737 MAX planes, which were involved in two accidents that killed everyone on board. Inquiry into the causes of these accidents by a panel of experts from the Federal Aviation Administration revealed a widespread culture of fear of retaliation if workers were to raise safety concerns.

The second way psychological safety prepares the terrain for creativity is by helping team members capitalize on what scientists call *task conflict*. Task conflict refers to disagreements among team members about the nature of the problem on which they are working and how to approach it. When teams debate or even clash over their work, they have to hash out divergent opinions about which ideas to pursue and critically evaluate ideas or approaches. All of this means more problem exploration and development. Bottom line, when team members have a sense of psychological safety, they tend to see disagreements about tasks and how to tackle them as *beneficial* to their work.

Third, when teams perceive disagreements as productive, they do not experience them as personal criticism or attack. In this way, psychological safety prevents conflict about ideas from turning into personality clashes and personal antagonism among team members, which are the bane of creative work. The same action—suggesting new ideas that depart from the team consensus or pointing to weaknesses or limitations of existing ideas—can be interpreted in different ways. If people feel safe on their team, they will likely welcome new perspectives. But if they do not feel safe on their team, they can perceive these suggestions as undermining their personal efforts.

The first and most important tip when aspiring to a climate for creativity is obvious—build a foundation of psychological safety.

LEADING FOR CREATIVITY

As anyone who has ever had a boss or worked in an organization with more than a handful of people intimately knows, leaders set the tone for our experience of work. Leaders—from supervisors, to project principals, to unit directors, to vice presidents and chief officers—make decisions that affect the daily work of those they lead. Their approach to motivating people and implementing decisions colors how employees feel and interact with others at work, what their goals are, and how they think and solve problems in their jobs. And this is the case regardless of industry, whether a leader is a school principal setting the vision for other educators, a creative director working with a team of designers, a founder of a technology start-up, or a production director at a major theater.

In studies of leadership approaches and their role in creativity and innovation, researchers recruit leaders at various levels as well as their employees. The employees answer questions about what their leaders do and how—from how they motivate others, to how they communicate their decisions, to how they guide others' work. These questions uncover patterns that describe specific leadership styles. Employees are also asked about the emotional climate on their teams, how they explore and solve problems, what motivates them, and what they do in their jobs. Do they come up with original but effective ideas? Do they think of creative solutions to work problems?

After getting the employee side, researchers ask leaders about the creative performance of individual employees and teams. How often are they coming up with new ideas to address work challenges? Do they fight to get approval for their ideas? Do they systematically introduce new ideas into their work?

Collectively, research shows that leaders who boost the creativity of those they work with adopt transformational, empowering, and entrepreneurial styles. These leadership styles are not mutually exclusive; rather, they focus on different aspects of leader behavior.

Transformational leaders communicate an attractive vision based on organizational values and ideals. In relating to others, they stimulate people's interests and encourage the exploration of problems, the habit of challenging assumptions, and thinking in novel ways to address problems. They provide individual consideration to those with whom they work by expressing concern for others, striving to understand individual needs and abilities, and investing in developing their team members' skills.

Empowering leaders support their workers' autonomy and provide opportunities for their development. They give authority to people over issues within their department, encourage them to take initiative, and support them in pursuing goals. Empowering leaders also discuss their own goals and those of others, review shared work, and make visible their planning of work tasks. In this way, they serve as role models of how work can be successfully accomplished.

Entrepreneurial leaders are risk takers. They challenge others to act in innovative ways and urge people to rethink their current ways of approaching problems or doing their jobs. They encourage them to think outside the proverbial box and pursue novel ideas and methods.

If we step back from this list and squint to see how these leadership styles relate to what we know about creativity from everything covered in this book so far, it becomes clear why all three types of leaders boost the creativity of those around them. The list of their behaviors is virtually identical to the list of conditions for creativity.

Consider the most basic precondition: psychological safety. Transformational leaders establish psychological safety by purposefully building a climate in which people can openly question assumptions about how work is done. Empowering and entrepreneurial leaders encourage people to take risks and approach work challenges in original ways. When they also provide individualized consideration, they enable employees to cope with any potential discomfort and anxiety associated with voicing bold opinions.

These leaders also heighten others' motivation for creativity. In an analysis of transformational leadership across 127 separate studies, management scholar Dohyoung Koh and his colleagues found that these leaders increase employee creative performance by enhancing their creative self-efficacy and intrinsic motivation. Because these leaders communicate a positive vision for the future and instill pride and respect in their teams, their employees tend to identify with them. This in turn can persuade employees to trust leaders' confidence that their teams are working on something important and meaningful and are able to rise to the occasion to solve problems creatively.

Similarly, empowering leaders aim to create the right conditions for people to take initiative in their work. Studies consistently find that those who work with empowering leaders indeed feel more able to take initiative and trust that leaders have their best interests in mind. In turn, workers who take initiative to pursue challenging goals become more likely to show creativity in what they do at work. This was very much the case with Meredith when she described encouraging engineers and designers on her team to raise their hands—literally or symbolically—and volunteer for projects or tasks for which they have interest, skill, and bandwidth. She acts primarily as a facilitator by directing people to relevant team members when someone comes to her with questions.

Entrepreneurial leaders who stress the necessity of measured risk taking and who encourage others to question the basic assumptions of how work is done create a culture that values and enables problem finding and exploration. Scientists at the University of Mannheim surveyed people in a range of industries—from information technology and technical support, to research and development, to public relations, to executive management and strategy. First, they answered questions about their supervisors to assess how much they reflect transformational leadership practices. They were also asked about their own approach to work. To what extent are their work priorities shaped by personal vision and aspirations? How focused are they on accomplishing work that furthers their advancement? Do they tend to take risks at work to pursue their goals? The final set of questions measured how frequently people engage in creative work and what their creative accomplishments at work are.

The results affirmed that those who work for transformational leaders decide to take risks at work and spend more of their work time exploring problems and considering different ideas. This ensures that they both dare to be original and don't prematurely settle on ideas.

Research is clear that leaders who aim to inspire and enable creativity in their teams should adopt transformational, empowering, and entrepreneurial styles. But the story does not end there. These leaders are inspirational and energizing, but we do not live and work based on inspiration alone. To be fully effective, leaders have to find a way to combine these inspirational styles with acknowledging and rewarding their team members' creative ideas and accomplishments. This communicates in tangible ways that creative work is not only encouraged but truly valued. In my consulting, a common theme from workers is that leaders invite new ideas and create ways for staff to share them, but then these ideas disappear into a black box and are never implemented. To transform the creative suggestions into innovations and make use of them as a leader, you will need to move from encouragement to acknowledgement, reward, and championing of creativity.

FROM CREATIVITY SCIENCE TO CREATIVITY PRACTICE

As we've seen, building the conditions for creativity in workplaces starts with the sense of psychological safety. Leaders direct what people do and how and set a tone for what is valued. Because of this they have an outsized influence on building the basis for a sense of safety (versus a sense of exposure), as well as engendering a creative climate by encouraging initiative and supporting the creative drive. The question becomes how to build this psychological infrastructure for creative work.

Establishing the Climate for Creativity

I have come across leaders who are proud of their "Don't bring me problems, bring me solutions" attitude. They reason that bringing up problems or concerns with how something is done signals a negative attitude and lack of prerequisite vision or optimism about what is possible. By asking for solutions, these leaders believe they are nudging people toward greater autonomy.

Alas, the "bring me solutions" attitude is not a creative problem-solving approach. Although perhaps intended to empower others, this is not a basis for a creativity climate. The message employees hear, rightly or not, is that leaders are not interested in engaging in the problem-solving process. The first issue with this leader attitude is that it nudges employees not to raise problems they see. It is safer not to rock the boat and invite displeasure by raising concerns. Another issue concerns solutions that can arise in this atmosphere. When they have to come up with solutions, people do. However, even with the best individual effort, these solutions do not have the benefit of being debated, analyzed, and elaborated on from multiple individual perspectives. They do not have a chance to be fully developed. Leaders who ask for solutions, and not problems, get solutions, but not the best possible ones.

So, what are the building blocks of a creative climate in which people's potential can be realized and ideas can be fully developed?

Organizational psychologist Samuel Hunter and his colleagues were able to identify organizational, relational, and job attributes that build the climate for creativity and innovation at work. On the organizational level, this climate grows from the following:

Creativity mission. Organizations often explicitly formulate and publish their mission statements. Lived climate for creativity depends on people's awareness that the organization aspires to creativity.

Top leadership support for creativity. When organizations see creativity as their mission, the additional challenge is clearly communicating this mission so that employees understand expectations of creative performance.

Flexibility and risk taking. When employees see their organization as willing to take risks and be flexible in dealing with the uncertainties of creative work, they themselves become better able and more willing to cope with the unpleasant ambiguities of creative work.

Product emphasis. This entails a conviction that the organization is committed to both the originality and the quality of work.

Availability of resources for creativity and innovation. People will judge how serious the organization is about creativity by how much it is willing to supply resources to make creative work possible. These can be financial and material resources, as well as human resources. Of course, these kinds of resources are closely related. Space, equipment, and tools are the scaffold onto which people build. Organizations need to be willing and able to recruit and keep workers who have necessary skills and can achieve creativity goals.

Rewards for creativity. Organizations make their mission visible and credible by rewarding creative contributions. Missions can attract people, but creative work needs to also be acknowledged and rewarded.

While organizations establish and communicate their priorities in formal and informal ways, people experience the climate for creativity and innovation most directly through their interactions with coworkers and leaders. On this level, climate for creativity is based on the following:

Psychological safety. This is an expectation of open exchange of thoughts, opinions, and ideas, whether proposing something new, developing products, or pointing to potential issues, without fear of reprisal.

Positive interpersonal exchange. This is an overall sense of togetherness, a feeling that we in this company, laboratory, school, hospital, or firm are united by a shared set of goals. This experience of cohesion creates emotional attachment to the place where people work, making employees take initiative in their jobs and engage in creative work.

Positive relations with coworkers. In a climate for creativity, relationships with peers are marked by trust and respectful interactions. People perceive team members and coworkers as both engaging and emotionally supportive.

Positive relations with supervisors. Most direct signs about support for creativity come from immediate supervisors and managers and their ability and willingness to engage with and act on unconventional and original ideas. People evaluate how real the stated invitation to creativity is by judging whether supervisors both encourage new ideas and are open to fully considering and implementing them.

Finally, a climate for creativity and innovation is also based on people's perceptions of the nature of their jobs:

Autonomy. Employees perceive that they have a measure of independence in deciding how they perform their job tasks.

Intellectual stimulation. A stimulating atmosphere enables debate. Unlike the emphasis on coming to project meetings with pre-prepared solutions that are formally presented and defended, an atmosphere of intellectual stimulation makes space for the collective dissection of ideas, building on them, and polishing them.

Challenge. Creativity thrives when people perceive their jobs as challenging and interesting. This is key to intrinsic motivation, which drives workers beyond literal job and task requirements toward thinking deeply about what can be done and how. Intrinsically motivated workers dare to imagine what is or could be possible. There is an art to structuring what people are tasked with to be complex and stretch their skills but not to such a degree that it crosses over into being so stressful that it becomes chronically overwhelming.

Resolving the Paradox of Creativity and Innovation

Leading innovative organizations poses two opposing challenges. On the one hand, leaders have to create an inspiring vision and enable exploration and experimentation. And on the other hand, they need to strive for efficiency and, once they have successful products and processes, continue to improve them and exploit them in full. These processes of exploration and exploitation are by their very nature in conflict with each other. Problem exploration and construction requires time and resources. "Time is money" is not just a trite saying. Taking time (and money) necessary for problem exploration does not seem efficient, even though it is indispensable. The challenge of leading innovative organizations is to find a way to excel on both sides of this tension. Successful leaders have to unite the "explore and play" and "build on what we have" messages.

The paradoxical demands of leading innovative organizations call for creative solutions. One option is structural—creating a physically separate space that focuses on new and emerging products. This is the case with the TwoTwenty innovation lab at Pinterest. The lab is not at its mother company headquarters. The name "TwoTwenty" reflects the location of Pinterest's first office, creating a symbolic connection to its early start-up days, with employees working remotely across the globe. With distance from the mothership, the innovation lab can operate similarly to a start-up and recapture the thirst for building new and innovative products without having to fit them into the existing ones.

Another way to resolve the contradiction of leading innovative organizations is through dual leadership. Instead of a single leader who has to balance the voice on one shoulder that insists on more time to play with novel ideas and the voice on the other shoulder that orders greater efficiency, two leaders can split responsibilities and negotiate between them the right balance between contradictory pulls. Dividing and conquering between two leaders can be implicit and rely on their unique strengths, and it can evolve over time. Leaders can turn to each other and rely on each other for both emotional support and partnership in solving problems that come along. When the partnership is built on a shared vision and on a mutual appreciation for learning from different perspectives, leaders can build a foundation for clearer communication with those with whom they work, enabling greater creative and innovative performance.

For creativity at work to take shape, organizational decisions have to be in sync with individual aspirations and abilities. Leaders can embody this link and put together disparate pieces of the creativity puzzle by challenging employees and empowering them, by inspiring and rewarding creative work. They can develop conditions in which individuals and teams can make the choice to pursue creative ideas and conditions enabling them to recommit to that creativity choice as many times as necessary to bring ideas to life.

All the Creativity Choices

This book took you on a journey of choosing creativity—making the decision to embark on the often long process of putting your creative ideas to work, turning them into action, and finding strategies to persist through the times when building those ideas and transforming them into products and performances becomes challenging or flat-out stalls. It asks three big questions and provides science-based answers to them.

WHAT IS THE TRUE NATURE OF CREATIVITY AND WHAT CAN START YOU ON THE PATH OF CREATIVITY?

Creativity is a choice. A choice to devise something original and effective. And a choice that is repeated over and over again as you work to build ideas into something tangible.

Creativity involves risk. In addition to likely financial and material risks, there are two major psychological risks that we need to contend with. Creative work requires you to accept a certain level of intellectual risk (*Can I do what I have not done before?*) and social or reputational risk (*What will people think about this?*).

The belief that you can be creative is not an all-or-nothing proposition. You do not have to be "born creative" or convinced you have creative abilities. Rather, the conviction will grow from your actions. As you see others around you being successful in their creative endeavors, as you receive encouragement from others, as you notice your actions growing into achievements, and as you feel more effective, your sense of creative self-confidence will get stronger.

WHAT ARE THE STRATEGIES FOR SUCCESSFUL CREATIVE WORK?

Your creative drive will thrive on the love of the challenge of building something and a little push from rewards along the way. As you channel the drive, find ways to direct your attention in unexpected directions.

The key to creativity is asking questions and exploring the problems they pose. This process of problem finding is not something that happens just in the beginning of a creative project. Identifying and constructing problems happens throughout our creative process.

Creative work is a roller coaster of emotions. Each emotion is a piece of data about what is going on with you and around you, and each can help you think in a particular way. You can often harness the power of emotions, whether they are pleasant or not, to boost different ways of thinking.

When emotions get in your way—they are too strong or the wrong feeling happens at the wrong time—you can do something to manage them and soften their sharp edges. Strategies for preventing those feelings, modifying the situations in which they occur, distracting yourself temporarily, changing how you think about them, and managing your reactions can all help at different times.

Creative block is a common experience. It is not a sign that you cannot do it. Remind yourself this is part of creative work and carry on.

WHAT IS THE SOCIAL SIDE OF CREATIVITY?

Creativity is social even when we think we create alone. Weak ties—people in your broader social circle whom you do not regularly communicate with—can provide valuable help coming up with new ideas and seeing new perspectives. And your strong ties can provide support and encouragement when you work to elaborate, develop, and make your ideas happen.

The climate for creativity around you matters. Psychological safety—the sense that you can share opinions and ideas without fear of consequences—is the foundation on which long-term creativity is built. It enables you to take necessary intellectual and reputational risks and consistently engage in the creative process not just when necessity demands invention but also to proactively pursue and develop new possibilities. The climate for creativity is the nutrient-rich soil in which many flowers can bloom.

My conversation with Ben Silbermann, founder and executive chair of Pinterest, touched on all the keys to creativity choices in this book, from getting started to getting there (in his case, a very successful there!), as well as the social side that is crucial to the process. Ben led Pinterest as a CEO from start-up to publicly traded company in 2017, at which time it was valued at $10 billion. At the end of January 2024, that value was two and a half times higher.

Ben's decision to start a company was not a given. His parents are ophthalmologists; they greatly prized reasonableness but not the risk taking that could threaten a good and stable life. Growing up, Ben was competitive and interested in technology, even attending the highly selective Research Summer Institute at the Massachusetts Institute of Technology for high school students. Yet, in college at Yale he did not study engineering or computer science but opted for political science.

When we spoke, above all, Ben highlighted the social nature of the creativity and innovation process. Innovative ideas do not emerge and get built into products that people can use and enjoy in a vacuum. After graduation, he moved to Washington, DC. This made sense for a political science major. But the thought of starting a business kept nagging at him. This idea only got puzzled looks in both his personal and professional circles. Why not stick with his training and work in government? everyone said. Washington, DC, is the seat of government, and the collective intelligence and imagination of the culture was about government. It was the right place for a political science major who wanted to follow a reasonable path but the wrong place for his aspiration.

Ben intuitively knew that he would need to be in a place that could support starting a business. So, he did the obvious—he moved to the San Francisco Bay Area. He describes it as akin to landing on a new world. The spirit of building a business is in the air everyone is breathing. Inescapable. Even at bars, Ben would hear people talking about the latest technology, and most social events were opportunities to bounce around new ideas. He came to appreciate this cultural and social aspect of innovation. "People overemphasize individual differences," he said. "Everyone is subject to social influences."

Once in the Bay Area, Ben got a job as a product specialist at Google, which gave him a front-row seat from which he was able to see what success in tech looked like. He witnessed the rewards of being risk-forward and being adept at turning academic ideas into products. Seeing risks turn into rewards helped him overcome the internalized voices of his parents whispering on his shoulder about the value of safe and reasonable life decisions. At the same time, Ben also became aware of the tailwinds that helped Google become what it is today and the power of the internet itself to lift a company. Being at the right place at the right time certainly mattered.

The job at Google was by every measure a good one, and Ben appreciated it. But after a while he kept coming home frustrated. "I was in the airshow," he said, "but I was the groundcrew." This feeling of dissatisfaction was a signal to reflect and take action toward something new. He contemplated the lessons he'd learned from working at Google to help clarify his next steps. "The first lesson was being able to see how big you can go when ambition and scale are prized," he said. And the second lesson turned into his first big creativity choice. "I realized I had to go and build something on my own."

With a push and support from his wife, Ben left Google in 2008. The time was right. The release of the first iPhone the year before and the rise of social media put a computer in everyone's pocket and stimulated the desire for self-expression. The question was how to ride those tailwinds.

Ben did not lack ideas. In fact, the idea that would eventually become Pinterest was not even the first one he tried. He reflected how there are many ways to good ideas. "Some people consider technology trends, some people think of markets, and I started with *Wouldn't it be cool if* . . . ," he said. One idea started with his noticing catalogs collecting around the house, followed by his growing unease that they were wasteful. So, he asked, "Wouldn't it be cool if there was an internet-based catalog of catalogs?" It took time to raise money and then, as the first version of the app was built, more time to get it approved by the App Store. Through this process, Ben and his team realized that the idea might be good, but they couldn't make it work in the way they imagined.

The inspiration for what would become Pinterest came from Ben's love for collecting. This time he asked, "Wouldn't it be cool if there was a visual way to organize what you find online?" Although collecting can reveal a lot about who a person is, at the time there were no places on the internet where one could share this kind of self-expression. Motivation to help more people do this kept Ben going. How to do it and whether it would attract users were uncertainties, but he saw them as challenges to overcome.

How to visually organize one's internet finds was a problem to solve. Ben's cofounder, Evan Sharp, provided an elegant solution.

A skillful designer, he conceived of and coded Pinterest's signature visual grid in which items are presented.

Ben stressed that no matter how big a goal, it comes down to a series of small steps. And a major part of creating something involves not getting permanently stuck on any one of these steps. He noticed that people often get overwhelmed by a big goal and run aground on steps one or two. He implicitly knew he had to manage these feelings preventively. "Well," Ben said, "if you do not know how to do something, it means you need to find someone who does know how to do that something. Once you do, the next step is figuring out how to pay them."

Each of the individual steps is manageable on its own. Focusing on one step at a time transforms the process from one that is overwhelming (so why even start?) to one that is challenging, sometimes even stressful, but workable. Ben does not consider himself necessarily patient, but he would perhaps call himself stubborn and certainly determined.

Ben attributes his creative persistence to a combination of ingredients. The most important one was his drive to see if what he, his cofounders, and their team built would work. And once they had a team, Ben was driven by a sense of obligation and responsibility to them. They dreamed of going big, and their belief that they actually could do it grew with each step taken, each problem solved, and each small win. Building creative self-efficacy went hand in hand with building a company.

The sense of togetherness was central throughout the process of building and growing Pinterest. The most crucial element was a partnership with his cofounder and co-leader. Ben considers himself lucky to have had a cofounder who is a friend and someone who was at the same stage in life. "Some commonality creates a base for what you want, such as a shared purpose or even a sense of humor." But as important as shared values are, complementary skills are crucial too. To Ben's big picture and inspiration, Evan brought the design and technology know-how. The equation is not one of simple addition;

rather, together they became more than the sum of their individual attributes and abilities.

Early on, Ben and his team introduced their product to several women who were lifestyle bloggers. They did not have a preconceived notion of how Pinterest would be used but were open to being surprised and paid attention to where users were taking it. They recognized the excitement in users and used it to fuel growth in unanticipated directions. Slow growth gave way to steady growth, which turned into rapid growth.

Told in the space of a few pages, the story of Pinterest sounds like smooth sailing. On the level of daily work and decision-making, the story is, of course, more complex. Ben shared, "The hard thing about a new business is uncertainty of outcome and the feeling that you are fully responsible." In looking back to these stresses, Ben circles again to the social side of creativity. "This is why the culture is so important. There are other people who went through the same journey." And he leaned on those who could understand the experience firsthand. To handle the challenges, Ben said, "You want to be on the optimistic side of realism to take an assessment of where things are and what is the right next step." But he also remarked, "Having a partner is a good thing. It is very easy to be an inaccurate assessor of your situation when you are in it."

Knowing the inner workings of the creative process does not mean that your work will be free of doubt or discomfort (it will not). It does not mean that your sailing will be smooth and free of turbulence. But it means that you will be equipped to make that first crucial decision to embark on a creative process, that you will have the tools and strategies to persist, and that you will have a sense of when to reach out and to whom.

In Ben's words, he and his cofounder were driven to build something that people love, and the result was Pinterest, a visual engine for stockpiling pieces of found inspiration. Just as its founders moved from an idea to building it and growing it, you might write that novel or create that picture book that's been in your mind for years, take a risk to share your ideas at work and champion a project, support your employees in their work, coach clients on how to develop and apply their creative potential, or think again about your very own idea for some new daiquiri. And make a creativity choice.

Acknowledgments

I am a passionate gift conceiver and giver. With every occasion I think of individual people, what they love and how I love them, and have a smile on my face as I do. This book is a gift. A gift to myself as a new challenge to put together various threads of creativity science for everyone who is interested in building creative ideas into something real in the world. And a gift that was made possible by many, directly or indirectly. Creativity is always social, even if at times it might not appear to be. I cannot mention all by name, but to all I am grateful.

This book is dedicated to my grandparents. They made me wonder about the world and showed me love beyond words. Baka Radojka could draw and fix anything and believed in me in a way I felt in every cell of my body. She taught me to go for it, whether "it" was my college choice or a Rolling Stones concert. Dida Mate created the most intense sense of awe of my childhood with his *ćiribi* game. I can still picture myself saying the magic words he invented, pulling on a tree branch, and then feeling the excitement of treats raining from the sky. Nono Pjero is the first who made me think I could write when he read an essay I wrote in ninth grade (on the *Dead Poets Society* movie). Nona Vinka's pasta sauce is to this day not only a fond childhood memory but one of the most amazing and intense experiences I have had. Nona Katy showed me the power of belief and open-mindedness; also, the sheer exhilaration of driving fast and enjoying the ride.

I want to thank my parents, Dragana and Zoran. I marveled seeing them build many things from an idea into something concrete (from their boat to engineering solutions at work). And I will never forget how my brother Dragan tried to teach me creative cooking. He said that you first imagine the flavors you want and then just execute it. This book is thinking through what it takes to "just execute it."

I have gratitude beyond words for my husband, Jamie, without whom this book quite literally would not be possible. He is a role model of creativity to me, both as an interdisciplinary scientist and as someone who approaches every life situation with a "How could we look at this creatively?" attitude, often saying those exact words. He took on much more than his fair share of cooking and homework help so that I could spend afternoons and evenings in our local Barnes & Noble bookstore writing. And he also (mostly) patiently dealt with emotional side effects of writing a book and all that is associated with it.

It has been a privilege to watch my son, Alex, grow and see his creativity in action, from all the stories of Mousey, his once-upon-a-time imaginary alter ego (and international entrepreneurial mastermind), to his pretend play story lines (animal rescue! Moomins in space!), to building whole Lego cities, to growing into a creative photographer and future environmental engineer.

I am grateful for my friends more than I know how to put into words. Tatjana Potkonjak is a performance artist at heart and always up for what others consider crazy but I think absolutely natural. Thank you for that long-ago 5 a.m. walk to Vis and for Trieste. And everything in between. Vlatka Filipović-Marijić is my role model of what a wonderful and psychologically healthy human is. When I grow up, I want to be more like you. Tanja Kućan Floyd, thank you for dreaming with me about possible lives. Also, *The Mousetrap* and

Paddington. Pallavi Mittal, thank you for being Pallavi and spreading joy everywhere around you. Branka Dečković got me interested in creativity before that word entered my vocabulary. What you did when we were in elementary school was a longtime inspiration. And I am grateful for my groups of support—women who gather around the political table: Terie Norelli, Sharon Nichols, Bernice Brody, Joan Jacobs, Leslie Cartier, and the Balkan ladies, Sanela Suljić Orsino and Nevenka Kozomora.

Elif Gökçiğdem expanded my thinking and keeps doing so. We met by lucky chance but continued to work together, driven by a common purpose. It is an honor to know you. One day we will make it to Göbekli Tepe together!

My professional network has been a source of great intellectual stimulation and inspiration, helping me transform ideas into workshops, courses, and, well, this book. First among many colleagues from the world of creativity studies is James Kaufman, whose intellectual leadership and friendship nourish me. Thank you for signing the review for one of my dissertation research papers and everything since. I cherish our breakfasts at Ken's that grow into all-day thinking and writing sessions. I love and have cited work by many colleagues who keep me asking more questions—Robert Sternberg, Izabela Lebuda, Maciej Karwowski, Aleksandra Zielińska, Scott Barry Kaufman, Sandy Russ, Vlad Glăveanu, Roni Reiter-Palmon, Paul Silvia, Giovanni Corazza, Pablo Tinio, Katherine Cotter, Jennifer Drake, Kaile Smith, Magdalena Grohman, Jean Pretz, and many others.

None of this would have happened without mentors, who taught me about psychology and research. Denis Bratko was the first to make me consider research as a career path, and Vladimir Takšić was my constant cheerleader. Jack Mayer's capacity to integrate disparate areas of research and build puzzles of 10,000 pieces is unprecedented and a continuing source of inspiration and aspiration. His work shows that narrow specializations do not work if our goal is to really understand people. Becky Warner has taught me not only to use statistics but also how to think about it as a tool in the service of research. And I am grateful to my postdoc mentors, David Pillemer, whose work on autobiographical memory truly had a directive function in my life, and Nalini Ambady, who believed in me when I did not and from whom I learned much about what is now my personal philosophy of science.

And then there are my colleagues at the Yale Center for Emotional Intelligence who have been there at important beginnings. Marc Brackett has been a friend since the first day of graduate school. It has been quite a journey. And Robin Stern's "You should write a book" got me started. You are my Sophia from *The Golden Girls*. You have the best one-liners that make me think. Postdocs and research assistants through the years made me consider new perspectives. Jessica Hoffmann was my first postdoc and continues to be a collaborator; thank you. Eliana Grossman helped me realize more than anyone the many powers of art. Thank you for the chats walking to the kati roll cart in New Haven and those walking to the kati roll stall in India on the way to the summit with His Holiness the Dalai Lama. Let's continue to talk.

Many thanks to my literary agent, Jill Marsal, a trusted guide and ally on this project. I am grateful that you reached out just as I was contemplating this book. I appreciate your connecting me with Catherine Knepper. Writing a book is a creative process and, as such, full of twists and turns and questions like "What did you mean here?" Catherine, I am grateful to you for pulling me out of my head and helping me communicate the message effectively. And I am grateful to the whole team at PublicAffairs, led by editors Kimberly Meilun and Emily Taber. I appreciate all the help in crafting the structure and narrative flow.

I am grateful to all the funders who have supported and continue to support my research. The long-standing collaboration with Fundación Botín in Santander, Spain, has been full of discovery and inspiration. Chairman Emilio Botín made me see firsthand how much difference a bold vision can make. It has been a great joy to work with Íñigo Sáenz de Miera and Fátima Sánchez Santiago and see Centro Botín grow from an idea into a home for creativity. The Faas Foundation and the Ontario Hospital Association enabled me to ask the big question about how people feel at work and in what ways that makes a difference to what they can do. Working with Annie Tobias at the Proximity Institute showed me the power of putting theory and research into practice in leadership development. The National Endowment for the Arts allowed me to study the apparent contradictions in creative individuals. The John Templeton Foundation grant to the Imagination Institute made it possible for me to dive deep to understand self-regulation of creative action, which was foundational in understanding the process of transforming ideas into something tangible. As I write this, the grant from the Templeton Religion Trust opened a new door to examine the creative process inside and out as it unfolds.

Last, but by no means least, I am grateful that a long time ago I came across the work of Frank Barron. His insight into the nature of creativity, creative individuals, and the process of creation keeps inspiring me. If time travel became possible, I would hope to meet in person. So much to chat about.

References

Introduction

Baas, M., De Dreu, C. K. W., & Nijstad, B. A. (2008). A meta-analysis of 25 years of mood-creativity research: Hedonic tone, activation, or regulatory focus? *Psychological Bulletin, 134*(6), 779–806. https://doi.org/10.1037/a0012815.

Barron, F. (1963). *Creativity and psychological health: Origins of personal vitality and creative freedom.* Van Nostrand.

Csikszentmihalyi, M. (1996). *Creativity: Flow and the psychology of discovery and invention.* Harper Perennial.

Feist, G. J. (1998). A meta-analysis of personality in scientific and artistic creativity. *Personality and Social Psychology Review, 2*(4), 290–309.

Ivcevic, Z., Grossman, E., & Ranjan, A. (2022). Patterns of psychological vulnerabilities and resources in artists and nonartists. *Psychology of Aesthetics, Creativity, and the Arts, 16*(1), 3–15. https://doi.org/10.1037/aca0000309.

Ivcevic, Z., & Mayer, J. D. (2009). Mapping dimensions of creativity in the life-space. *Creativity Research Journal, 21,* 152–165. https://doi.org/10.1080/10400410902855259.

Ivcevic, Z., & Nusbaum, E. C. (2017). From having an idea to doing something with it: Self-regulation for creativity. In M. Karwowski & J. C. Kaufman (Eds.), *The creative self: Effect of beliefs, self-efficacy, mindset, and identity* (pp. 343–365). Academic Press.

Kerr, S. P., Kerr, W. R., & Dalton, M. (2019). Risk attitudes and personality traits of entrepreneurs and venture team members. *Proceedings of the National Academy of Sciences, 116*(36), 17712–17716. https://doi.org/10.1073/pnas.1908375116.

Scott, G., Leritz, L. E., & Mumford, M. D. (2004). The effectiveness of creativity training: A quantitative review. *Creativity Research Journal, 16*(4), 361–388. https://doi.org/10.1207/s15326934crj1604_1.

Sio, U. N., & Lortie-Forgues, H. (2024). The impact of creativity training on creative performance: A meta-analytic review and critical evaluation of 5 decades of creativity training studies. *Psychological Bulletin, 150*(5), 554–585. https://doi.org/10.1037/bul0000432.

Yamada, K. (2013). *What do you do with an idea?* Compendium.

Chapter 1: Creativity Is a Choice

Amabile, T. M. (1996). *Creativity in context: Update to the social psychology of creativity.* Westview Press.

Can "creative" be a noun? When adjectives drift into noun territory. (n.d.). Merriam-Webster. https://www.merriam-webster.com/grammar/can-creative-be-a-noun-usage-history.

Child, J., with Prud'homme, A. (2007). *My life in France.* Anchor Books.

Cramer, P. (2015). Defense mechanisms: 40 years of empirical research. *Journal of Personality Assessment, 97*(2), 114–122. https://doi.org/10.1080/00223891.2014.947997.

Daiquiri. (n.d.). Wikipedia. Retrieved January 21, 2023. https://en.wikipedia.org/wiki/Daiquiri.

Difford, S. (n.d.). Daiquiri history and story of its creation. Difford's Guide. Retrieved on January 21, 2023. https://www.diffordsguide.com/g/1083/daiquiri-cocktail/story.

Foster, B. (2005, January). Einstein and his love of music. *Physics World.* http://www.gci.org.uk/Documents/einstein&music.pdf.

Glăveanu, V. P. (2011). Is the lightbulb still on? Social representations of creativity in a Western context. *International Journal of Creativity & Problem-solving, 21*(1), 53–72.

Glăveanu, V., Lubart, T., Bonnardel, N., Botella, M., De Biaisi, P. M., Desainte-Catherine, M., Georgsdottir, A., Guillou, K., Kurtag, G., Mouchiroud, C., Storme, M., Wojtczuk, A., & Zenasni, F. (2013). Creativity as action: Findings from five creative domains. *Frontiers in Psychology, 4,* Article 176. https://doi.org/10.3389/fpsyg.2013.00176.

Gould, E. (2017, November 20). An unabashed appreciation of Smitten Kitchen, the Ur-food blog. *New Yorker.* https://www.newyorker.com/culture/annals-of-gastronomy/an-unabashed-appreciation-of-smitten-kitchen-the-ur-food-blog.

Grossman, E., & Drake, J. E. (2023). The affective benefits of creative activities. In Z. Ivcevic, J. D. Hoffmann, & J. C. Kaufman (Eds.), *The Cambridge handbook of creativity and emotions* (pp. 376–393). Cambridge University Press.

Holinger, M., & Kaufman, J. C. (2023). Everyday creativity as a pathway to meaning and well-being. In Z. Ivcevic, J. D. Hoffmann, & J. C. Kaufman (Eds.), *The Cambridge handbook of creativity and emotions* (pp. 393–410). Cambridge University Press.

Ivcevic, Z. (2007). Artistic and everyday creativity: An act-frequency approach. *Journal of Creative Behavior, 41*(4), 271–290. https://doi.org/10.1002/j.2162-6057.2007.tb01074.x.

Ivcevic, Z., & Nusbaum, E. C. (2017). From having an idea to doing something with it: Self-regulation for creativity. In M. Karwowski & J. C. Kaufman (Eds.), *The creative self: Effect of beliefs, self-efficacy, mindset, and identity* (pp. 343–365). Academic Press.

Julia Child. (n.d.). Wikipedia. Retrieved January 20, 2023. https://en.wikipedia.org/wiki/Julia_Child.

Kaufman, J. C., & Beghetto, R. A. (2009). Beyond big and little: The four c model of creativity. *Review of General Psychology, 13*(1), 1–12. https://doi.org/10.1037/a0013688.

La Duke, P. (2019, December 10). Ten entrepreneurs share how they turned their hobbies into successful careers. *Authority Magazine.* https://medium.com/authority-magazine/ten-entrepreneurs-share-how-they-turned-their-hobbies-into-successful-careers-22e574e35e2.

Marques Brownlee. (n.d.). Wikipedia. Retrieved May 17, 2024. https://en.wikipedia.org/wiki/Marques_Brownlee.

Monti, F. (2016, June 28). Cuba's overlooked role in cocktail history. *Punch.* https://punchdrink.com/articles/cuban-cocktails-history-and-recipes-little-known-contributions-to-cocktail-culture.

Pardilla, C. (2016, May 12). Cocktails 101: The daiquiri. *Eater.* https://www.eater.com/drinks/2016/5/12/11327350/daiquiri-cocktail-recipe-rum-lime-cuban-drink.

Organ, D. W., & Konovsky, M. (1989). Cognitive versus affective determinants of organizational citizenship behavior. *Journal of Applied Psychology, 74*(1), 157–164. https://doi.org/10.1037/0021-9010.74.1.157.

Proudfoot, D., Kay, A. C., & Koval, C. Z. (2015). A gender bias in the attribution of creativity: Archival and experimental evidence for the perceived association between masculinity and creative thinking. *Psychological Science, 26*(11), 1751–1761. https://doi.org/10.1177/0956797615598739.

Said-Metwaly, S., Taylor, C. L., Camarda, A., & Barbot, B. (2022). Divergent thinking and creative achievement—How strong is the link? An updated meta-analysis. *Psychology of Aesthetics, Creativity, and the Arts.* Advance online publication. https://doi.org/10.1037/aca0000507.

Scott, G., Leritz, L. E., & Mumford, M. D. (2004). The effectiveness of creativity training: A quantitative review. *Creativity Research Journal, 16*(4), 361–388. https://doi.org/10.1207/s15326934crj1604_1.

Silvia, P. J. (2009). Looking past pleasure: Anger, confusion, disgust, pride, surprise, and other unusual aesthetic emotions. *Psychology of Aesthetics, Creativity, and the Arts, 3*(1), 48–51. https://doi.org/10.1037/a0014632.

Sternberg, R. J. (2002). "Creativity as a decision": Comment. *American Psychologist, 57*(5), Article 376. https://doi.org/10.1037/0003-066X.57.5.376a.

Sternberg, R. J. (2003). Development of creativity as a decision making process. In R. K. Sawyer, V. John-Steiner, S. Moran, R. J. Sternberg, D. H. Feldman, J. Nakamura, & M. Csikszentmihalyi (Eds.), *Creativity and development* (pp. 91–138). Oxford University Press.

Tierney, P., Farmer, S. M., & Graen, G. B. (1999). An examination of leadership and employee creativity: The relevance of traits and relationships. *Personnel Psychology, 52*(3), 591–620. https://doi.org/10.1111/j.1744-6570.1999.tb00173.x.

Tinio, P. P. L. (2013). From artistic creation to aesthetic reception: The mirror model of art. *Psychology of Aesthetics, Creativity, and the Arts, 7*(3), 265–275. https://doi.org/10.1037/a0030872.

Zhou, J., & George, J. M. (2001). When job dissatisfaction leads to creativity: Encouraging the expression of voice. *Academy of Management Journal, 44*(4), 682–696. https://doi.org/10.5465/3069410.

Chapter 2: Creativity Takes Risk

Abad-Santos, A. (2019, November 11). Martin Scorsese's fight against Marvel isn't really about Marvel movies. *Vox.* https://www.vox.com/2019/11/8/20950451/martin-scorsese-marvel-movies-cinema-feige.

Asch, S. E. (1956). Studies of independence and conformity: I. A minority of one against a unanimous majority. *Psychological Monographs: General and Applied, 70*(9), 1–70. https://doi.org/10.1037/h0093718.

Aten, J. (2021, January 19). This is Steve Jobs's most controversial legacy. It is also his most brilliant. *Inc.* https://www.inc.com/jason-aten/this-was-steve-jobs-most-controversial-legacy-it-was-also-his-most-brilliant.html.

Beghetto, R. A., Karwowski, M., & Reiter-Palmon, R. (2021). Intellectual risk taking: A moderating link between creative confidence and creative behavior? *Psychology of Aesthetics, Creativity, and the Arts, 15*(4), 637–644. https://doi.org/10.1037/aca0000323.

Blais, A. R., & Weber, E. U. (2006). A domain-specific risk-taking (DOSPERT) scale for adult populations. *Judgment and Decision Making, 1*(1), 33–47. https://doi.org/10.1017/S1930297500000334.

Brandstetter, J., Rácz, P., Beckner, C., Sandoval, E. B., Hay, J., & Bartneck, C. (2014, September). A peer pressure experiment: Recreation of the Asch conformity experiment with robots. In *2014 IEEE/RSJ International Conference on Intelligent Robots and Systems* (pp. 1335–1340). IEEE.

Brown, T., Ordona, M., & Phillips, J. (2023, May 3). Marvel is doing just fine—for now. But some L.A.-area fans are at a "tipping point." *Los Angeles Times*. https://www.latimes.com/entertainment-arts/movies/story/2023-05-03/marvel-studios-movies-mcu-box-office-reviews-fan-reactions.

de Vet, A. J., & de Dreu, C. K. W. (2007). The influence of articulation, self-monitoring ability, and sensitivity to others on creativity. *European Journal of Social Psychology*, *37*(4), 747–760. https://doi.org/10.1002/ejsp.386.

El-Murad, J., & West, D. C. (2003). Risk and creativity in advertising. *Journal of Marketing Management*, *19*(5–6), 657–673. https://doi.org/10.1080/0267257X.2003.9728230.

Freud, A. (1946). *The ego and the mechanisms of defense*. International Universities Press. (Original work published 1936.)

Freud, S. (1962). The neuro-psychoses of defense. In J. Strachey (Ed. and Trans.), *The standard edition of the complete works of Sigmund Freud* (Vol. 3, pp. 45–61). Hogarth Press. (Original work published 1894.)

Freud, S. (1966). Further remarks on the neuro-psychoses of defense. In J. Strachey (Ed. and Trans.), *The standard edition of the complete works of Sigmund Freud* (Vol. 3, pp. 161–185). Hogarth Press. (Original work published 1896.)

Hunter, S. T., Blocker, L. D., Gutworth, M. B., & Allen, J. (2023). Why we support some original ideas but reject others: An application of signaling theory. *Journal of Creative Behavior*, *57*(2), 199–220. https://doi.org/10.1002/jocb.570.

Ivcevic, Z., & Hoffmann, J. D. (2021). The creativity dare: Attitudes toward creativity and prediction of creative behavior in school. *Journal of Creative Behavior*, *56*(2), 239–257. https://doi.org/10.1002/jocb.527.

Kois, D. (2021, August 1). "This is going to change the world!" *Slate*. https://slate.com/human-interest/2021/08/dean-kamen-viral-mystery-invention-2001.html.

Mahmoud, N. E., Kamel, S. M., & Hamza, T. S. (2020). The relationship between tolerance of ambiguity and creativity in architectural design studio. *Creativity Studies*, *13*(1), 179–198. https://doi.org/10.3846/cs.2020.9628.

Mueller, J., Melwani, S., Loewenstein, J., & Deal, J. J. (2018). Reframing the decision-makers' dilemma: Towards a social context model of creative idea recognition. *Academy of Management Journal*, *61*(1), 94–110. https://doi.org/10.5465/amj.2013.0887.

Mueller, J. S., Melwani, S., & Goncalo, J. A. (2012). The bias against creativity: Why people desire but reject creative ideas. *Psychological Science*, *23*(1), 13–17. https://doi.org/10.1177/0956797611421018.

Merit review facts. (n.d.). National Science Foundation. https://www.nsf.gov/bfa/dias/policy/merit_review/facts.jsp#5.

Stevens, G. A., & Burley, J. (1997). 3,000 raw ideas = 1 commercial success! *Research Technology Management, 40*(3): 16–27. https://www.jstor.org/stable/24131400.

Stoycheva, K. (2024). Tolerance of ambiguity and the creative action: To engage and endure. *Journal of Creative Behavior.* Advance online publication. https://doi.org/10.1002/jocb.1506.

Toh, C. A., & Miller, S. R. (2016). Creativity in design teams: The influence of personality traits and risk attitudes on creative concept selection. *Research in Engineering Design, 27,* 73–89. https://doi.org/10.1007/s00163-015-0207-y.

Tyagi, V., Hanoch, Y., Hall, S. D., Runco, M., & Denham, S. L. (2017). The risky side of creativity: Domain specific risk taking in creative individuals. *Frontiers in Psychology, 8,* Article 145. https://doi.org/10.3389/fpsyg.2017.00145.

Whiting, K. (2021, October 21). These are the top 10 job skills of tomorrow—and how long it takes to learn them. World Economic Forum. https://www.weforum.org/agenda/2020/10/top-10-work-skills-of-tomorrow-how-long-it-takes-to-learn-them.

Chapter 3: Yes, You Can

Bandura, A. (1997). *Self-efficacy: The exercise of control.* W. H. Freeman.

Curtis, B. (2013, May 16). The Dan Brown code: In a court filing, the best-selling author reveals all the secrets of a pulp novelist. *Slate.* https://slate.com/news-and-politics/2013/05/dan-brown-inferno-in-a-court-filing-the-best-selling-author-reveals-the-secrets-to-his-success.html.

Farmer, S. M., & Tierney, P. (2017). Considering creative self-efficacy: Its current state and ideas for future inquiry. In M. Karwowski & J. C. Kaufman (Eds.), *The creative self: Effect of beliefs, self-efficacy, mindset, and identity* (pp. 23–47). Elsevier Academic Press. https://doi.org/10.1016/B978-0-12-809790-8.00002-9.

Feist, G. J. (2017). The creative personality: Current understandings and debates. In J. A. Plucker (Ed.), *Creativity and innovation: Theory, research, and practice* (pp. 181–198). Prufrock Press, Inc.

Haase, J., Hoff, E. V., Hanel, P. H. P., & Innes-Ker, Å. (2018). A meta-analysis of the relation between creative self-efficacy and different creativity measurements. *Creativity Research Journal, 30*(1), 1–16. https://doi.org/10.1080/10400419.2018.1411436.

Helson, R., Soto, C. J., & Cate, R. A. (2006). From young adulthood through the middle ages. In D. K. Mroczek & T. D. Little (Eds.), *Handbook of personality development* (pp. 337–352). Lawrence Erlbaum Associates Publishers.

Hon, A. H. Y., & Chan, W. W. H. (2013). Team creative performance: The roles of empowering leadership, creative-related motivation, and task interdependence. *Cornell Hospitality Quarterly, 54*(2), 199–210. https://doi.org/10.1177/1938965512455859.

Karwowski, M., Han, M.-H., & Beghetto, R. A. (2019). Toward dynamizing the measurement of creative confidence beliefs. *Psychology of Aesthetics, Creativity, and the Arts*, *13*(2), 193–202. https://doi.org/10.1037/aca0000229.

Karwowski, M., & Lebuda, I. (2016). The big five, the huge two, and creative self-beliefs: A meta-analysis. *Psychology of Aesthetics, Creativity, and the Arts*, *10*(2), 214–232. https://doi.org/10.1037/aca0000035.

Karwowski, M., Lebuda, I., Wisniewska, E., & Gralewski, J. (2013). Big five personality traits as the predictors of creative self-efficacy and creative personal identity: Does gender matter? *Journal of Creative Behavior*, *47*(3), 215–232. https://doi.org/10.1002/jocb.32.

Li, C.-R., Yang, Y., Lin, C.-J., & Xu, Y. (2021). Within-person relationship between creative self-efficacy and individual creativity: The mediator of creative process engagement and the moderator of regulatory focus. *Journal of Creative Behavior*, *55*(1), 63–78. https://doi.org/10.1002/jocb.435.

Lindquist, M. J., Sol, J., & van Praag, M. C. (2012). Why do entrepreneurial parents have entrepreneurial children? Working paper no. 6740. Institute of Labor Economics (IZA). https://hdl.handle.net/11245/1.395582.

Myers, F. R. (2022, October). The James Webb Space Telescope, from concept to commissioning. Talk presented at the Cambridge Science Festival. Massachusetts Institute of Technology Museum, Cambridge, MA. https://mitmuseum.mit.edu/programs/cambridge-science-festival.

Puente-Díaz, R., & Cavazos-Arroyo, J. (2017). Creative self-efficacy: The influence of affective states and social persuasion as antecedents and imagination and divergent thinking as consequences. *Creativity Research Journal*, *29*(3), 304–312. https://doi.org/10.1080/10400419.2017.1360067.

Puente-Díaz, R., & Cavazos-Arroyo, J. (2022). Creative self-efficacy and metacognitive feelings as sources of information when generating, evaluating, and selecting creative ideas: A metacognitive perspective. *Journal of Creative Behavior*, *56*(4), 647–658. https://doi.org/10.1002/jocb.557.

Ross, C. E. (2000). Occupations, jobs, and the sense of control. *Sociological Focus*, *33*(4), 409–420. https://doi.org/10.1080/00380237.2000.10571177.

Royston, R., & Reiter-Palmon, R. (2019). Creative self-efficacy as mediator between creative mindsets and creative problem-solving. *Journal of Creative Behavior*, *53*(4), 472–481. https://doi.org/10.1002/jocb.226.

Salanova, M., Llorens, S., & Schaufeli, W. B. (2011). "Yes, I can, I feel good, and I just do it!" On gain cycles and spirals of efficacy beliefs, affect, and engagement. *Applied Psychology: An International Review*, *60*(2), 255–285. https://doi.org/10.1111/j.1464-0597.2010.00435.x.

Schwaba, T., Luhmann, M., Denissen, J. J. A., Chung, J. M. H., & Bleidorn, W. (2018).

Openness to experience and culture-openness transactions across the lifespan. *Journal of Personality and Social Psychology, 115*(1), 118–136. https://doi.org/10.1037/pspp0000150.

Swarm, W. B., Jr. (1985). The self as architect of social reality. In B. Sehlenker (Ed.), *The self and social life* (pp. 100–125). McGraw-Hill.

Tierney, P., & Farmer, S. M. (2002). Creative self-efficacy: Its potential antecedents and relationship to creative performance. *Academy of Management Journal, 45*(6), 1137–1148. https://doi.org/10.2307/3069429.

Tierney, P., & Farmer, S. M. (2004). The Pygmalion process and employee creativity. *Journal of Management, 30*(3), 413–432. https://doi.org/10.1016/j.jm.2002.12.001.

Tierney, P., & Farmer, S. M. (2011). Creative self-efficacy development and creative performance over time. *Journal of Applied Psychology, 96*(2), 277–293. https://doi.org/10.1037/a0020952.

Yar, D. H., Wennberg, W., & Berglund, H. (2008). Creativity in entrepreneurship education. *Journal of Small Business and Enterprise Development, 15*(2), 304–320. https://doi.org/10.1108/14626000810871691.

Zielińska, A., Lebuda, I., & Karwowski, M. (2023). Dispositional self-regulation strengthens the links between creative activity and creative achievement. *Personality and Individual Differences, 200*, Article 111894. https://doi.org/10.1016/j.paid.2022.111894.

Chapter 4: Driven to Create

Acar, S., Runco, M. A., & Park, H. (2020). What should people be told when they take a divergent thinking test? A meta-analytic review of explicit instructions for divergent thinking. *Psychology of Aesthetics, Creativity, and the Arts, 14*(1), 39–49. http://dx.doi.org/10.1037/aca0000256.

Aleksić, D., Škerlavaj, M., & Dysvik, A. (2016). The flow of creativity for idea implementation. In M. Škerlavaj, M. Černe, A. Dysvik, & A. Carlsen (Eds.), *Capitalizing on creativity at work: Fostering the implementation of creative ideas in organizations* (pp. 29–38). Edward Elgar Publishing. https://doi.org/10.4337/9781783476503.

Amabile, T. M. (1997). Entrepreneurial creativity through motivational synergy. *Journal of Creative Behavior, 31*(1), 18–26. https://doi.org/10.1002/j.2162-6057.1997.tb00778.x.

Amabile, T. M., Hill, K. G., Hennessey, B. A., & Tighe, E. M. (1994). The Work Preference Inventory: Assessing intrinsic and extrinsic motivational orientations. *Journal of Personality and Social Psychology, 66*(5), 950–967. https://doi.org/10.1037/0022-3514.66.5.950.

References

Amabile, T. M., & Kramer, S. J. (2011). *The progress principle: Using small wins to ignite joy, engagement, and creativity at work*. Harvard Business Press.

Baer, M. (2012). Putting creativity to work: The implementation of creative ideas in organizations. *Academy of Management Journal, 55*(5), 1102–1119. https://doi.org/10.5465/amj.2009.0470.

Benedek, M., Karstendiek, M., Ceh, S. M., Grabner, R. H., Krammer, G., Lebuda, I., Silvia, P. J., Cotter, K. N., Li, Y., Hu, W., Martskvishvili, K., & Kaufman, J. C. (2021). Creativity myths: Prevalence and correlates of misconceptions on creativity. *Personality and Individual Differences, 182*, Article 111068. https://doi.org/10.1016/j.paid.2021.111068.

Blake Mycoskie (n.d.). Wikipedia. Retrieved August 15, 2023. https://en.wikipedia.org/w/index.php?title=Blake_Mycoskie&oldid=1172207124.

Boova, L., Pratt, M. G., & Lepisto, D. A. (2019). Exploring work orientations and cultural accounts of work: Toward a research agenda for examining the role of culture in meaningful work. In R. Yeoman, C. Bailey, A. Madden, and M. Thompson (Eds), *The Oxford handbook of meaningful work* (pp. 185–207). Oxford University Press.

Breugst, N., Domurath, A., Patzelt, H., & Klaukien, A. (2012). Perceptions of entrepreneurial passion and employees' commitment to entrepreneurial ventures. *Entrepreneurship Theory and Practice, 36*(1), 171–192. https://doi.org/10.1111/j.1540-6520.2011.00491.x.

Cardon, M. S., & Kirk, C. P. (2015). Entrepreneurial passion as mediator of the self-efficacy to persistence relationship. *Entrepreneurship Theory and Practice, 39*(5), 1027–1050. https://doi.org/10.1111/etap.12089.

Caughron, J. J., & Mumford, M. D. (2008). Project planning: The effects of using formal planning techniques on creative problem-solving. *Creativity and Innovation Management, 17*(3), 204–215. https://doi.org/10.1111/j.1467-8691.2008.00484.x.

Chi, A. (2018, April). The most advanced prosthetic in the world. TEDxPortland. https://www.ted.com/talks/albert_chi_the_most_advanced_prosthetic_in_the_world.

Corazza, G. E., & Agnoli, S. (2022). The DA VINCI model for the creative thinking process. In T. Lubart, M. Botella, S. Bourgeois-Bougrine, X. Caroff, J. Guegan, C. Mouchiroud, J. Nelson, & F. Zenasni (Eds.), *Homo creativus: The 7 C's of human creativity* (pp. 49–67). Springer International Publishing.

Csikszentmihalyi, M. (1996). *Creativity: Flow and the psychology of discovery and invention*. Harper Perennial.

Csikszentmihalyi, M., & LeFevre, J. (1989). Optimal experience in work and leisure. *Journal of Personality and Social Psychology, 56*(5), 815–822. https://doi.org/10.1037/0022-3514.56.5.815.

Drnovsek, M., Cardon, M. S., & Patel, P. C. (2016). Direct and indirect effects of passion on growing technology ventures. *Strategic Entrepreneurship Journal, 10*(2), 194–213. https://doi.org/10.1002/sej.1213.

Fetzer, G., & Pratt, M. G. (2020). Meaningful work and creativity: Mapping out a way forward. In R. Reiter-Palmon, C. M. Fisher, and J. S. Mueller (Eds.), *Creativity at work*. Palgrave Studies in Creativity and Innovation in Organizations. Palgrave Macmillan. https://doi.org/10.1007/978-3-030-61311-2_13.

Forgeard, M. (2022). Prosocial motivation and creativity in the arts and sciences: Qualitative and quantitative evidence. *Psychology of Aesthetics, Creativity, and the Arts, 18*(2), 222–244. https://doi.org/10.1037/aca0000435.

Forgeard, M. (2023). Motivations, emotions, and creativity. In Z. Ivcevic, J. D. Hoffmann, & J. C. Kaufman (Eds.), *The Cambridge handbook of creativity and emotions* (pp. 149–166). Cambridge University Press.

Haught-Tromp, C. (2017). The *Green Eggs and Ham* hypothesis: How constraints facilitate creativity. *Psychology of Aesthetics, Creativity, and the Arts, 11*(1), 10–17. http://dx.doi.org/10.1037/aca0000061.

Jacob Lawrence: The migration series. (n.d.). Phillips Collection. https://lawrence migration.phillipscollection.org.

Kellogg, R. T. (1988). Attentional overload and writing performance: Effects of rough draft and outline strategies. *Journal of Experimental Psychology: Learning, Memory, and Cognition, 14*(2), 355–365. https://doi.org/10.1037/0278-7393.14.2.355.

Koole, S., & Spijker, M. (2000). Overcoming the planning fallacy through willpower: Effects of implementation intentions on actual and predicted task-completion times. *European Journal of Social Psychology, 30*(6), 873–888. https://doi.org/10.1002/1099-0992(200011/12)30:6<873::AID-EJSP22>3.0.CO;2-U.

Liu, D., Jiang, K., Shalley, C. E., Keem, S., & Zhou, J. (2016). Motivational mechanisms of employee creativity: A meta-analytic examination and theoretical extension of the creativity literature. *Organizational Behavior and Human Decision Processes, 137*, 236–263. https://doi.org/10.1016/j.obhdp.2016.08.001.

Locke, E. A., & Latham, G. P. (Eds.). (2013). *New developments in goal setting and task performance*. Routledge/Taylor & Francis Group. https://doi.org/10.4324/97802 03082744.

Lucas, B. J., & Nordgren, L. F. (2020). The creative cliff illusion. *PNAS: Proceedings of the National Academy of Sciences of the United States of America, 117*(33), 19830–19836. https://doi.org/10.1073/pnas.2005620117.

Malik, M. A. R., Butt, A. N., & Choi, J. N. (2015). Rewards and employee creative performance: Moderating effects of creative self-efficacy, reward importance, and locus of control. *Journal of Organizational Behavior, 36*(1), 59–74. https://doi.org/10.1002/job.1943.

Mayer, J. D., Caruso, D. R., & Salovey, P. (2016). The ability model of emotional intelligence: Principles and updates. *Emotion Review*, 8(4), 290–300. https://doi.org/10.1177/1754073916639667.

Moeller, J. (2014). Passion as concept of the psychology of motivation. Conceptualization, assessment, inter-individual variability and long-term stability. Doctoral dissertation, University of Erfurt. http://www.db-thueringen.de/servlets/Derivate Servlet/Derivate-29036/DissJuliaMoeller.pdf.

Moeller, J., Ivcevic, Z., White, A. E., Taylor, C., Menges, J. I., Caruso, D., & Brackett, M. A. (2019, August 7). Passion for work: What is it, who has it, and does it matter? OSF Preprints. https://doi.org/10.31219/osf.io/xhbu7.

Nakamura, J., & Csikszentmihalyi, M. (2002). The concept of flow. In S. J. Lopez & C. R. Snyder (Eds.), *The Oxford handbook of positive psychology* (pp. 89–105). Oxford University Press.

Nusbaum, E. C., Silvia, P. J., & Beaty, R. E. (2014). Ready, set, create: What instructing people to "be creative" reveals about the meaning and mechanisms of divergent thinking. *Psychology of Aesthetics, Creativity, and the Arts*, 8(4), 423–432. http://dx.doi.org/10.1037/a0036549.

O'Keefe, P. A., Dweck, C. S., & Walton, G. M. (2018). Implicit theories of interest: Finding your passion or developing it? *Psychological Science*, 29(10), 1653–1664. https://doi.org/10.1177/0956797618780643.

Onarheim, B. (2012). Creativity from constraints in engineering design: Lessons learned at Coloplast. *Journal of Engineering Design*, 23(4), 323–336. https://doi.org/10.1080/09544828.2011.631904.

Pratt, M. G., Pradies, C., & Lepisto, D. A. (2013). Doing well, doing good, and doing with: Organizational practices for effectively cultivating meaningful work. In B. Dik, Z. Byrne, & M. Steger (Eds.), *Purpose and meaning in the workplace* (pp. 173–196). American Psychological Association.

Root-Bernstein, R., Allen, L., Beach, L., Bhadula, R., Fast, J., Hosey, C., Kremkow, B., Lapp, J., Lonc, K., Pawelec, K., Podufaly, A., Russ, C., Tennant, L., Vrtis, E., & Weinlander, S. (2008). Arts foster scientific success: Avocations of Nobel, National Academy, Royal Society, and Sigma Xi members. *Journal of Psychology of Science and Technology*, 1(2), 51–63. https://doi.org/10.1891/1939-7054.1.2.51.

Schellenberg, B. J. I., Verner-Filion, J., Gaudreau, P., Bailis, D. S., Lafrenière, M.-A. K., & Vallerand, R. J. (2019). Testing the dualistic model of passion using a novel quadripartite approach: A look at physical and psychological well-being. *Journal of Personality*, 87(2), 163–180. https://doi.org/10.1111/jopy.12378.

Sellier, A.-L., & Dahl, D. W. (2011). Focus! Creative success is enjoyed through restricted choice. *Journal of Marketing Research*, 48(6), 996–1007. https://doi.org/10.1509/jmr.10.0407.

Shally, C. E., Gilson, L. L., & Blum, T. C. (2009). Interactive effects of growth need strength, work context, and job complexity on self-reported creative performance. *Academy of Management Journal, 52*(3), 489–505. https://doi.org/10.5465/AMJ.2009.41330806.

Stokes, P. D. (2008). Creativity from constraints: What can we learn from Motherwell? From Mondrian? From Klee? *Journal of Creative Behavior, 42*(4), 223–236. https://doi.org/10.1002/j.2162-6057.2008.tb01297.x.

Stollberger, J., & Debus, M. E. (2020). Go with the flow, but keep it stable? The role of flow variability in the context of daily flow experiences and daily creative performance. *Work & Stress, 34*(4), 342–358. https://doi.org/10.1080/02678373.2019.1695293.

Tromp, C., & Baer, J. (2022). Creativity from constraints: Theory and applications to education. *Thinking Skills and Creativity, 46*, Article 101184. https://doi.org/10.1016/j.tsc.2022.101184.

Vallerand, R. J., Blanchard, C., Mageau, G. A., Koestner, R., Ratelle, C., Léonard, M., Gagné, M., & Marsolais, J. (2003). Les passions de l'âme: On obsessive and harmonious passion. *Journal of Personality and Social Psychology, 85*(4), 756–767. https://doi.org/10.1037/0022-3514.85.4.756.

Vallerand, R. J., Chichekian, T., Verner-Filion, J., & Bélanger, J. J. (2023). The two faces of persistence: How harmonious and obsessive passion shape goal pursuit. *Motivation Science, 9*(3), 175–192. https://doi.org/10.1037/mot0000303.

Vallerand, R. J., Paquet, Y., Philippe, F. L., & Charest, J. (2010). On the role of passion for work in burnout: A process model. *Journal of Personality, 78*(1), 289–312. https://doi.org/10.1111/j.1467-6494.2009.00616.x.

Zielińska, A., Forthmann, B., Lebuda, I., & Karwowski, M. (2023). Self-regulation for creative activity: The same or different across domains? *Psychology of Aesthetics, Creativity, and the Arts*. Advance online publication. https://doi.org/10.1037/aca0000540.

Chapter 5: Problem Finding

Abdulla, A. M., Paek, S. H., Cramond, B., & Runco, M. A. (2020). Problem finding and creativity: A meta-analytic review. *Psychology of Aesthetics, Creativity, and the Arts, 14*(1), 3–14. https://doi.org/10.1037/aca0000194.

Ananth, P., & Harvey, S. (2023). Ideas in the space between: Stockpiling and processes for managing ideas in developing a creative portfolio. *Administrative Science Quarterly, 68*(2), 465–507. https://doi.org/10.1177/00018392231154909.

Augmented reality (n.d.). Wikipedia. Retrieved January 18, 2024. https://en.wikipedia.org/wiki/Augmented_reality.

Baas, M., Nevicka, B., & Ten Velden, F. S. (2014). Specific mindfulness skills differentially predict creative performance. *Personality and Social Psychology Bulletin, 40*(9), 1092–1106. https://doi.org/10.1177/0146167214535813.

Botella, M., Zenasni, F., & Lubart, T. (2018). What are the stages of the creative process? What visual art students are saying. *Frontiers in Psychology, 9*, Article 2266. https://doi.org/10.3389/fpsyg.2018.02266.

Brooks, K. (2016, April 28). Here's a rare glimpse inside Salvador Dalí's unpublished diaries. *HuffPost.* https://www.huffpost.com/entry/salvador-dali-diary _n_572235c7e4b0f309baeffb47.

Catmull, E., & Wallace, A. (2014). *Creativity, Inc.: Overcoming the unseen forces that stand in the way of true inspiration.* Random House.

Csikszentmihalyi, M. (1988). Motivation and creativity: Toward a synthesis of structural and energistic approaches to cognition. *New Ideas in Psychology, 6*(2), 159–176. https://doi.org/10.1016/0732-118X(88)90001-3.

Csikszentmihalyi, M., & Getzels, J. W. (1971). Discovery-oriented behavior and the originality of creative products: A study with artists. *Journal of Personality and Social Psychology, 19*(1), 47–52. https://doi.org/10.1037/h0031106.

Da Vinci, L. (1956). *Treatise on painting: Codex urbinas latinus 1270* (Vol. 2). Princeton University Press.

Dorst, K. (2019). Co-evolution and emergence in design. *Design Studies, 65,* 60–77. https://doi.org/10.1016/j.destud.2019.10.005.

Dorst, K., & Cross, N. (2001). Creativity in the design process: Co-evolution of problem-solution. *Design Studies, 22*(5), 425–437. https://doi.org/10.1016/S0142 -694X(01)00009-6.

Einstein, A., & Infeld, L. (1938). *The evolution of physics.* Simon & Schuster.

Gläveanu, V., Lubart, T., Bonnardel, N., Botella, M., De Biaisi, P. M., Desainte-Catherine, M., Georgsdottir, A., Guillou, K., Kurtag, G., Mouchioud, C., Storme, M., Wojtczuk, A., & Zenasni, F. (2013). Creativity as action: Findings from five creative domains. *Frontiers in Psychology, 4,* Article 176. https://doi.org/10.3389 /fpsyg.2013.00176.

Green, J. (2021). *The Anthropocene reviewed: Essays on a human-centered planet.* Dutton.

Harrabin, R. (2017, August 3). Device could make washing machines lighter and greener. *BBC.* https://www.bbc.com/news/uk-40821915.

Kolata, G. (2021, April 8; updated October 3, 2023). Long overlooked, Kati Kariko helped shield the world from the coronavirus. *New York Times.* https://www .nytimes.com/2021/04/08/health/coronavirus-mrna-kariko.html.

Kritsky, G., Mader, D., & Smith, J. J. (2013). Surreal entomology: The insect imagery of Salvador Dalí. *American Entomologist, 59*(1), 28–37. https://doi.org/10.1093/ae/59.1.28.

Lee, S. R., & Kim, J. D. (2023). When do startups scale? Large-scale evidence from job postings. *Strategic Management Journal.* Advanced online publication. http://dx.doi.org/10.2139/ssrn.4015530.

Leone, S., Japp, P., & Reiter-Palmon, R. (2023). The emergence of problem construction at the team-level. *Small Group Research, 54*(5), 639–670. https://doi.org/10.1177/10464964231152877.

Raz, G. (Host). (2017, April 9). Instacart: Apoorva Mehta. *How I built this* (podcast). Wondery. https://podcasts.apple.com/za/podcast/instacart-apoorva-mehta/id1150510297?i=1000384196518.

Pablo Picasso. (n.d.). Oxford Reference. https://www.oxfordreference.com/display/10.1093/acref/9780191826719.001.0001/q-oro-ed4-00008311.

Paton, B., & Dorst, K. (2011). Briefing and reframing: A situated practice. *Design Studies, 32*(6), 573–587. https://doi.org/10.1016/j.destud.2011.07.002.

Pokémon Go. (n.d.). Wikipedia. Retrieved January 18, 2024. https://en.wikipedia.org/wiki/Pok%C3%A9mon_Go.

Reiter-Palmon, R. (2018). Creative cognition at the individual and team level: What happens before and after idea generation. In R. Sternberg & J. C. Kaufman (Eds.), *The nature of human creativity* (pp. 184–208). Cambridge University Press. http://dx.doi.org/10.1017/9781108185936.015.

Reiter-Palmon, R., Japp, P., Christenson, K., Allen, J., Shuffler, M., Summers, J., & Murugavel, V. (2023). *The effect of debriefs on team creative behaviors and outcomes.* Paper presented at the Marconi Institute of Creativity conference, Trieste, Italy.

Reiter-Palmon, R., Leone, S., & Schreiner, E. (2023). Conflicting problem representations and creativity: Effects on problem construction. *Creativity Research Journal, 36*(3), 521–531. https://doi.org/10.1080/10400419.2023.2234720.

Reiter-Palmon, R., & Murugavel, V. (2018). The effect of problem construction on team process and creativity. *Frontiers in Psychology, 9*, Article 2098. https://doi.org/10.3389/fpsyg.2018.02098.

Root-Bernstein, R., Allen, L., Beach, L., Bhadula, R., Fast, J., Hosey, C., Kremkow, B., Lapp, J., Lonc, K., Pawelec, K., Podufaly, A., Russ, C., Tennant, L., Vrtis, E., & Weinlander, S. (2008). Arts foster scientific success: Avocations of Nobel, National Academy, Royal Society, and Sigma Xi members. *Journal of Psychology of Science and Technology, 1*(2), 51–63. https://doi.org/10.1891/1939-7054.1.2.51.

Ruiz, C. (2010). Salvador Dalí and science: Beyond a mere curiosity. Gala-Salvador Dalí Foundation. https://www.salvador-dali.org/en/research/archives-en-ligne/download-documents/16/salvador-dali-and-science-beyond-a-mere-curiosity.

Silk, E. M., Rechkemmer, A. E., Daly, S. R., Jablokow, K. W., & McKilligan, S. (2021). Problem framing and cognitive style: Impacts on design ideation perceptions. *Design Studies, 74*, Article 101015. https://doi.org/10.1016/j.destud.2021.101015.

Smith, K., & Drake, J. (2023). Investigating daily inspiration and creativity in creative and non-creative individuals. Paper presented at the Marconi Institute of Creativity conference, Trieste, Italy.

Suh, A. (2013). *Leonardo's notebooks*. Black Dog & Leventhal Publishers.

Taylor, M. (2016). God and the atom: Salvador Dalí's mystical manifesto and the contested origins of nuclear painting. Dalí Museum. https://thedali.org/wp-content/uploads/2016/12/proceedings-TAYLOR-en_edits_12.19.16_final.pdf.

Wigert, B. G., Murugavel, V. R., & Reiter-Palmon, R. (2022). The utility of divergent and convergent thinking in the problem construction processes during creative problem-solving. *Psychology of Aesthetics, Creativity, and the Arts*. Advance online publication. https://doi.org/10.1037/aca0000513.

Chapter 6: Harnessing the Power of Emotions

Adam, N. A., & Alarifi, G. (2021). Innovation practices for survival of small and medium enterprises (SMEs) in the COVID-19 times: The role of external support. *Journal of Innovation and Entrepreneurship, 10*(1), Article 15. https://doi.org/10.1186/s13731-021-00156-6.

Allison, T. H., Warnick, B. J., Davis, B. C., & Cardon, M. S. (2022). Can you hear me now? Engendering passion and preparedness perceptions with vocal expressions in crowdfunding pitches. *Journal of Business Venturing, 37*(3), Article 106193. https://doi.org/10.1016/j.jbusvent.2022.106193.

Baas, M. (2023). Experimental methods in the study of emotions and creativity. In Z. Ivcevic, J. D. Hoffmann, & J. C. Kaufman (Eds.), *The Cambridge handbook of creativity and emotions* (pp. 11–29). Cambridge University Press.

Barrett, L. F. (2004). Feelings or words? Understanding the content in self-report ratings of experienced emotion. *Journal of Personality and Social Psychology, 87*(2), 266–281. https://doi.org/10.1037/0022-3514.87.2.266.

Byron, K., Khazanchi, S., & Nazarian, D. (2010). The relationship between stressors and creativity: A meta-analysis examining competing theoretical models. *Journal of Applied Psychology, 95*(1), 201–212. https://doi.org/10.1037/a0017868.

Cardon, M. S., Sudek, R., & Mitteness, C. (2009). The impact of perceived entrepreneurial passion on angel investing. *Frontiers of Entrepreneurship Research, 29*(2), Article 1. http://digitalknowledge.babson.edu/fer/vol29/iss2/1.

Clore, G. L., & Huntsinger, J. R. (2009). How the object of affect guides its impact. *Emotion Review, 1*(1), 39–54. https://doi.org/10.1177/1754073908097185.

Cohen, J. B., & Andrade, E. B. (2004). Affective intuition and task-contingent affect regulation. *Journal of Consumer Research, 31*(2), 358–367. https://doi.org/10.1086/422114.

Fisher, D. R. (2022, July 22). Lessons learned from the post–George Floyd protests. Brookings. https://www.brookings.edu/blog/fixgov/2022/07/22/lessons-learned -from-the-post-george-floyd-protests.

Forgas, J. P., & Koch, A. S. (2013). Mood effects on cognition. In M. D. Robinson, E. Watkins, & E. Harmon-Jones (Eds.), *Handbook of cognition and emotion* (pp. 231– 251). Guilford Press.

Fredrickson, B. L. (2001). The role of positive emotions in positive psychology: The broaden-and-build theory of positive emotions. *American Psychologist, 56*(3), 218– 226. https://doi.org/10.1037/0003-066X.56.3.218.

Han, E. (2022). 5 examples of design thinking in business. *Harvard Business School On- line*. https://online.hbs.edu/blog/post/design-thinking-examples.

King, A. (2021, June 23). How Lip Bar founder Melissa Butler achieves a "carefree" blowout. *Vogue*. https://www.vogue.com/article/how-lip-bar-founder-melissa -butler-achieves-a-carefree-blowout.

Kühnel, J., Bledow, R., & Kiefer, M. (2022). There is a time to be creative: The align- ment between chronotype and time of day. *Academy of Management Journal, 65*(1), 218–247. https://doi.org/10.5465/amj.2019.0020.

Mayer, J. D., Gaschke, Y. N., Braverman, D. L., & Evans, T. W. (1992). Mood-congruent judgment is a general effect. *Journal of Personality and Social Psychology, 63*(1), 119–132. https://doi.org/10.1037/0022-3514.63.1.119.

Mayer, J. D., & Salovey, P. (1997). What is emotional intelligence? In P. Salovey & D. Sluyter (Eds.), *Emotional development and emotional intelligence: Educational implica- tions* (pp. 3–31). Basic Books.

Morse, K. F., Fine, P. A., & Friedlander, K. J. (2021). Creativity and leisure during COVID-19: Examining the relationship between leisure activities, motivations, and psychological well-being. *Frontiers in Psychology, 12*, Article 609967. https://doi .org/10.3389/fpsyg.2021.609967.

Palfai, T. P., & Salovey, P. (1993–1994). The influence of depressed and elated mood on deductive and inductive reasoning. *Imagination, Cognition and Personality, 13*(1), 57–71. https://doi.org/10.2190/FYYA-GCRU-J124-Q3B2.

Posner, J., Russell, J. A., & Peterson, B. S. (2005). The circumplex model of affect: An integrative approach to affective neuroscience, cognitive development, and psychopathology. *Development and Psychopathology, 17*(3), 715–734. https://doi .org/10.1017/S0954579405050340.

Ram, J., & Atkisson, E. (n.d.). "I'll do it myself." United States Patent and Trademark Office. https://www.uspto.gov/learning-and-resources/journeys-innovation/historical -stories/ill-do-it-myself.

Raz, G. (Host). (2022, October 31). Tripadvisor: Steve Kaufer. *How I built this* (podcast).

Wondery. https://wondery.com/shows/how-i-built-this/episode/10386-tripadvisor -steve-kaufer/.

Schwarz, N. (2012). Feelings-as-information theory. In P. A. M. Van Lange, A. Kruglanski, & E. T. Higgins (eds.), *Handbook of theories of social psychology* (pp. 289–308). Thousand Sage.

Strasberg, L. (1988). *A dream of passion: The development of the method.* Methuen.

Tang, M., Hofreiter, S., Reiter-Palmon, R., Bai, X., & Murugavel, V. (2021). Creativity as a means to well-being in times of COVID-19 pandemic: Results of a cross-cultural study. *Frontiers in Psychology, 12,* Article 601389. https://doi.org/10.3389 /fpsyg.2021.601389.

Tugade, M. M., & Fredrickson, B. L. (2002). Positive emotions and emotional intelligence. In L. F. Barrett & P. Salovey (Eds.), *The wisdom in feeling: Psychological processes in emotional intelligence* (pp. 319–340). Guilford Press.

van Tilburg, W. A., Sedikides, C., & Wildschut, T. (2015). The mnemonic muse: Nostalgia fosters creativity through openness to experience. *Journal of Experimental Social Psychology, 59,* 1–7. https://doi.org/10.1016/j.jesp.2015.02.002.

Wilson, M. (2018). The untold story of the vegetable peeler that changed the world. *Fast Company.* https://www.fastcompany.com/90239156/the-untold-story-of-the -vegetable-peeler-that-changed-the-world.

Wright, A. G. C., Aslinger, E. N., Bellamy, B., Edershile, E. A., & Woods, W. C. (2020). Daily stress and hassles. In K. L. Harkness & E. P. Hayden (Eds.), *The Oxford handbook of stress and mental health* (pp. 27–44). Oxford University Press.

Chapter 7: When Emotions Get in the Way

Barsade, S. G., Coutifaris, C. G., & Pillemer, J. (2018). Emotional contagion in organizational life. *Research in Organizational Behavior, 38,* 137–151. https://doi.org/10.1016 /j.riob.2018.11.005.

Berg, J. M., Wrzesniewski, A., & Dutton, J. E. (2010). Perceiving and responding to challenges in job crafting at different ranks: When proactivity requires adaptivity. *Journal of Organizational Behavior, 31*(2–3), 158–186. https://doi.org/10.1002/job.645.

Bledow, R., Rosing, K., & Frese, M. (2013). A dynamic perspective on affect and creativity. *Academy of Management Journal, 56*(2), 432–450. https://doi.org/10.5465 /amj.2010.0894.

Bonanno, G. A., & Burton, C. L. (2013). Regulatory flexibility: An individual differences perspective on coping and emotion regulation. *Perspectives on Psychological Science, 8*(6), 591–612. https://doi.org/10.1177/1745691613504116.

De Cock, R., Denoo, L., & Clarysse, B. (2020). Surviving the emotional rollercoaster called entrepreneurship: The role of emotion regulation. *Journal of Business Venturing, 35*(2), Article 105936. https://doi.org/10.1016/j.jbusvent.2019.04.004.

Ebrahimi, O. V., Pallesen, S., Kenter, R. M., & Nordgreen, T. (2019). Psychological interventions for the fear of public speaking: A meta-analysis. *Frontiers in Psychology, 10*, Article 488. https://doi.org/10.3389/fpsyg.2019.00488.

Famous quotes by Thomas Edison. (n.d.). Thomas A. Edison. https://www.thomas edison.org/edison-quotes.

Fang He, V., Sirén, C., Singh, S., Solomon, G., & von Krogh, G. (2018). Keep calm and carry on: Emotion regulation in entrepreneurs' learning from failure. *Entrepreneurship Theory and Practice, 42*(4), 605–630. https://doi.org/10.1177/1042258718783428.

Folkman, S. (2013). Stress: Appraisal and coping. In J. R. Turner and M. Gellman (Eds.), *Encyclopedia of behavioral medicine* (pp. 1913–1915). Springer.

Gocłowska, M. A., Damian, R. I., & Mor, S. (2018). The diversifying experience model: Taking a broader conceptual view of the multiculturalism-creativity link. *Journal of Cross-Cultural Psychology, 49*(2), 303–322. https://doi.org/10.1177 /0022022116650258.

Geng, Z., Liu, C., Liu, X., & Feng, J. (2013). Effects of emotional labor strategies on job stress and creativity. *Academy of Management Proceedings, 2013*(1), 15098.

Gross, J. J. (2013). Emotion regulation: Taking stock and moving forward. *Emotion, 13*(3), 359–365. https://doi.org/10.1037/a0032135.

Gross, J. J. (Ed.). (2013). *Handbook of emotion regulation.* Guilford Press.

Headrick, L., Newman, D. A., Park, Y. A., & Liang, Y. (2023). Recovery experiences for work and health outcomes: A meta-analysis and recovery-engagement-exhaustion model. *Journal of Business and Psychology, 38*(4), 821–864. https://doi .org/10.1007/s10869-022-09821-3.

Ivcevic, Z., & Brackett, M. A. (2015). Predicting creativity: Interactive effects of openness to experience and emotion regulation ability. *Psychology of Aesthetics, Creativity, and the Arts, 9*(4), 480–487. https://doi.org/10.1037/a0039826.

Ivcevic, Z., Moeller, J., Menges, J., & Brackett, M. A. (2021). Supervisor emotionally intelligent behavior and employee creativity. *Journal of Creative Behavior, 55*(1), 79–91. https://doi.org/10.1002/jocb.436.

Kaufman, J. C. (2023). *Creativity advantage.* Cambridge University Press.

Lazazzara, A., Tims, M., & De Gennaro, D. (2020). The process of reinventing a job: A meta-synthesis of qualitative job crafting research. *Journal of Vocational Behavior, 116*, 103267. https://doi.org/10.1016/j.jvb.2019.01.001.

Leung, A. K.-y., Liou, S., Qiu, L., Kwan, L. Y.-Y., Chiu, C.-y., & Yong, J. C. (2014). The role of instrumental emotion regulation in the emotions-creativity link: How worries render individuals with high neuroticism more creative. *Emotion, 14*(5), 846–856. https://doi.org/10.1037/a0036965.

Li, H., Jin, H., & Chen, T. (2020). Linking proactive personality to creative performance: The role of job crafting and high-involvement work systems. *Journal of Creative Behavior, 54*(1), 196–210. https://doi.org/10.1002/jocb.355.

Li, N., Sun, Y., Jiang, D., & Yang, X. (2021). Exploring the moderating effect of interpersonal emotion regulation between the integration of opportunity and resource and entrepreneurial performance. *Frontiers in Psychology, 12,* Article 756767. https://doi.org/10.3389/fpsyg.2021.756767.

Ma, C., Wang, B., Sun, C., & Lin, L. (2023). The spillover effect of emotional labor: How it shapes frontline employees' proactive innovation behavior. *SAGE Open, 13*(3), 21582440231191791. https://doi.org/10.1177/21582440231191791.

Maden-Eyiusta, C., & Alten, O. (2023). Expansion-oriented job crafting and employee performance: A self-empowerment perspective. *European Management Journal, 41*(1), 79–89. https://doi.org/10.1016/j.emj.2021.10.012.

Madjar, N., & Shalley, C. E. (2008). Multiple tasks' and multiple goals' effect on creativity: Forced incubation or just a distraction? *Journal of Management, 34*(4), 786–805. https://doi.org/10.1177/0149206308318611.

Madore, K. P., & Wagner, A. D. (2019, March). Multicosts of multitasking. *Cerebrum, 2019.* Dana Foundation. https://www.ncbi.nlm.nih.gov/pmc/articles/PMC7075496.

Opoku, M. A., Kang, S. W., & Kim, N. (2023). Sleep-deprived and emotionally exhausted: Depleted resources as inhibitors of creativity at work. *Personnel Review, 52*(5), 1437–1461. https://doi.org/10.1108/PR-09-2021-0620.

Riepenhausen, A., Wackerhagen, C., Reppmann, Z. C., Deter, H.-C., Kalisch, R., Veer, I. M., & Walter, H. (2022). Positive cognitive reappraisal in stress resilience, mental health, and well-being: A comprehensive systematic review. *Emotion Review, 14*(4), 310–331. https://doi.org/10.1177/17540739221114642.

Sheppes, G., & Gross, J. J. (2012). Emotion regulation effectiveness: What works when. In H. A. Tennen & J. M. Suls (Eds.), *Handbook of psychology* (2nd ed., pp. 391–406). Wiley Blackwell Press.

Shin, I., Hur, W. M., & Oh, H. (2015). Essential precursors and effects of employee creativity in a service context: Emotional labor strategies and official job performance. *Career Development International, 20*(7), 733–752. https://doi.org/10.1108/CDI-10-2014-0137.

Sirén, C., He, V. F., Wesemann, H., Jonassen, Z., Grichnik, D., & von Krogh, G. (2020). Leader emergence in nascent venture teams: The critical roles of individual emotion regulation and team emotions. *Journal of Management Studies, 57*(5), 931–961. https://doi.org/10.1111/joms.12563.

Tamir, M. (2016). Why do people regulate their emotions? A taxonomy of motives in emotion regulation. *Personality and Social Psychology Review, 20*(3), 199–222. https://doi.org/10.1177/1088868315586325.

Tamir, M., Vishkin, A., & Gutentag, T. (2020). Emotion regulation is motivated. *Emotion, 20*(1), 115–119. https://doi.org/10.1037/emo0000635.

Wang, J., Zhang, Z., & Jia, M. (2017). Understanding how leader humility enhances employee creativity: The roles of perspective taking and cognitive reappraisal. *Journal of Applied Behavioral Science, 53*(1), 5–31. https://doi.org/10.1177/0021886316678907.

Wilkinson, A. (2015, February 1). A pursuit of beauty. *New Yorker.* https://www.new yorker.com/magazine/2015/02/02/pursuit-beauty.

Wrzesniewski, A., & Dutton, J. E. (2001). Crafting a job: Revisioning employees as active crafters of their work. *Academy of Management Review, 26*(2), 179–201. https://doi.org/10.5465/amr.2001.4378011.

Zhu, L. Y. (2022). Linking anxiety to passion: Emotion regulation and entrepreneurs' pitch performance. Doctoral dissertation, University of California, Irvine.

Chapter 8: Overcoming Creative Blocks

Barrett, L. F., Lewis, M., & Haviland-Jones, J. M. (Eds.). (2016). *Handbook of emotions* (4th ed.). Guilford Press.

De Dreu, C. K. W., Bass, M., & Nijstad, B. A. (2008). Hedonic tone and activation in the mood-creativity link: Towards a dual pathway to creativity model. *Journal of Personality and Social Psychology, 94*(5), 739–756. https://doi.org/10.1037/0022-3514.94.5.739.

Dewey, A., Steinberg, H., & Coulson, M. (1998). Conditions in which British artists achieve their best work. *Creativity Research Journal, 11*(4), 275–282. https://doi.org/10.1207/s15326934crj1104_1.

Fleck, J. I., & Weisberg, R. W. (2004). The use of verbal protocols as data: An analysis of insight in the candle problem. *Memory & Cognition, 32*(6), 990–1006. https://doi.org/10.3758/BF03196876.

Gable, S. L., Hopper, E. A., & Schooler, J. W. (2019). When the muses strike: Creative ideas of physicists and writers routinely occur during mind wandering. *Psychological Science, 30*(3), 396–404. https://doi.org/10.1177/0956797618820626.

Gaiman, N. (2011). *Writers on a New England Stage.* https://overcast.fm/+BED4EqKDgs.

Glăveanu, V., Lubart, T., Bonnardel, N., Botella, M., de Biaisi, P.-M., Desainte-Catherine, M., Georgsdottir, A., Guillou, K., Kurtag, G., Mouchiroud, C., Storme, M., Wojtczuk, A., & Zenasni, F. (2013). Creativity as action: Findings from five creative domains. *Frontiers in Psychology, 4*, Article 176. https://doi.org/10.3389/fpsyg.2013.00176.

Higgins, E. T. (2011). Accessibility theory. In P. A. M. Van Lange, A. W. Kruglanski, & E. T. Higgins (Eds.), *Handbook of theories of social psychology* (Vol. 1, pp. 75–96). Sage.

Hirst, B. (1992). How artists overcome creative blocks. *Journal of Creative Behavior*, *26*(2), 81–82. https://doi.org/10.1002/j.2162-6057.1992.tb01163.x.

Gallay, L. H. (2013). Understanding and treating creative block in professional artists. Doctoral dissertation, Alliant International University.

Ivcevic, Z., Grossman, E. R., Cotter, K. N., & Nusbaum, E. (2023). Self-regulation of creativity: Toward measuring strategies of creative action. *Creativity Research Journal*, *36*(3), 491–507. https://doi.org/10.1080/10400419.2023.2226494.

Ivcevic, Z., & Hoffmann, J. (2020, August). The role of emotions across the creative process of artists. In Z. Ivcevic (Chair), *Creativity and emotions: From the decision to be creative to reactions to creative products*. Symposium conducted at the Annual Convention of the American Psychological Association.

Montero-Marín, J., Gaete, J., Demarzo, M., Rodero, B., Lopez, L. C. S., & García-Campayo, J. (2016). Self-criticism: A measure of uncompassionate behaviors toward the self, based on the negative components of the Self-Compassion Scale. *Frontiers in Psychology*, *7*, Article 1281. https://doi.org/10.3389/fpsyg.2016.01281.

Neff, K. D. (2023). Self-compassion: Theory, method, research, and intervention. *Annual Review of Psychology*, *74*, 193–218. https://doi.org/10.1146/annurev-psych-032420-031047.

Neff, K. D., Tóth-Király, I., Knox, M. C., Kuchar, A., & Davidson, O. (2021). The development and validation of the State Self-Compassion Scale (long- and short form). *Mindfulness*, *12*(1), 121–140. https://doi.org/10.1007/s12671-020-01505-4.

Ovington, L. A., Saliba, A. J., Moran, C. C., Goldring, J., & MacDonald, J. B. (2018). Do people really have insights in the shower? The when, where and who of the aha! moment. *Journal of Creative Behavior*, *52*(1), 21–34. https://doi.org/10.1002/jocb.126.

Prescott, V. (Host). (2011, June 29). Neil Gaiman [Audio podcast episode]. In *Writers on a New England Stage*. New Hampshire Public Radio.

Sawyer, R. K. (2018). Teaching and learning how to create in schools of art and design. *Journal of the Learning Sciences*, *27*(1), 137–181. https://doi.org/10.1080/10508406.2017.1381963.

Vohs, K. D., Redden, J. P., & Rahinel, R. (2013). Physical order produces healthy choices, generosity, and conventionality, whereas disorder produces creativity. *Psychological Science*, *24*(9), 1860–1867. https://doi.org/10.1177/0956797613480186.

Youmans, R. J. (2011). The effects of physical prototyping and group work on the reduction of design fixation. *Design Studies*, *32*(2), 115–138. https://doi.org/10.1016/j.destud.2010.08.001.

Youmans, R. J., & Arciszewski, T. (2014). Design fixation: Classifications and modern methods of prevention. *Artificial Intelligence for Engineering Design, Analysis and Manufacturing, 28*, 129–137. https://doi.org/10.1017/S0890060414000043.

Zabelina, D. L., & Robinson, M. D. (2010). Don't be so hard on yourself: Self-compassion facilitates creative originality among self-judgmental individuals. *Creativity Research Journal, 22*(3), 288–293. https://doi.org/10.1080/10400419.2010.503538.

Chapter 9: With a Little Help from Your Friends

Academy Awards Acceptance Speech Database. (n.d.). https://aaspeechesdb.oscars.org.

Carmeli, A., Dutton, J. E., & Hardin, A. E. (2015). Respect as an engine for new ideas: Linking respectful engagement, relational information processing and creativity among employees and teams. *Human Relations, 68*(6), 1021–1047. https://doi.org/10.1177/0018726714550256.

Carmeli, A., Levi, A., & Peccei, R. (2021). Resilience and creative problem-solving capacities in project teams: A relational view. *International Journal of Project Management, 39*(5), 546–556. https://doi.org/10.1016/j.ijproman.2021.03.007.

Dutton, J. E., Debebe, G., & Wrzesniewski, A. (2015). Being valued and devalued at work: A social valuing perspective. In K. Elsbach & B. Betchky (Eds.), *Qualitative organizational research.* Vol. 3: *Best papers from the Davis Conference on Qualitative Research* (pp. 54–61). Information Age.

Iacurci, G. (2003, February 1). 2022 was the "real year of the Great Resignation," says economist. *CNBC.* https://www.cnbc.com/2023/02/01/why-2022-was-the-real-year-of-the-great-resignation.html.

Lee, A., Legood, A., Hughes, D., Tian, A. W., Newman, A., & Knight, C. (2020). Leadership, creativity and innovation: A meta-analytic review. *European Journal of Work and Organizational Psychology, 29*(1), 1–35. https://doi.org/10.1080/1359432X.2019.1661837.

Liden, R. C., & Maslyn, J. M. (1998). Multidimensionality of leader-member exchange: An empirical assessment through scale development. *Journal of Management, 24*(1), 43–73. https://doi.org/10.1016/S0149-2063(99)80053-1.

Madjar, N. (2008). Emotional and informational support from different sources and employee creativity. *Journal of Occupational and Organizational Psychology, 81*(1), 83–100. https://doi.org/10.1348/096317907X202464.

Mannucci, P. V., & Perry-Smith, J. E. (2022). "Who are you going to call?" Network activation in creative idea generation and elaboration. *Academy of Management Journal, 65*(4), 1192–1217. https://doi.org/10.5465/amj.2019.0333.

Mascareño, J., Rietzschel, E., & Wisse, B. (2020). Leader-member exchange (LMX) and innovation: A test of competing hypotheses. *Creativity and Innovation Management, 29*(3), 495–511. https://doi.org/10.1111/caim.12390.

Perry-Smith, J., & Mannucci, P. V. (2015). Social networks, creativity, and entrepreneurship. In C. E. Shalley, M. A. Hitt, & J. Zhou (Eds.), *The Oxford handbook of creativity, innovation, and entrepreneurship* (pp. 205–224). Oxford University Press. https://doi.org/10.1093/oxfordhb/9780199927678.013.0016.

Perry-Smith, J. E., & Mannucci, P. V. (2017). From creativity to innovation: The social network drivers of the four phases of the idea journey. *Academy of Management Review, 42*(1), 53–79. https://doi.org/10.5465/amr.2014.0462.

Shefer, N., Carmeli, A., & Cohen-Meitar, R. (2018). Bringing Carl Rogers back in: Exploring the power of positive regard at work. *British Journal of Management, 29*(1), 63–81. https://doi.org/10.1111/1467-8551.12247.

Taylor, C., Ivcevic, Z., Moeller, J., & Brackett, M. A. (2020). Gender and creativity at work. *Creativity and Innovation Management, 29*(3), 453–464. https://doi.org/10.1111/caim.12397.

Taylor, C. L., Ivcevic, Z., Moeller, J., Menges, J. I., Reiter-Palmon, R., & Brackett, M. A. (2022). Gender and emotions at work: Organizational rank has greater emotional benefits for men than women. *Sex Roles, 86*(1–2), 127–142. https://doi.org/10.1007/s11199-021-01256-z.

Zhou, J., & George, J. M. (2001). When job dissatisfaction leads to creativity: Encouraging the expression of voice. *Academy of Management Journal, 44*(4), 682–696. https://doi.org/10.2307/3069410.

Zhou, J., Shin, S. J., Brass, D. J., Choi, J., & Zhang, Z.-X. (2009). Social networks, personal values, and creativity: Evidence for curvilinear and interaction effects. *Journal of Applied Psychology, 94*(6), 1544–1552. https://doi.org/10.1037/a0016285.

Chapter 10: Building Creativity at Work

Amundsen, S., & Martinsen, Ø. L. (2014). Empowering leadership: Construct clarification, conceptualization, and validation of a new scale. *Leadership Quarterly, 25*(3), 487–511. https://doi.org/10.1016/j.leaqua.2013.11.009.

Baas, M., & Paletz, S. (2025). Conflict, creativity, and crisis. In Z. Ivcevic, R. Reiter-Palmon, M., Grohman, & M. Tang (Eds.), *Crisis, creativity, and innovation.* Palgrave.

Bradley, B. H., Postlethwaite, B. E., Klotz, A. C., Hamdani, M. R., & Brown, K. G. (2012). Reaping the benefits of task conflict in teams: The critical role of team psychological safety climate. *Journal of Applied Psychology, 97*(1), 151–158. https://doi.org/10.1037/a0024200.

Chen, L., Wadei, K. A., Bai, S., & Liu, J. (2020). Participative leadership and employee creativity: A sequential mediation model of psychological safety and creative process engagement. *Leadership & Organization Development Journal, 41*(6), 741–759. https://doi.org/10.1108/LODJ-07-2019-0319.

Choo, A. S., Linderman, K. W., & Schroeder, R. G. (2007). Method and psychological effects on learning behaviors and knowledge creation in quality improvement projects. *Management Science, 53*(3), 437–450. https://www.proquest.com/scholarly-journals/method-psychological-effects-on-learning/docview/213264016/se-2.

Chokshi, N. (2024, February 26). Boeing's safety culture faulted by F.A.A. in new report. *New York Times.* https://www.nytimes.com/2024/02/26/business/boeing-faa-safety-culture.html.

Curşeu, P. L., & Schruijer, S. G. (2010). Does conflict shatter trust or does trust obliterate conflict? Revisiting the relationships between team diversity, conflict, and trust. *Group Dynamics: Theory, Research, and Practice, 14*(1), 66–79. https://doi.org/10.1037/a0017104.

Edmondson, A. (1999). Psychological safety and learning behavior in work teams. *Administrative Science Quarterly, 44*(2), 350–383. https://doi.org/10.2307/2666999.

Giorno, T. (2024, April 17). Boeing whistleblower: "Absolutely" a culture of retaliation. *The Hill.* https://thehill.com/business/4599995-boeing-whistleblower-absolutely-a-culture-of-retaliation.

Hunter, S. T., Bedell, K. E., & Mumford, M. D. (2007). Climate for creativity: A quantitative review. *Creativity Research Journal, 19*(1), 69–90. https://doi.org/10.1080/10400410709336883.

Hunter, S. T., Cushenbery, L. D., & Jayne, B. (2017). Why dual leaders will drive innovation: Resolving the exploration and exploitation dilemma with a conservation of resources solution. *Journal of Organizational Behavior, 38*(8), 1183–1195. https://doi.org/10.1002/job.2195.

Janssen, O. (2000). Job demands, perceptions of effort-reward fairness and innovative work behaviour. *Journal of Occupational and Organizational Psychology, 73*(3), 287–302. https://doi.org/10.1348/096317900167038.

Jehn, K. A., & Bendersky, C. (2003). Intragroup conflict in organizations: A contingency perspective. *Research in Organizational Behavior, 25*, 189–244. https://doi.org/10.1016/S0191-3085(03)25005-X.

Kark, R., & Carmeli, A. (2009). Alive and creating: The mediating role of vitality and aliveness in the relationship between psychological safety and creative work involvement. *Journal of Organizational Behavior, 30*(6), 785–804. https://doi.org/10.1002/job.v30:610.1002/job.571.

Kasemaa, A., & Suviste, R. (2020). Comparing two instruments of transformational leadership. *Central European Management Journal, 28*, 2–31. https://doi.org/10.7206/cemj.2658-0845.13.

Kessel, M., Kratzer, J., & Schultz, C. (2012). Psychological safety, knowledge sharing, and creative performance in healthcare teams. *Creativity and Innovation Management, 21*(2), 147–157. https://doi.org/10.1111/j.1467-8691.2012.00635.x.

References

Kim, W. (2024, January 31). How Boeing put profits over planes. *Vox*. https://www.vox.com/money/24052245/boeing-corporate-culture-737-airplane-safety-door-plug.

Koh, D., Lee, K., & Joshi, K. (2019). Transformational leadership and creativity: A meta-analytic review and identification of an integrated model. *Journal of Organizational Behavior, 40*(6), 625–650. https://doi.org/10.1002/job.2355.

Lee, A., Legood, A., Hughes, D., Tian, A. W., Newman, A., & Knight, C. (2020). Leadership, creativity and innovation: A meta-analytic review. *European Journal of Work and Organizational Psychology, 29*(1), 1–35. https://doi.org/10.1080/1359432X.2019.1661837.

Lee, A., Willis, S., & Tian, A. W. (2018). Empowering leadership: A meta-analytic examination of incremental contribution, mediation, and moderation. *Journal of Organizational Behavior, 39*, 306–325. https://doi.org/10.1002/job.2220.

Liu, Y., Keller, R. T., & Bartlett, K. R. (2021). Initiative climate, psychological safety and knowledge sharing as predictors of team creativity: A multilevel study of research and development project teams. *Creativity and Innovation Management, 30*(3), 498–510. https://doi.org/10.1111/caim.12438.

Reiter-Palmon, R., & Millier, M. (2023). Psychological safety and creativity: The glue that binds a creative team. In Z. Ivcevic, J. D. Hoffmann, & J. C. Kaufman (Eds.), *The Cambridge handbook of creativity and emotions* (pp. 559–576). Cambridge University Press.

Renko, M., El Tarabishy, A., Carsrud, A. L., & Brännback, M. (2015). Understanding and measuring entrepreneurial leadership style. *Journal of Small Business Management, 53*(1), 54–74. https://doi.org/10.1111/jsbm.12086.

Shefrin, H. (2024, January 28). Boeing's weak corporate culture underlies difficulties with 737 MAX 9. *Forbes*. https://www.forbes.com/sites/hershshefrin/2024/01/28/boeings-weak-corporate-culture-underlies-difficulties-with-737-max-9.

Zhou, Q., & Pan, W. (2015). A cross-level examination of the process linking transformational leadership and creativity: The role of psychological safety climate. *Human Performance, 28*(5), 405–424. https://doi.org/10.1080/08959285.2015.1021050.

Index

Dr. Zorana Ivcevic Pringle is a senior research scientist at Yale University's Center for Emotional Intelligence. She is a regular contributor to *Psychology Today* and *Creativity Post* and coeditor of *The Cambridge Handbook of Creativity and Emotions* and *Crises, Creativity, and Innovation*. She lives in Portsmouth, New Hampshire.